ERICA ARMSTRONG DUNBAR

A Fragile Freedom

AFRICAN AMERICAN WOMEN
AND EMANCIPATION IN
THE ANTEBELLUM CITY

Yale University Press
New Haven &
London

Society and the Sexes in the Modern World
Christine Stansell, Series Editor

Published with assistance from the foundation established in memory of Philip
Hamilton McMillan of the Class of 1894, Yale College.

Set in Sabon by IBT Global.

Printed in the United States of America.

Library of Congress Cataloging-in-Publication Data

Dunbar, Erica Armstrong.
A fragile freedom : African American women and emancipation in the antebellum
city / Erica Armstrong Dunbar.
    p. cm. — (Society and the sexes in the modern world)
    Includes bibliographical references and index.
    ISBN 978-0-300-12591-7 (cloth : alk. paper)
    1. African American women—Pennsylvania—Philadelphia—History—19th
century.   2. African American women—Pennsylvania—Philadelphia—Social
conditions—19th century.   3. Free African Americans—Pennsylvania—
Philadelphia—History—19th century.   4. Free African Americans—Pennsylvania—Philadelphia—Social conditions—19th century.   5. Slaves—Emancipation—Pennsylvania—Philadelphia—History.   6. Antislavery movements—
Pennsylvania—Philadelphia—History—19th century.   7. Slavery—Pennsylvania—Pennsylvania—Philadelphia—History.   8. Philadelphia (Pa.)—History—
19th century.   9. Philadelphia (Pa.)—Social conditions—19th century.
10. Philadelphia (Pa.)—Race relations—History—19th century.   I. Title.
    F158.9.N4D86 2008
    973.7'1140974811—dc22   2007036454

A catalogue record for this book is available from the British Library.

The paper in this book meets the guidelines for permanence and durability of
the Committee on Production Guidelines for Book Longevity of the Council on
Library Resources.

10   9   8   7   6   5   4   3   2   1

This book is dedicated to the memory of my Nana
Elsie Harewood Armstrong
and to
Christian Andrew Dunbar
My sweet bud of promise

Contents

Illustrations

Acknowledgments

There are a great number of people who have, in some way, played a supportive role in the completion of this project. I owe so very much to many colleagues, institutions, friends, and my family.

I learned to read, write, and think at Germantown Friends School. I spent fourteen years of my life experiencing life-changing educational moments. My education, steeped in Quaker values, allowed me to feel safe and confident as I developed from a child into a teenager. Though many teachers nurtured and supported me, one in particular helped to shape me into a "good student." Geoffrey Selling, my fourth- and fifth-grade teacher, taught me how to organize my schoolwork and my thoughts. My work with him created a solid foundation for my primary, secondary, and collegiate education. Thank you, Geoffrey.

I can honestly say that my undergraduate years at the University of Pennsylvania changed my life and introduced me to the discipline of American history. In 1990 I met my mentor, inspiration, and role model, Evelyn Brooks Higginbotham. She took the time to gently mold me into an academic, allowing me to tag along at national conferences, inviting me to her home for meals, and permitting me to enroll in every undergraduate course she offered at Penn. When she left for Harvard she did not abandon me; she continued to advise and encourage me. When I left Philadelphia for graduate school in

New York, she continued to support me, eventually serving as a reader on my dissertation committee. I stand in awe of her tremendous contribution to the discipline and to the fields of African American and women's history.

There were many other extremely supportive people with whom I worked as an undergraduate. I am very appreciative of the Mellon Mays Undergraduate Fellowship Program, a unique program that also changed my life. It gave me the opportunity to begin independent research, to attend conferences, and to support my journey to and through graduate school. I would like to thank Valarie Swain-Cade McCoullum, Vice Provost for University Affairs at Penn and director of the MMUF program. Val has stood in my corner and in the corner of all MMUF fellows since my undergraduate years. I would also like to thank Pat Ravenell, aka "the bank," for supporting me and Susan Peterson Pace, who left this world much too soon, but not without leaving her mark. Susan stood as a constant source of motherly support for all fellows; I miss her and I thank her. Herman Beavers began this journey with me as one of my professors, and since then he has become a colleague and dear friend. Farah Griffin came to Penn in my senior year and allowed me to work with her on her own work—I thank her for her support and friendship. In my junior year at Penn I took a course from Mary Frances Berry; she taught me a great deal about the history of African Americans and the law.

As an undergraduate I was given the opportunity to work with the Martin Luther King Jr. Papers Project at Stanford University. It was there that I met and became good friends with Clay and Susan Carson. Clay opened up the world of Martin Luther King Jr., as well as the editorial process, to me. I met great friends and colleagues at the King Papers Project, including Crystal Feimster, Elizabeth Baez, Angela Earnest, and Leslie Harris. Crystal and I have journeyed together through the graduate school application process, qualifying exams, the dissertation, the job market, marriage, childbirth, and finally the manuscript. Her humor and support have periodically kept me moving forward. Leslie Harris became my friend in 1993; I have watched her grow from a graduate student to a leading scholar in nineteenth-century African American history. I have learned so very much from her steadfast dedication to social history, and I have modeled my own work after hers.

I would like to thank the Ford Foundation for its support through the first years of my graduate education at Columbia University. I went there to work with Eric Foner. His monumental contribution to American history, his brilliant lecturing skills, and his helpfulness allowed me to navigate the murky waters of graduate school. Elizabeth Blackmar impressed me with her incredible helpfulness and support as I held fast to researching African

American women's history. Daryl Scott served as an adviser and mentor throughout my entire six years at Columbia. He taught me a great deal about the academy and remains a good friend. Judith Weisenfeld read many versions of my unpolished dissertation, offering extremely helpful advice and suggestions for the final draft. Judith's own work also serves as an inspiration. There were several other friends and colleagues who were of great assistance and support to me during my years at Columbia. I would like to thank Deborah Mcoullum as well as the Graduate School of Arts and Sciences Merit Fellowship Program for their help. I would also like to thank the Leadership Alliance for their assistance in my final year of the program and the Library Company of Philadelphia for their fellowship support, which allowed me to finish my dissertation.

I met a handful of inspirational good friends while at Columbia. Adrienne Petty Roberts became my friend on the first day of graduate student orientation. We have survived coursework, orals, the dissertation, and the job market together. We have supported each other along the way and will continue to do so in the future. Martha Jones entered my life in New York and continues to be a constant friend and colleague. We have also navigated the hurdles of the academy together, and her work serves as an inspiration. I value her candor, insight, and humor.

A scholar cannot live on books alone. I am extremely indebted to my "New York Crew" for taking me to parties and reminding me that there is life outside nineteenth-century America. Dana Baxter, Dawn Baxter, Christine Bussey Singleton, Nikki Bussey, Kysha Harris, Shena Hickman, and Dana Thomas migrated from Penn to New York City with me and forced me to enjoy my twenties. Jessica Davis Ba and Robin Watkins always kept in touch and cheered me along in all of my endeavors, as did Rhea, James, Bryce, and Nolan Williams. Rhea's cheery "hellooooooo" always brightened my mood, and our friendship has been a constant support. My friend Lisa Langhart's work ethic serves as an inspiration, and her friendship is irreplaceable. I am certain that she will be the first of my friends to make a million dollars all on her own. Keep doing your thang, girl! My dear friend Marjorie DeLaCruz has been a constant source of support, love, and laughter for almost fifteen years. Our time together on Tiemann Place represents some of the highlights of my life, and I grew into the woman that I wanted to be while living with her. Her family cared for me and opened up their home and dinner table to me on many occasions. Dr. Raphael DeLaCruz and his wife, Gladys, became my New York parents, offering packages of orange juice, diet Coke, toilet paper, and platanos on a consistent basis. Marjorie offered me shelter when I literally had no place to live, companionship through good times and bad, and fantastic vacations to the Dominican Republic, and she has always been there for me. Thank you from the bottom of my heart, amiga.

I graduated from Columbia University in May 2000 and began teaching that August at the University of Delaware. I am extremely indebted to the university, my colleagues, and my friends who have allowed me to transition from a green twenty-eight-year-old to a more seasoned scholar and teacher. The history department has been extremely helpful to me, and I would like to thank my chair, Carole Haber, for making Delaware a great place to work. The university granted me leave to work on the manuscript in my third year, and this, combined with the Woodrow Wilson Career Enhancement Fellowship, gave me eighteen months to move my project from a dissertation to a book manuscript. Barbara Savage served as a mentor and friend while I was on leave, reading drafts of a very rough manuscript and pouring me tea in her kitchen in Mt. Airy, while becoming a dear friend and role model. Her own work astounds me, and her constant support is invaluable. Anne Boylan and Peter Kolchin welcomed me into the Department of History, prepared dinner for me, took me to jazz concerts, and worked hard to make me feel welcome. They were successful. Anne continues to be a friend and mentor. Her knowledge regarding nineteenth-century American and women's history is monumental, and her work informs my own. I am grateful for the encouragement and the many conversations, pep talks, and recommendations she has offered. Susan Strasser was the first person to send me an e-mail welcoming me to the department, and we have become good friends. She reminds me that the core values of the discipline should not be forgotten. Her attention to graduate and undergraduate teaching is remarkable and does not deter her from publication. We talk on the phone, eat lunch together, and laugh . . . a lot. Thank you, Susie. Wyunbari Maloba has also been a supportive friend and colleague. Maloba always checked in with me, made certain that things were going well, and offered counsel, Indian food, and friendship.

I would also like to thank Yale University Press for their support. I don't know how to thank Christine Stansell for her help and faith in my work. Her careful reading of the manuscript has pushed me to produce a better book. Her own work stands as a model for anyone interested in U.S. women's history. I would also like to thank Lara Heimert and Ellie Goldberg for guiding me through the early phases of manuscript preparation. I need also to thank my editor, Chris Rogers, and my copy editor, Ann Twombly. Ann's unapologetic edits were exactly what I needed and her insightful comments and questions have helped me to produce a much better book. My Germantown Friends School intern, Kate Mercogliano, spent the month of January 2005 helping me to prepare the manuscript for review. Leslie Harris read my manuscript and offered an unbiased critique of my work, for which I will always be in her debt. Not many scholars would offer as detailed a review as did Leslie. Every hour I spent editing and revising improved my book and strengthened our friendship. Many thanks and love to you, Leslie!

My accomplishments mean nothing without my family. So many of my family members have supported me, and my accomplishments, from childhood to the present. I would like to thank my father, Jacob Armstrong, for the periodic conversations about nineteenth-century Philadelphia, my grandfather Albert Armstrong, my uncles Stanley and the Reverend Albert Armstrong, my aunt, the Reverend Cathy Armstrong, and my cousins Tina, Yvette, and Jeanine. My extended kin consists of Mr. Willie and Mrs. Catherine Cromartie, Lisa Cromartie, my "play sister," Nneka Giles, my godparents, Frances and Peter Smith, and their daughter, Johari. Jamal and Natalie Smith have proven to be wonderful godparents to my son, showering him with attention and now a new playmate, Evan Parker Smith. Aichlee Bushnell saved my academic life by caring for my son in the summers of 2005 and 2006.

Ultimately this book is about hard-working women, and I have been surrounded by them my entire life. My grandmother Elsie Dorrington Harewood Armstrong, to whom this book is dedicated, showed me how to get something from nothing. She came to this country from Barbados as a young girl, was orphaned at an early age, and eventually married and raised a family. Although she did not complete a formal education, I have learned a great deal from her. Her ability to overcome family hardships, racism, sexism, and poverty always checks my momentary discontent. I miss her and think of her every day. I have learned similar lessons from my twin sister, Nicole Armstrong. She is the example of perseverance and determination, and she has refused to let anyone hold her back. As I finish this book, Nicole is completing her graduate degree from Bryn Mawr College. Many people told her this would be an impossibility, and she proved them all wrong. It has taken many years, but Nicole and I are now good friends, and I cherish the time and love she has given to me and my son. My mother, Frances Chudnick Armstrong, has been my backbone and rock for my entire life. She has always put her needs second to mine, always found a way to afford me the very best, from private school and ivy league educations to child care. She too is an example of hard work and dedication to the betterment of family. My mother always encouraged me, always nurtured me, and always supported me. In many ways, this book is as much hers as it is mine.

There are two important men in my life. Jeffrey Kim Dunbar entered my life in 1998 and made me believe in love again. His sensitivity, intellect, and deep commitment to family restored my faith in mankind. As a physician, he heals the sick; as a husband, he has healed my soul. I know how very fortunate I am to have found him and I love and cherish our life together.

And to my sweet bud of promise—Christian Andrew Dunbar, who arrived on this planet in July 2004 and has done nothing but enrich my life—I dedicate this book to you and your future. Mommy will do what her mother and grandmother have done—I will love you, nurture you, and move mountains for you if need be. Thank you for the gift of motherhood—loving you makes me complete.

Introduction

By the 1830s Amy Matilda Cassey was a well-known member of Philadelphia's African American elite. Cassey had grown up in New York, the daughter of a leading New York minister. She moved to Philadelphia, where she met and married a prominent barber, Joseph Cassey.[1] A member of the Philadelphia Female Anti-Slavery Society and several other philanthropic organizations, Cassey kept a friendship album—one of only four created by black Philadelphians still in existence today. It is a rare object that allows entrance into the personal sphere of "the higher classes of colored society," a social sphere whose inner life has largely been closed to historians. As friends inscribed thoughts in her album, they imbued poetry and prose with both personal and political meaning. Cassey's friend Sarah Louise Forten, a writer, activist, and the daughter of the wealthy sailmaker and entrepreneur James Forten, contributed several entries wishing Cassey happiness and success in motherhood:

> May those sweet buds of promise who sport at the knee,
> Be all that a mother could wish them to be,
> And those loved ones, who twine themselves close round the heart,
> From the counsels of virtue, may never depart.[2]

These were more than sentimental clichés. Happiness and a tightly knit family were not circumstances to be taken for granted among free African

American women of antebellum America. In the eyes of Forten, Cassey, and many other women of African descent, virtue, respectability, and autonomous motherhood had long been denied. Forten requested that all of Cassey's friends and family, especially those who contributed to her album, keep close to the "counsels of virtue."

Forten and Cassey represent the minority of antebellum African American women, as their class status and rigorous education positioned them in a burgeoning black elite and entitled them to its benefits. Free of the many burdens of poverty, Forten, Cassey and a handful of African American women in Philadelphia had the opportunity to engage in political and social activism, the most important of which was the antislavery movement. These women would enter an arena of politics inhabited by white men and women and contribute to the definition of abolition in its formative moments. Even though their own freedom, although precarious, had been secured shortly after the American Revolution, these women worked to secure the freedom of all men and women of African descent.

These elite women were unusual. Without the benefits of family wealth and reputation, the majority of African American women in Philadelphia gained freedom and its advantages through their own long and arduous work. As domestics, washerwomen, seamstresses, and fruit hucksters, they experienced emancipation in the later years of their lives, spending much of their energy securing the freedom of their children, their own "sweet buds of promise."

The pursuit of freedom took varied forms for African American women of the urban North; emancipation was a complex and time-consuming process. Whether elite or poverty-stricken, African American women regardless of their social or economic position embodied the great promise of emancipation.

This book explores how African American women in Philadelphia journeyed from enslavement to the precarious status of "free persons" during the decades preceding the Civil War. Current histories of the antebellum United States tell us much about the lives of free northern women from the colonial era through the Civil War. We have the pioneering work of historians such as Dorothy Sterling, Shirley Yee, and Julie Winch, which examine the careers of African American female activists; yet little has been written about the experiences of "regular women." Mine is the first book to focus on the experiences of northern African American women during the early years of the republic.[3]

I have chosen Philadelphia, but at the same time have kept in mind similar developments in New York and Boston. I argue that early nineteenth-century Philadelphia served as a rehearsal for emancipation in the post–Civil War era across the nation. Much of what took place in the decades following the Civil War had already taken shape in Philadelphia throughout the earlier part of the century. In many ways, antebellum Philadelphia represented a northern version of what the historian Willie Lee Rose called "a rehearsal for Reconstruction."

Tens of thousands of African American women occupied the streets, homes, alleys, churches, and organizations of the urban North. Indeed, throughout much of the antebellum period, they were the majority of Philadelphia's African American population. Their experiences as enslaved, indentured, and free people were different from those of their male counterparts and varied according to class. This book attempts to connect the forgotten to the remembered and bridge the gap between the illiterate indentured servant and the well-read antislavery activist. To do this, I incorporate new sources as well as provide different readings of well-known primary documents. Black women's friendship albums, made public only a few years ago, are multivocal sources on which to draw. Eighteenth-century labor contracts, personal correspondence, and church records explore the experience of the early republic through the eyes of African American women.

The generation of free black women who came of age in the 1830s were the recipients of freedom: its privileges, its terrible disappointments. Freedom for black Philadelphia dated back to the Revolutionary War: slaves were emancipated by Patriots through military service or were set free by slave masters unable to make a profit from the "peculiar institution." For most, however, slavery began to draw to a close in 1780 with the enactment of the Gradual Abolition Act, which initiated the process of formal emancipation in Pennsylvania.[4] Its effects were far from immediate. Everywhere in the North, gradual emancipation was halting and fitful. Although it was one of the first abolition bills passed in America, the 1780 law in fact did not free one single slave. The law stated that any person born in bondage on or before March 1, 1780, would remain enslaved for life; every child born of a slave mother after that date would be held in bondage for no more than twenty-eight years. The effects of what had been, until then, an ironclad, naturalized status were notable. Slavery slowly frayed and then unraveled. Most African Americans were free or had freed themselves by the end of the first decade of the nineteenth century; slavery continued to decline over a period of fifty years, and only eleven slaves lived in the city of Philadelphia by 1830.[5] Pennsylvania's system of gradual emancipation was similar to the abolition process in Massachusetts.

Although the institution of slavery in the North declined during the years of the early republic, African Americans were often released from enslavement and shuffled into temporary contracts of servitude. The transition was not from slavery to freedom but from slavery to forced servitude. As white indentured servitude had come to an end, African Americans were forced into a moribund system.[6] For many blacks, slavery was simply transformed into a new system of quasi freedom. Indentured servitude represented the end of enslavement, but it was a far cry from freedom.

Pennsylvania was the first state south of New England to dismantle slavery fairly quickly, and compared to New York, the effects were expeditious and dramatic. Yet for black Philadelphians fifty years was far from swift. The ending of slavery was a difficult and frustrating road for most African Americans.[7] Although the nation's birthplace moved quickly to join the antislavery movement of the 1830s, "freedom arrived by degrees" for African Americans in Philadelphia, as black women were among the last of its recipients.[8] The system of slavery and, later, servitude clung to the skirts of African American women in the city of brotherly love.

Philadelphia was arguably the most important community of free blacks, the largest in the North and an exciting, even exhilarating venture in free black community building. Black institutions created a unique space in which black women could mobilize, the first space in which African American women would organize themselves in postrevolutionary political culture.

In 1800 both enslaved and free African Americans numbered a little over four thousand. By 1830 the black population of Philadelphia had more than tripled, approaching fourteen thousand residents. By the eve of the Civil War, black residents of the city numbered more than twenty thousand, approximately 3.7 percent of the total population.[9] Visitors and inhabitants of Philadelphia have left behind descriptions of black Philadelphia, most of which are fairly bleak. It is true that many blacks lived in small shanties located in the crowded, dirty alleys of the city. But the early decades of the nineteenth century also witnessed a free black community rising above the degradation of abject poverty. Many free black families lived in the North and South Mulberry wards, a fairly poor district filled with small homes and a smattering of retailers. Blacks also lived in the Northern Liberties, which lay just outside the city and bordered North Mulberry. The Cedar Street corridor, located on the southern side of the city, became a hotspot for black families when cheap tenements were constructed in the Cedar and Locust wards as well as in West Southwark and Moyamensing. An additional attraction to this area was the presence of St. Thomas African Episcopal Church and Mother Bethel African Methodist Episcopal Church. These churches created a vibrant black community that continued to grow.[10]

The ratio of black women to men increased over time. Of the 14,000 black residents in Philadelphia in 1830, approximately 9,200 were women.[11] One historian estimates that in 1820 there were 1.40 black women for every black man. In 1830 the ratio increased to 1.43, and by 1840 there were 1.63 black women for every black man in the city of Philadelphia. Many African American men left the city for rural areas looking for farmwork. Some took to the open seas, finding employment as seamen, and returned to Philadelphia only for brief periods. In contrast to black men, women found domestic work much more available in the city; this work, and the opportunity for advancement, is most likely the cause of the imbalanced sex ratio in the city. Similar statistics hold true for New York during the antebellum years; there were two black women for every black man in that city.[12] Because African American women constituted the majority of the black population, their experiences and struggles for freedom deserve attention.

The infrastructure of free black institutions took root in Philadelphia during the early republic and paved the way for future generations of free blacks to build schools, churches, and mutual aid societies over the course of the entire nineteenth century. Other cities such as New York and Boston contained relatively large numbers of African Americans, who likewise began the business of building free black communities. The black elite of Philadelphia most likely owned their own homes, but their neighbors were a mixed sort, ranging from blacks who owned modest homes to the desperately poor who rented dark rooms in alleys.[13] Although elite societies and organizations created social barriers, geographic boundaries drew the wealthy and the poverty-stricken together within the African American community.

This book begins with the development of slavery in colonial Philadelphia. Like the other mid-Atlantic colonies, Pennsylvania evolved with the aid of slave labor, yet its capital and main port city attracted a settler very different from the ones drawn to New York and New Jersey. Pennsylvania provided an environment for settlers of modest backgrounds to find opportunity away from the backbreaking labor of tobacco cultivation in the South and the strict social codes of Puritan New England. Those who settled in "the best poor man's country," many of whom were Quakers, enjoyed the benefits of slave labor without becoming solely dependent upon it. The first chapter examines Philadelphia's relationship with the peculiar institution, the decline of slavery, and a new set of concerns and issues for black men and women in nineteenth-century Philadelphia.

The second chapter explores the end of slavery and the transition from black bondage to black servitude during the early years of the republic. As men and women of African descent moved toward partial freedom, they did so as indentured servants. Chapter 2 examines the ways in which black women maneuvered their manumission from indentured servitude. Demanding privileges such as education, autonomy regarding their children's lives, skills necessary for survival after emancipation and eventual freedom, African American women navigated the road to manumission through indenture contracts and the courts.

Chapter 3 illustrates the responsibility of freedom and the creation of respectability forged by black Philadelphians. As African American women organized mutual aid societies and built their churches, they policed themselves and the larger free black community through disciplinary tribunals within the black church. Black women used the church to protect the sanctity of marriage, protect women from abusive husbands, and maintain order and civility within the free black community. By threatening members of the church with expulsion for bad behavior or breach of church custom, these women used the might of the early black church to protect the image of free black Philadelphia.

Chapter 4 takes up the political work assumed by a generation of elite African American women. It examines the creation of the first women's interracial antislavery society in the country and the experiences of black women abolitionists. As women of African descent moved from slaves to servants to political activists, their experiences were frustrating yet rewarding. As members of the black elite, women such as Margaretta Forten and Sarah Mapps Douglass were invited to participate in the work of the Philadelphia Female Anti-Slavery Society. Focusing on abolition and improving conditions for free blacks in the city, black and white women worked together in a political organization for the first time. African American women, however, became frustrated with the racism they found in abolitionist circles and whites' loss of interest in protecting the civil liberties of free black men and women in the city.

Chapter 5 explores the social and political demands made by African American women in antebellum Philadelphia and beyond. By examining periodicals and spiritual narratives, I explore the diverse ways in which black women of the urban North used print culture.

As political and social organizations brought African American women together, elaborate networks of friends and colleagues created a private social community that often overlapped with the political. Chapter 6 provides a window into these private worlds through examining black friendship albums. As the albums were passed from friend to friend along the East Coast, the display of immaculate penmanship, proper grammar and spelling, and respectable prose allowed African Americans to reinforce their respectability within their own social circles. Because the albums themselves traveled from Baltimore to Philadelphia and as far north as Boston, educated African Americans established a national protocol regarding discussions about freedom, womanhood, and respectability. The private arena of the album not only served as a badge of respectability but also provided black women with an additional platform on which to reconstruct their image and expand their sentimental relationships.

The conclusion stresses the political, social, and economic gains made by African American women of the urban North, highlighting the end of American slavery and the acknowledgment of new problems and concerns that would persist well into the twentieth century. This, then, is a book about how slavery, servitude, and freedom informed the lives of African American women both rich and poor.

I

Slavery and the "Holy Experiment"

Black Alice was born in Pennsylvania in 1686, just five years after William Penn received a charter for the "new world." She lived for 116 years and recounted her life's story shortly before her death. Early settlers in Pennsylvania knew Alice as a griot, or trusted storyteller, who recounted not only her own story but also the history of Philadelphia, as an enslaved woman of African descent.

Her tale began with her parents, who were brought from Barbados aboard the ship *Isabella;* Alice was thus one of the earliest black settlers born in Philadelphia. She lived within the city's limits until the age of ten, when her master relocated her to nearby Dunk's Ferry, where she lived out the remainder of her life.[1] Alice watched the infant colony become the nation's birthplace while witnessing the transformation of the land, inhabitants, and customs. She told of the days when the wilderness of Philadelphia was filled with its indigenous inhabitants and later by men such as William Penn, James Logan, and other well-known settlers. She lived through the French and Indian War, the American Revolution, and the signing of the Constitution while watching hundreds and then thousands of black men and women come into the port city as slaves, servants, refugees, and free people. At the time of her death in 1802, Alice lived in one of the largest free black communities in the new nation, one in which the final and feeble hold of African slavery had all but ended.

The majority of monographs that examine the early history of Philadelphia focus on prominent colonists such as William Penn and Benjamin Franklin, or the city that eventually became home to the Constitution. Alice's account, as well as court documents and indenture papers, provides historians with a "different" Philadelphia. Race, gender, enslavement, and geographical location played a crucial role in shaping the experiences of these early Philadelphians. For Alice and many other enslaved women of African descent, life was unstable at best. To be an African slave woman in early Philadelphia meant that one had to work hard, be flexible, and think shrewdly. The experiences of black women, who had little power and authority over their own lives and those of their family members, hinged on domestic labor, kinship networks, and the ability to bear children. These factors, as well as the development of Philadelphia into a major seaport, a war, and a shift in the law, would influence black women's eventual transition from slavery to freedom.

Slavery found its way to the Delaware Valley before the arrival of William Penn in 1682. Enslaved by the Dutch, Swedes, and Finns, men and women of African descent first lived and worked along the shores of the Delaware River as well as in the hinterland some fifty years before Penn founded his colony. The first significant European settlement in the region was New Sweden, governed by Johan Printz, known to have an African in his service. The Dutch West India Company also used African slaves along the Delaware River throughout the 1660s.[2] Historians have been able to recover very little regarding the lives of these men and women or of their African ancestors, for no census was ever taken in Philadelphia during the very early period. We can assume, however, that African slaves who cleared the land and engaged in domestic work were relatively few in number and that they were brought against their will to the Americas. Indeed, very little changed for the men and women of African descent upon the arrival of Penn and his fellow Quakers. Although Penn proclaimed the colony to be a holy experiment, a refuge from religious intolerance and economic disparity in England, African slavery was an acceptable institution among the founding fathers of the young colony. By 1770 there were approximately six thousand slaves living in Pennsylvania.[3]

The end of the colonial period, however, did bring about widespread change for African Americans. As the Revolutionary War neared its end, Pennsylvanians began to manumit their slaves. The Gradual Abolition Act of 1780 convinced those residents who were hesitant that they had no choice but to release their slaves. Although details are difficult to uncover, African Americans experienced a tremendous transformation during the colonial period as they moved from slavery to freedom. Philadelphia, home to the Constitutional

Convention, took the lead in this metamorphosis, becoming the bedrock of free black communities throughout the urban North.

The women of African descent who lived in colonial Philadelphia experienced these changes while they began the early phases of creating free motherhood and womanhood, for themselves and generations of women not yet born. Although African American women such as Black Alice generally spent most of their lives as domestics in the employ of a white master, their lives differed greatly according to their residence and the decades in which they lived.[4] It is clear that by the eve of the Revolution, African American women had more advantages than did their mothers and grandmothers. Although slavery clung to the apron strings of its female residents, its grasp was eventually loosened, which gave new meaning to William Penn's holy experiment.

Life in Colonial Pennsylvania

In 1684 a ship named the *Isabella* docked on the Delaware, and its cargo of 150 Africans was quickly unloaded. The ship had come from Bristol, England, and its cargo had more than likely been purchased somewhere in the West Indies, perhaps Barbados. European colonists had settled in Pennsylvania only some three years earlier, yet they were eager to sift through and eventually purchase the ship's merchandise.[5] There was a great deal of work to be accomplished in the infant colony, and the majority of Quaker settlers found themselves ill prepared to complete the work without the use of slave and servant labor.

The colony of Pennsylvania began when the Crown granted a charter to the young William Penn in March 1681. Penn managed to persuade the financially strapped Charles II to grant him approximately 45,000 square miles of land as payment for a debt owed to Penn's father. Later Penn would convince six hundred investors to support the colony and approximately four thousand people to emigrate to Pennsylvania.[6] By the eighteenth century, Penn had sold nearly three-quarters of a million acres of Pennsylvania land, and the colony was an instant success.[7]

Penn began to map out the holy experiment, which would prove different from the New England colonies to the north and the plantation societies of the south. Pennsylvania would become a colony for the "common person," allowing the second sons of Englishmen a chance for prosperity, as well as the sons and daughters of the impoverished a chance for survival. In addition to securing the charter from the king, Penn convinced the Duke of York to concede the land known as Delaware.[8] This addition would give the colony an outlet to the sea and would thus secure the future of a vibrant economy that was based on a mix of trade and agriculture. By the eighteenth century, Philadelphia would become a major seaport, engaged in all aspects of commercial trade, including the sale of Africans.

Penn set out to attract settlers to his new colony through understated advertisement. A brochure explained the design of the colony and the financial success and religious tolerance to be found there. But Penn was quite honest with his potential residents about the difficulties presented to early colonists. Though opportunities for success would be afforded to the settlers, life in a young colony would most likely be difficult—but surely Penn's colony would be more tolerable than the swampy, malaria-ridden marshes of Virginia or the religious rigidity of New England. Pennsylvania was a middle colony in many ways.[9]

Having sent his cousin William Markham to govern the colony in his stead during the first year, Penn prepared himself for his first trip to Pennsylvania in 1682. His journey to the New World was similar to many of the other sojourns made by the English across the Atlantic Ocean. It took three months to complete the journey, and Penn was fortunate to have survived the trip: while he was on board the *Welcome,* a smallpox epidemic killed thirty passengers. Penn had escaped the dreaded disease as a child, and, according to passenger accounts, he went to the aid of his fellow passengers who succumbed to it.[10] Having survived that first trip to Pennsylvania, Penn would remain in the colony for two years before returning to England. The proprietor of Pennsylvania would not return until 1699, when he stayed only a brief time before going home.[11]

Penn demonstrated notable concern regarding the relationship between English colonists and the Lenni-Lenape, also known as the Delaware Indians. Penn appeared less hostile to the Indians than other colonial proprietors, specifically those in the Chesapeake region. Interested in an amicable relationship, Penn sent word to the Delaware that he intended to treat them "fairly" in the hopes of avoiding tension and, even worse, bloodshed. Penn appeared interested in the culture of his new neighbors, and he spent a significant amount of time studying the lives and communal rituals of local Native Americans. As the relationships between early settlers and Native Americans in places such as Virginia and New England grew steadily worse, Pennsylvanians and the Delaware kept up a fragile, more cordial exchange with each other. Many Native Americans from the Chesapeake region fled to Pennsylvania during the later years of the seventeenth century, attempting to avoid the conflict and bloodshed between southeastern natives and the English brought about by Bacon's Rebellion.[12] There were fewer English settlers migrating to Pennsylvania than to other infant colonies and that fact, along with a more gradual period of expansion, combined with Penn's peace-keeping efforts to maintain a relatively stable relationship between European settlers and natives of the Delaware Valley.[13] This stability would, however, change by the early decades of the eighteenth century.

Penn spent very little time in the new colony, and after he set sail in 1684 for England, he left much of the governing of Pennsylvania in the hands of his secretary, James Logan, a businessman and extremely successful land speculator. Like many new colonists, Logan purchased large tracts of land, and as immigrants began to pour into Philadelphia and the surrounding territory, Native American villages were gradually displaced.[14] By the second quarter of the eighteenth century, the Delaware Indians had been pushed toward the Susquehanna River, and the tension between white settlers and the Lenape grew worse as the fur trade in New York and western Pennsylvania brought the Iroquois Indians to great prominence. European settlers convinced the Iroquois to use their immense power in controlling the smaller Delaware villages, eventually forcing them to abandon their land. By 1742 a series of unscrupulous treaties and laws absorbed the last bit of land that belonged to the Delaware Indians between the Lehigh and Delaware Rivers. They were driven off in borrowed wagons in disgrace and despair.[15]

As the Delaware Indians were dispossessed of their land, colonists found a new need for agricultural laborers, a need met by a simultaneous increase in the number of imported African slaves to Pennsylvania. Although the absolute numbers remained relatively low throughout the early decades of the century, the increase over the course of twenty-five years was fivefold. In 1730 approximately twenty slaves were imported annually, the majority of whom came from the West Indies or South Carolina. The number jumped to thirty slaves per year by the 1740s and rose to one hundred slaves annually by 1756.[16] A preference for European indentured servants explains the small increase in slave imports from 1730 to 1750, and many shopkeepers and city merchants sought out English servants, already familiar with the language and customs of the early colonists. In addition, a population explosion in Europe prompted a massive influx of European men and women to the colonies. Thus, white labor was plentiful in the early eighteenth century.

Innkeepers and widows preferred slave women to slave men in the city. This of course was due to their need for domestic help for housekeeping and child-care duties. Although slave men were preferred among merchants and craftsmen, slave women were always needed to assist in the home and occasionally in the shops. Female slaves had to be flexible, for their work was always multifaceted; the majority of enslaved women, however, worked as domestics in Philadelphia, creating a concentration of female slaves in the city. Male slaves residing in Philadelphia were often involved in the trades. If a slaveholder owned a residence in the city and a farm in the country, it was likely that he kept female slaves in a domestic capacity in the city, whereas he used male slaves for farmwork.[17]

As African slavery became entrenched within the colony, the Pennsylvania Assembly passed the first codes regarding its practice in the commonwealth in 1700. There was to be no confusion regarding the legality of slave ownership, lifelong servitude was to be permitted, and special courts were established to try African slaves as well as a handful of free black men and women.[18] Regional and international events also affected the African slave trade in Pennsylvania. In 1712 a slave conspiracy in New York alarmed many slaveholders throughout the mid-Atlantic colonies. In April of that year a group of approximately twenty slaves set fire to a building in New York City, later attacking any white man who attempted to put out the fire. With knives, axes, and guns, the slaves murdered nine whites and injured many others. As white New Yorkers gained control of the situation, thirteen slaves were hanged, three were burned at the stake, one was broken on the wheel, one starved to death in chains, and six committed suicide before their assigned deaths. Although horrified by the violence, white Pennsylvanians remained committed to the right of property ownership, specifically the right to own slaves. Pennsylvanians chose not to terminate human bondage, but to curtail it. To discourage the importation of Africans into the colony, an import duty was placed on each slave brought into Pennsylvania. The tax proved successful in maintaining a relatively small African population among an influx of European indentured servants to the colony.[19]

A few Pennsylvanians beginning to rethink the moral and economic problems of slaveholding found themselves confronting that institution already deeply embedded in Pennsylvania. Manumitting one's slave in the eighteenth century was no simple act, which made the possibility of black freedom difficult. By 1726 the Pennsylvania Assembly demanded that a bond be placed on the head of every emancipated African. If a slaveholder wished to manumit his slave, for religious or financial reasons, he was forced to present a £30 bond, since free blacks in colonial Pennsylvania were considered to be a nuisance or, worse, a danger. Pennsylvania lawmakers made their opinions regarding free blacks clear: "'tis found by experience that free Negroes are an idle, slothful people and often prove burdensome to the neighborhood and afford ill examples to other Negroes."[20]

The 1726 law also allowed all able-bodied men and women of African descent to be bound out to labor without pay; justices were permitted to bind out emancipated or freeborn black children without the consent of their parents, girls until the age of twenty-one and boys until the age of twenty-four.[21] Blacks who were considered vagrants could be indentured, and a free black man could be sold back into slavery if he married a white woman. Additionally, the tax on the importation of black slaves to Pennsylvania was lowered from £5 to £2, which made slaveholding more affordable for middle-income Philadelphians. The Quaker Ralph Sandiford wrote, "We have Negroes flocking in upon us since the duty on them is reduced to 40s per head for their importation, which makes a revenue of the evil instead of removing it; for we have frequently slaves sold twice a week in sight of my habitation which is in the center of the city."[22] Thus, although European labor continued to be preferred during the early and middle decades of the eighteenth century, African slavery slowly gained acceptance. This acceptance would eventually place slavery and freedom at the center of Philadelphia's religious, political, and philosophical debates.

The French and Indian War prompted a drastic increase in the number of slaves living in Philadelphia and its environs. As the war dragged on, many English servants either enlisted or ran off to join the military campaign, often without the permission or knowledge of their masters. The scarcity of available free white workers forced owners to turn to African slaves. Between 1756 and 1766 approximately thirteen hundred slaves arrived on the banks of the Delaware River.[23] Before the war, the majority of African slaves who resided in Pennsylvania had been "seasoned" in the West Indies, normally for a period of several years. The mid-eighteenth century, however, saw a rise in the number of slaves shipped directly from Africa, most of whom were purchased by wealthy artisans who resided close to or within the commercial center of the city.[24]

Slavery in Colonial Pennsylvania

In 1751 Ben Franklin explained the supposed benefits of slaveholding over the servant trade when he wrote, "Slaves may be kept as long as Man pleases, or has Occasion for their Labour; while hired Men are continually leaving their Master."[25] Although this premise pushed southern plantation owners and small farmers to cling to the institution of slavery, this was not exactly the case for white Pennsylvanians. Economic factors prompted many, especially in Philadelphia County, to invest in servants rather than African slaves. There was a significant investment involved in purchasing a slave; the necessary capital was simply not available to all Philadelphians. Throughout the eighteenth century, the average price for a servant was £14, but the actual purchase price could be more than three times that amount.[26]

Those in need of service were often discouraged by the cost, and they opted for white servants instead.

Slaveholders acknowledged the additional financial drawback of feeding and clothing slaves, as well as providing basic necessities to any offspring they produced. Unable to participate in hard labor, children were often seen as a financial drain, yet another drawback. The alternative was to hire European indentured servants for three to four years. The short term appealed both to those lacking the initial capital necessary to purchase an African slave and to those who were in search of short-term investments. Aside from the day-to-day responsibilities of caring for slaves or servants, there were taxes imposed on both slaves and servants. In Philadelphia County, masters who owned servants over the age of fifteen were forced to pay a tax of 2s 3d. If a master owned a slave in Philadelphia, however, the tax was 6s; the financial risk and loss were greater.[27]

The young colony also held slaveholders responsible for the lives of their slaves; if a slave became ill or aged, the financial loss could be great. Masters often dismissed elderly slaves, leaving them to care for themselves in the alleys of Philadelphia. Residents of the city must have complained about the growing number of discarded slaves, for in 1726 the Pennsylvania Assembly passed a law forcing slaveholders to care for their slaves who were elderly or infirm.

Despite a relatively small slave trade, traders in colonial Pennsylvania received lucrative profits from the sale of human cargo. Although the number of African slaves was small before the 1730s, the middle decades of the century brought financial gain to slave catchers and traders alike. The majority of slaves received in Philadelphia were "waste" slaves, poor in quality and more than likely unsuitable for the arduous life of a southern farm slave.[28] Farmers in the colonial South needed slaves who were healthy and strong, able to work the cash crops of tobacco and rice. Southern planters purchased these valuable slaves; left behind to populate northern colonies such as Pennsylvania were men and women who were physically less desirable. The increased demand for slave labor throughout the era of the French and Indian War resulted in the shipping of larger cargoes of slaves to the Philadelphia port. During the 1750s and 1760s many of Philadelphia's black residents came directly from the shores of West Africa, bringing with them the memories and practices of life across the Atlantic Ocean.

African slaves were expected to be versatile and complete any and all work demanded of them. The nature of their work depended on their location. Slaves who were suited for labor in both the city and the countryside were seen as especially valuable. One of the earliest colonial newspapers, the *Pennsylvania Gazette,* concentrated on news in Philadelphia and the surrounding areas, advertising the sale of property such as homes, horses, and slaves. A 1747 advertisement appeared in the *Gazette* for a "Likely young Negro Wench, fit for town or country."[29] As a young female slave familiar with the varied skills necessary for domestic work, she most likely would have fetched a reasonable price. Also mentioned in the advertisement was her proficiency as a "good cook." Superior culinary skills as well as the ability to iron, wash, and sew were seen as necessary in both the city and the country, and a deficiency in any of these skills could lead to the sale of a slave, as seen in a 1758 advertisement: "A Likely handy Negroe Wench, about 30 years old, very healthy, has been bred up both to Town and Country Work, she is Country born and is sold by her master because she does not answer for a Cook, for which she was bought. Enquire at the New printing Office."[30] Strong performance was essential, for the lives of female slaves could be uprooted at a moment's notice.

Within the fairly large colony of Pennsylvania, slavery in the hinterland proved to be a very different experience from that in the city. In rural Pennsylvania, the majority of owners were wealthy farmers, dependent on slave labor for fieldwork. Although few rural tavern keepers and craftsmen held African men and women in bondage, most slaves did farmwork: chopping wood, plowing fields, and picking apples and harvesting other produce, as well as domestic work.

Unlike the city of Philadelphia, which saw a decline in slave ownership following the French and Indian War, rural Pennsylvania at that time witnessed signs of increased slaveholding. As early abolitionist sentiment grew in Philadelphia, it eventually made its way to the hinterland, led by the Society of Friends in Chester, Pennsylvania. The Friends of Chester was one of the first local meetings before 1730 to suggest a ban on slavery.[31] This suggestion did not take root, however, and many whites outside the city turned their demand from European indentured servants to African slaves.

In the city, slave owners held on average two to three slaves per household. This statistic demonstrates how improbable it was that a slave family would live together under the same roof.[32] Whereas several slave families might reside together on the larger farms of the colonial South, slave families in Philadelphia had to visit one another, which, depending on one's master, could be a difficult undertaking. Although Philadelphia was a "walking city," masters often set strict guidelines for visitation. Visits were usually infrequent and brief; if a member of an urban slave family was sold to the country, it was unlikely that family members would be able to see him or her. According to Philadelphia probate records, only two of every five black women lived in a household with a black man.[33] Marriage records from the Anglican Church indicate that very few married couples actually cohabited. In addition to high mortality rates due to disease and poor living conditions, lack of cohabitation prevented the black community from reproducing itself at a steady rate throughout the eighteenth century. Indeed, no slave population anywhere in colonial American reproduced itself until the end of the eighteenth century.

Although black men and women often did not live in the same households, it appears that a significant black community, both enslaved and free, had consolidated by the late eighteenth century, which kept African Americans in touch with each other. The same cannot be said for blacks in rural Pennsylvania, however, where large tracts of land often separated men and women. But country life had its benefits. There were more men in the country; the need for those who could handle hard physical labor placed black men in the majority. Throughout the middle decades of the eighteenth century, only one of every three black men lived with a black woman; fewer lived with their own children.[34] Women of African descent in rural Pennsylvania could expect to live with their children, but not with their husbands. For instance, 70 percent of black women listed in eastern Chester County (now Delaware County) appeared on household inventories that included black children, most likely their own children. Infant mortality rates in the countryside were significantly lower than those of the city.[35] In the city, in contrast, masters often sold black children to eliminate the expense of raising them. Thus, Robert Towers advertised in 1764: "A Likely Negroe woman, about 24 Years of Age and her Child, a Boy about three Years old, she has had the Small-pox, is a brisk handy Wench, can wash and iron, do any Kind of House–work and is fit for Town or Country Business. She is sold because of her having a Child, and not for any Fault, they will be sold together or separate."[36]

Towers explained that the woman was a good worker, but she had made the mistake of having a child. It is impossible to know whether her offspring was from a consensual union or a product of unwanted sexual advances from her master or some other male member of the Towers family. What we can see, though, is that her reproductive abilities proved to be a liability, and she would most likely be removed from her family and friends to the home of a new owner, possibly without her child—for who would want to take an infant or a toddler?

But although life in the city had its problems, many men and women of African descent preferred to reside within its borders, where there were better opportunities for freedom and the improvement of life's conditions. In the 1740s a handful of Quakers in the city reached out to the black community by offering educational instruction. Anthony Benezet and John Woolman, known for their strong antislavery sentiments, opened private academies for a small number of black pupils. As freedom became less elusive during the

later decades of the eighteenth century and as larger numbers of black Philadelphians pulled their resources together, the city became a place of refuge
and of hope for the future.

The Society of Friends served as the catalyst for the eventual destruction
of African slavery in Philadelphia. For nearly a century, Quakers in the Pennsylvania colony ran their businesses and governed townships with the assistance of slave labor. In the 1670s George Fox, cofounder of the Society
of Friends, advised his fellow Quakers eventually to move away from the
system of oppression against Africans. Most Quaker colonists agreed with
Fox's admonitions to treat their slaves humanely and to Christianize them,
yet they ignored his advice regarding emancipation.[37] In 1688 the Germantown Quakers were the first among Pennsylvania Friends to declare their
opposition to the institution of slavery. Those Quakers who saw slavery as
incompatible with a religion that valued equality and consensus building
were labeled troublemakers, were expelled from the Society, and watched
their small businesses run into financial ruin. Wealthy Quakers controlled the
Assembly, and it was the Assembly that restricted manumission throughout
the colonial era. However much the immorality of slavery may have tugged
at the consciences of Quakers, their need for labor far outweighed the cries
of righteous indignation heard from a minority of Pennsylvanians.

Quakers outside the city were the first to formally request mandatory African emancipation among the Friends. As early as 1711 Friends from Chester
County repeatedly asked the Yearly Meeting to stop members from purchasing new slaves. A definitive ruling on slavery was never issued, however,
and the Yearly Meeting simply urged fellow Quakers not to participate in
the trade. Several decades passed before the requests made by the Chester
County Friends and other Quakers began to receive wider support.

By the 1730s the revivalism of the Great Awakening encouraged some of
Pennsylvania's residents to rethink the morality of human bondage. A new
generation of Quaker leaders emerged in the 1750s, as a group of younger
men disheartened by past decisions of the Society became a cohort with considerable power. Bothered by boastful displays of wealth in homes, clothes,
and other material goods, this new generation of Quakers pushed for reform
in the Society that would return it to humility and piety.[38] Hundreds of members were disowned throughout the middle decades of the century, which created room for a new kind of Quakerism, a Quakerism that would eventually
refuse to allow members to participate in the slave trade.

In a campaign led by John Woolman and Anthony Benezet, the Yearly Meeting eventually accepted the requests made by the Chester County Friends

years earlier. John Woolman, a shopkeeper from Burlington County, New Jersey, who pared down his small business to devote much of his time to traveling in the ministry and spreading abolitionist sentiment, worked with Anthony Benezet. Benezet was born in France and immigrated to Pennsylvania from England in 1731.[39] Woolman launched a virulent attack against slaveholding and its evils. These two men, along with a handful of "radical" Quaker abolitionists, convinced Pennsylvania Friends to abandon slaveholding because it represented an affront to Quakerism. Slavery stood as a symbol of ostentation, creating a wealthy slave-owning elite that challenged the essential notion of Quaker egalitarianism. Emancipation was part of a larger effort to purify the Society, not necessarily for the sake of black equality.

They called not only for an end to the purchase of human chattel, but also for formal instruction of all Africans held in bondage. Woolman and Benezet argued that education would prepare the African man and woman for emancipation and thus allow for an easier transition into a free society for both white and black Pennsylvanians. In 1755 the Yearly Meeting warned Friends against importing slaves from abroad or purchasing them locally, and three years later it asked all the local monthly meetings to refrain from any involvement with the slave trade and to restrict all positions of authority to those who conformed to the new policies. Still, it was sixteen years before the Yearly Meeting expelled members of the Society for slave ownership.[40]

Although Anthony Benezet was one of the first Philadelphians to teach young black children in his home, the Anglican Church also paved the way for black education in Philadelphia. Through an introduction to Christian doctrine, marriage, and baptism, the Anglican Church gradually drew men and women of African descent into its fold. In the early years of the eighteenth century the Anglican-based Society for the Propagation of the Gospel (SPG) placed missionaries in the city and the countryside. Faced with hostility from slaveholders, missionaries reassured white Philadelphians that a Christian education would not "ruin" their property. According to SPG missionaries, Christian instruction would save souls and reinforce obedience, not emancipation. This was a hard concept for white slaveholders to follow, however, and very few Anglican ministers demonstrated an intense desire to Christianize the growing number of slaves before the 1740s.[41]

The First Great Awakening shifted religious attitudes across the country. The reconsideration of the morality of slavery placed some white slaveholders in a quandary: they attempted to follow a Christian path while holding on to their valuable property. For the first time significant numbers of Africans were Christianized, as Methodist evangelicals invited their slaves to participate in baptismal ceremonies and to attend church services. Methodists recognized anyone's conversion, regardless of economic status or race. New Light Presbyterians, Methodists, and Baptists also welcomed the opportunity to convert "black heathens," and although the majority of Africans would not convert until the later part of the century, many slaves were accepted into the Christian fold. Nevertheless, their inclusion did not release them from the shackles of slavery. Slave masters, particularly in the South, often forced their slaves to attend religious services on Sundays and to spend the rest of the week laboring. Still, slaves across the colonies who heard about or participated in these more egalitarian religious practices were influenced by a new religious dogma, and for the first time they saw their own rights to freedom in a European context. The revivals acknowledged divinity in every man and woman.[42]

The combination of Quaker antislavery sentiment and evangelicalism brought a religious energy to Philadelphia and its environs. The itinerant preacher George Whitefield arrived in 1740, reiterating the need to Christianize and educate the city's black residents. While in the city, Whitefield announced the opening of two schools for residents of African descent in Pennsylvania; one would be in Philadelphia. Although Whitefield never called for the eradication of slavery and in fact owned slaves himself, he remained concerned about the souls of all people, including black men and women. Robert Bolton, a musician and the leader of a well-known dancing ensemble, assisted Whitefield's call to education by dismantling his music school and opening a school intended for black children. His school soon enrolled several black children, but Philadelphia was not yet prepared to deal with the formal education of black youth. Bolton was arraigned on charges of ignoring the colony's slave codes.[43] Benezet continued to teach black children in his home, tutoring both enslaved and free children of color. From 1750 onward, he instructed black children in the same disciplines as their white Quaker counterparts. Although the number of his students was small, the mere existence of formal instruction for black children during the colonial era was promising.

Wartime chaos in the 1760s and 1770s brought change, hope, and disappointment to black Philadelphians. As white indentured servants left their masters to join in the military campaign of the French and Indian War, thousands of blacks poured into the seaport and were eagerly purchased by whites in the city and the countryside. Even so, many Philadelphia Quakers began to emancipate their slaves. By the 1780s freedom from British control was secured and emancipation for Philadelphia's men and women of African descent appeared imminent.

When the colonists revolted, the British threatened their economic stability by undermining slave ownership. In a bold proclamation in November 1775, Lord Dunmore, royal governor of Virginia, declared the colony of Virginia in a state of rebellion and placed it under martial law. His offer of freedom to slaves and bonded servants who gave their services to the king enraged slaveholders.[44] George Washington and his comrades initially refused to arm men of color, so thousands of slaves took flight throughout the Chesapeake in search of British camps and freedom. Although Dunmore's proclamation applied only to men old enough to bear arms, male slaves often took flight with their wives and children, hoping to secure freedom for their entire families.

The news of Dunmore's proclamation sent slaveholders across the colonies into a panic, turning what was, for some, mild animosity against the British control into rabid patriotism. If slavery was challenged in Virginia, it could also be threatened in Pennsylvania. After decades of Quaker antislavery agitation, and now this challenge to the practice, black men and women in Pennsylvania saw the door to manumission open wider. Philadelphia slaveholders feared rebellion and violence, and rumors spread quickly about angry slaves threatening to aid the British cause. But most slaves and servants simply waited, monitoring the progress of the war before they made any risky decisions. Offers of immediate freedom to slaves must have been attractive, but the decision for free black men and women about their allegiance was much more complex.

In 1776 British troops landed at Head of Elk, Maryland, and pushed north toward Philadelphia. On September 11, 1776, George Washington's Continental army was badly beaten at Brandywine, and Cornwallis quickly moved to occupy the city of Philadelphia. Many white residents fled to the countryside as three thousand British troops marched into the city.[45] Chaos and fear gripped the city as smallpox and camp fever devastated both British and Patriot troops. The cost of goods skyrocketed, and commodities such as coffee, flour, and salt were either too expensive to purchase or impossible to find.[46] When whites left the city, they took as much property as possible, including their slaves, many of whom knew the details of Lord Dunmore's proclamation. Freedom for Philadelphia's slaves would not entail walking hundreds of miles through the swampy marshes of war-torn Virginia. Instead, simply walking out of their masters' homes, down the narrow streets of the city to the British camps, could mean freedom.

It is certain that most slaves believed in the British promise of immediate emancipation, and the presence of all-black British regiments, such as the Black Guides and Pioneers, the Black Brigade, and the Ethiopian Regiment, must have been encouraging to African bondsmen. A slave could also take advantage of the chaos that accompanied the war, however, by simply running away and hiding until the end of the military campaign, thus avoiding having to choose sides. As black men and women left their masters in the South and the hinterland of the mid-Atlantic, many arrived in Philadelphia and New York looking for refuge. The fugitive slave population doubled in Philadelphia during the war and increased fourfold in New York City.[47] Although men were the first to take advantage of the chaos of war, women were quick to follow suit. The promise of freedom upon reaching British camps was certainly a daunting and dangerous wager: slave women and their children were vulnerable to cruel and inhumane treatment. But for some, freedom was worth the risk. Black women and children found ways to earn a subsistence living throughout the course of the Revolution. As washerwomen, cooks, and prostitutes, women did whatever was necessary to remain attached to the British camps.

For free men and women of color, the decision to support the British was just as difficult. Although these men and women were no longer or may never have been human chattel, they were not considered citizens, nor did they enjoy the majority of privileges allotted to white colonists. Men such as James Forten, a wealthy black sailmaker, would eventually proclaim allegiance to the Patriot cause.[48] Only a small number of free blacks participated in the revolutionary struggle by volunteering their services to American troops. A handful of free black men volunteered for the Pennsylvania navy; yet the assistance offered by the free black community of Philadelphia went unrecognized, since the army at first was unwilling to accept black men into the fledgling military. Only after 1779, when army officials had a difficult time recruiting and retaining white men, did they turn their attention to free blacks. The Continental army finally reversed its decision regarding the enlistment of blacks, slave or free. Although South Carolina and Georgia both objected to this reversal, nearly five thousand black men had served in the army by the war's end.[49]

Black men normally served in all-black brigades, but in the Continental army the Patriots interspersed black men among white troops. Often, though, black men in the mixed units were noncombatants, manual laborers who cleared roads and cooked and cleaned for white troops. Slaves were forced to work every day, whereas free blacks worked every other, and enslaved men, like those owned by confederates in the Civil War, fought in place of their masters.[50] Although a few black men such as James Forten were later revered as revolutionary heroes, the majority of black Philadelphians who fought in the war were never recognized for their contributions.

As the war came to a close and Patriot troops secured their independence from British control, black men and women attempted to grasp their own freedom from their masters. Between three thousand and four thousand blacks left America through the New York seaport. Many would find their way to England; others would relocate to Nova Scotia and Sierra Leone. Relocation was difficult: they confronted racism in Europe and the harsh life of pioneers in Africa. But for those several thousand men and women, the possibility of freedom outweighed any obstacle.[51]

Although historians attribute abolition in Pennsylvania to the principles behind the American Revolution, it was not the primary reason for slavery's demise. In Philadelphia slavery was in the process of being dismantled before the outbreak of the Revolution, for both white Quakers and men and women of African descent had begun to tear it down. The political ideology of the Revolution did provide a secular language to critique black slavery, but in itself it certainly did not provide for immediate emancipation in Pennsylvania. Available cheap and abundant white labor following the war pushed city residents to abandon the expensive practice of slaveholding. But slaveholders in the countryside, some of whom had talked of abolishing slavery in the early eighteenth century, held on to the peculiar institution through the 1770s.[52]

Philadelphians could purchase slaves at public auction throughout the 1770s. British ships captured by privateers were brought to the Philadelphia port to sell off their cargo. This was the case in 1779, when the ship *General Greene,* loaded with coffee, molasses, sugar, and slaves, found eager buyers.[53] And although Quakers were freeing their slaves, non-Quakers continued to import black men and women. As the Society of Friends released their slaves in rural Pennsylvania, Anglicans, Episcopalians, and Presbyterians remained detached from abolitionist sentiment, especially if their trade was dependent on human labor.

Still, it was a major shift. Throughout the chaos of the Revolutionary War, artisans ended their relationship with the system of bound labor. Many artisans served in the militia, but their businesses were disrupted and teetered on the brink of bankruptcy. Upon their return from war, artisans were much more willing to hire labor, now a cheaper alternative. With a glut of white laborers, owners found ways to end their connections to slave labor without manumitting their chattel: by death (either their own or the death of their slaves), by a slave's escape, or by selling their slaves to slave traders.[54]

Slavery would live on for only another twenty-five years in Pennsylvania. (It was more long-lived in the neighboring states of New Jersey and Delaware.) This was due to the Gradual Abolition Act of 1780. This monumental piece of legislation was one of the first legislative acts to abolish slavery in America or anywhere in the world. The act, along with the revival of the Pennsylvania Abolition Society in 1784, created a hostile environment for slaveholders in Philadelphia. Although founded earlier in the century, the Pennsylvania Abolition Society was revived and became a watchdog organization, ensuring that thousands of men and women of African descent were set free under the provisions of the new law.[55]

But how did the American Revolution and the birth of a new nation affect the lives of black women? The historian Linda Kerber's construct of the republican mother explains how, in the postrevolutionary years, Americans accommodated republican ideology. Kerber suggests that republican motherhood "merged the domestic domain . . . with the new public ideology of individual responsibility and civic virtue." Yet it was "a deeply ambivalent ideology," writes Anne Boylan, "with both progressive and conservative tendencies, requiring as it did that 'egalitarian society [would rest] on . . . deference among a class of people—women—who would devote their efforts to service,' especially to their families."[56]

Other historians of women in this era note the simultaneous rise of an ideology of "spheres" and of women's political activism in salons, women's organizations, female academies, and economic life. The ideology of "spheres" was new and part of the ideological reconstruction of the gender system following the Revolution. The ideal of republican motherhood supposedly included women on the periphery of political life in the new nation by giving women the duty of transmitting values. Women were to provide their children—more important, their sons—with strong morals, piety, and education in order to build the next generation of patriotic citizens, thereby enlarging the social significance of motherhood and women's influence at home.[57] Most free African American women remained outside the class barriers of republican motherhood; most women, black or white, were removed from it.

Free white and black women became much more politically active as the early national years moved forward; when issues such as suffrage and abolition took center stage for white women activists, additional concerns demanded the time and efforts of black women activists. Although the domestic sphere expanded to include the political, African American women found themselves simultaneously combating the vestiges of slavery, such as negative racial stereotypes, and protecting themselves from the physical and sexual abuse of their white employers. The desire for citizenship and equal rights became central for women activists of the nineteenth century, yet free African American women found their status as free people challenged every day as millions of black men and women remained enslaved. The domestic sphere was simply different for black women. Enslaved African American women faced even greater obstacles and remained focused on the goal of freedom.

By the turn of the century, the black community of Philadelphia began to gain strength in numbers and in spirit as the sharp population decline of black men and women reversed itself. As black families both enslaved and free began to piece themselves together, men and women would for a short time quickly create the largest urban free black population anywhere in the new nation. The number of free blacks grew steadily, augmented by an influx of newly emancipated (or self-emancipated) people from the countryside. From 1781 to 1790 Philadelphia slave owners manumitted 269 slaves, and several hundred more realized their freedom with the help of the Pennsylvania Abolition Society. The increase in Philadelphia's free black population from 1783 to 1790 was fourfold: in 1790 nearly two thousand free men and women resided within the city limits.[58]

Total freedom did not come quickly, nor did it come with ease. As African Americans moved into the nineteenth century, they found themselves in a new system of bound labor, indentured servitude. Servitude elongated the transition from slavery to freedom. For African American women in particular, servitude was a difficult and lengthy experience. They used their extended period in bondage, however, as a time to gain skills, rudimentary education, and the means to improve the future conditions of their own freeborn children.

Black Alice lived through the era of slavery and emancipation in Philadelphia watching the birth of a new nation coincide with freedom for many African Americans. For the lives of black men and women in nineteenth-century Philadelphia were drastically different from the lives of Black Alice's parents, brought from Barbados in 1684. For African American men and women much had changed, yet there was much more work to be done.

Maneuvering Manumission in Philadelphia
African American Women and Indentured Servitude

In 1803, one year after Black Alice died, eight-year-old Mary Kerr indentured herself to Mary Lewis of Philadelphia. Kerr's apprenticeship was to last a period of nine years and nine months, and she would thus achieve her freedom at the age of eighteen. Kerr's indenture agreement notes that she was "a mulatress and illegitimate" and did "voluntarily and of her own free will and accord put herself apprentice to Mary Lewis." According to the agreement, Lewis had raised this young girl from infancy "at her own expense" and in return for Kerr's service, Lewis would instruct her in the "art, trade, and mystery of Housewifery."[1]

At first glance the indenture of Mary Kerr appears to be quite normal. Many black men, women, and children straddled the worlds between freedom and slavery in a period of indentured servitude. Kerr was to serve her mistress faithfully, and in return she would receive "sufficient meat, drink, apparel, lodging and washing, fitting for an apprentice," as well as training in housewifery, a skill that would prepare Kerr to be a domestic. In addition to her receiving the basic necessities, Kerr's indenture also noted that she was to be instructed in how to read, write, and cipher. Upon completion of her term, she was to be given two suits of clothing, one of which was to be entirely new.[2]

All these conditions were fairly standard in late eighteenth- and early nine-teenth-century Philadelphia, yet there was one very large departure: Mary Lewis, the mistress, was a black woman.[3]

Kerr's contract of service tells us very little about her relationship with her mistress, yet it does offer several important clues regarding their life to-gether. It is clear that Lewis raised Kerr for nearly all her life: they may well have been related. Few people were willing to take on the responsibilities of raising an infant black girl at the turn of the nineteenth century, so we can assume that Lewis was a benevolent woman, a family member, or both. As the almshouses of Philadelphia often hired out abandoned black children, Lewis was most likely saving Kerr from decades of labor at the hands of un-familiar white Philadelphians. Lewis's handwritten signature on the contract of service demonstrates that she was able to read and write and could pass this skill on to Mary Kerr. Most black servants would have been fortunate to receive any education at all.

Although most black indentured servants entered into service with white masters or mistresses, Mary Kerr and Mary Lewis were emblematic of a dif-ferent set of experiences of African American women in the early republic. Mary Lewis's financial ability as a free black woman to own a servant was rare, yet she nonetheless illustrates the complex and creative ways in which African Americans, both male and female, maneuvered between slavery and freedom, eventually finding emancipation. Unlike Mary Kerr, most black women lived and worked under the constant supervision of a white master. Many, however, managed to negotiate for basic necessities: food and cloth-ing and even the eighteenth-century luxury of a formal education. Regard-less of their masters' race, black women struggled and bargained for the tools to improve their lives and those of their children. African American women drew upon their own resources as well as those of their friends, their families, and even their masters to protect their interests and to make the best of a bad situation. Although servitude was far from freedom, and its boundaries were never certain, African American women knew it wasn't slavery, and they viewed it as one step closer to complete emancipation.

The experience of emancipation in Philadelphia differed greatly between men and women. Black Philadelphians experienced freedom through an elongated process of indentured servitude, and black women found them-selves the last recipients of freedom. This was because in the dismantling of slavery the last to release their slaves were owners of domestic servants. Most domestic servants were women and they often had children of their own and thus were less likely to attempt escape. From 1780 to 1820, as indentured servitude drew to a close in Philadelphia, most servants were black women, a very different population from the servant population in the past. British men and women had eventually rejected the system of bound labor by the late eighteenth century, and by the 1780s black women filled the void the whites had left, serving longer periods of indenture than whites and thus spending the majority of their lives as bound servants.

Within the first five years of the enactment of Pennsylvania's emancipation law, artisans, merchants, and widows of Philadelphia emancipated their slaves evenly according to gender. Gentlemen and farmers, however, freed many more men and boys; professionals such as doctors and lawyers freed five times more males than females.[4] By the 1790s the sex ratio of manumissions was even more skewed, for artisans, merchants, and widows altered their pattern of manumission, releasing more men and boys than women.[5] Black women, in other words, remained as household slaves while their male counterparts were released and allowed to hire themselves out to work. Historians such as Edward Turner, Gary Nash, and Jean Soderlund have accurately described the emancipation process for black Philadelphians as one that occurred in stages. The process was also gendered. Black women remained enslaved for longer periods, entered into indentures for longer periods, and were less likely to run away.

Yet through the process of indentured servitude, African American women began to re-create themselves and their families, carving a space for themselves as semifree people who used friends and family, the Pennsylvania Abolition Society, and the Court of Common Pleas to gain some control over their contracts and over their lives. The legacy of the Revolution forced Philadelphians to think differently about concepts of freedom and republicanism. Enslaved and free black men and women began to act on what they saw as a window of opportunity. As white men and women used the word *freedom* constantly, it was also heard within the black communities of Philadelphia. Unable to free themselves outright, black women had no choice but to use the system of indentured servitude as a vehicle that moved them toward eventual freedom. Through the negotiation of their freedom, black women policed their own masters by questioning dubious indenture contracts and by creating indenture agreements that would best serve their own needs.

Ending Slavery: Gradual Emancipation in Philadelphia

Several factors led to the eventual dismantling of slavery in the state of Pennsylvania; however, the Quakers were largely responsible for early legislative movement toward abolition. Quakers remained uncomfortable with the institution of slavery for many reasons; primary among them was a growing hesitancy about owning other human beings and the view that slaveholding was a luxury. Luxury and ostentatious displays of wealth signified worldliness, antithetical to Quaker beliefs and traditions. Many Quakers accepted the racist rhetoric that Africans were inferior and perhaps dangerous to white men and women. This belief fueled strong opposition to the practice of Africans living with Quaker families.

The first legislative step toward abolition in Pennsylvania was the Gradual Abolition Act of 1780. Two years earlier, in 1778, talk of a gradual abolition bill began to circulate in the city. George Bryan, a merchant and Irish immigrant to Philadelphia, began to promote a bill that prompted the Assembly to establish a committee to draft a law by February 1779.[6] In deference to the property rights of slaveholders, the original act did not call for the actual emancipation of slaves in the state of Pennsylvania. Instead, Bryan's bill pushed for the emancipation of all children born to slaves only after serving a period of servitude: eighteen years for females and twenty-one years for males. All slaveholders in the state were required to register their slaves with their county, and those who remained unregistered were to gain manumission automatically.[7] As for new residents, any slaveholder entering the state with his or her slaves was required to release them within six months after their arrival, congressmen and foreign ministers being the only exception to the rule. The Assembly passed the Gradual Abolition Act of Pennsylvania on March 1, 1780, yet slavery would not entirely end in Pennsylvania until 1847.[8] Emancipation was a tricky business, and for slaveholders worried about financial loss, gradualism was the only remedy to their problems. Gradual emancipation allowed slave owners to exact as much free labor from their slaves as possible. Slaves would spend their early years, their most productive years, working for their masters, thereby reducing their masters' financial losses.

For slave owners in Philadelphia, gradual emancipation calmed the fears about black freedom. Many whites felt that blacks were simply unprepared for freedom, and if left to their own devices would become indolent and lazy and bring crime and agitation to the city. By ensuring that blacks were owned, in one form or another, well into adulthood, gradual emancipation and lengthy indentures eased whites' distrust of black freedom.

The chaos of the Revolution, however, did not allow the 1778–1779 Pennsylvania Assembly to vote on the abolition bill.[9] A second version was presented to the Assembly in October 1779, with several changes: one extended the time in bondage of children born of slaves to twenty-eight years. With this condition, the first children born to slave mothers would not experience freedom until 1808, which abolitionists could not know would be the year in which the transatlantic slave trade would draw to a close.[10]

Similar transitions from slavery to freedom would soon appear in other colonies and, most famously, with West Indian emancipation in 1833. In Massachusetts people began to talk about gradual emancipation. Seven slaves petitioned the Massachusetts legislature for an act to initiate gradual abolition. The bill was tabled, however, and it wasn't until 1783 that the state's supreme court ruled that slavery was incompatible with the state's 1780 constitution. New York followed the Pennsylvania model in 1799, allowing females born to slave women to receive freedom at the age of twenty-five, males at twenty-eight.[11] Gradual emancipation began in 1804 in the neighboring state of New Jersey, where female and male slaves remained in bondage until the age of twenty-one and twenty-five, respectively.

In places such as Jamaica and Barbados, emancipation would not come until 1834, prompting slave masters to release their slaves and to quickly apprentice them. In Barbados slaves under the age of six were immediately set free, perhaps because they were seen as more of a hindrance than a financially lucrative investment. Slaves older than six were forced to work under an apprentice system for twelve years. Ex-slaves did not receive wages, and planters were held responsible for the clothing, shelter, medical care, and food necessary to sustain newly apprenticed men and women.[12]

Slavery ended in 1833 in the Bahamas. Five years later, in 1838, the Bahamian government terminated all postabolition indentured servitude.[13] For the Bahamas, the self-hire system had always been more popular among planters than outright enslavement. Beginning in the eighteenth century, slaves were permitted to seek employment on their own in return for an agreed-upon payment to their masters. This agreement guaranteed steady income to slave owners without the responsibilities of slave maintenance while simultaneously allowing slaves the opportunity to select their own employers.[14]

As emancipation began to spread throughout the northern states, black men and women created their own freedom, despite the impediments. Many enslaved Philadelphians did not wait for the new act; instead, they seized freedom themselves. Many slaves ran away: between 1780 and 1784, approximately 122 slaves absconded, and in the next four years another 45 slaves escaped from their masters.[15] Most runaways were young black men.[16] The few women who did attempt escape in Philadelphia took flight with children in tow, or tried to join free husbands. Advertisements in the *Pennsylvania Gazette* often confirmed the age and marital status of fugitive female slaves: "FORTY SHILLINGS Reward. RAN away from the subscriber, on the 25th of June last, a Negroe woman, named HANNAH, about 35 years of age, pretty likely, about 5 feet 2 or 3 inches high, came from Guinea, has one mark each side of her eye, if examined, and a small lump or scar on the back of her neck; had on, when she went away, a red flannel jacket and petticoat, old blue quilt, with mixed cloth in the fore part, and some patches on the lower part behind, had on a course white shift, but expect her dress will be altered. Her husband is a free man, and it is expected he harbours her; his name is Big Bill, formerly belonging to Daniel Cooper, deceased."[17]

For enslaved African American women, marriage to a free man held many advantages and could on occasion expedite emancipation. In the case of Hannah, who was thirty-five years old in 1785, her status as a slave in Philadelphia would most likely never change: she was not affected by gradual abolition. Unless her master experienced regret or remorse, Hannah would remain enslaved through her master's life. This was a good reason to attempt escape. Hannah's husband, Big Bill, most likely gained his freedom when his former owner died, and he could offer refuge to his wife. Free black men could find work of their own and hide a fugitive wife among the growing black population in the city.

Several female slaves from the South who fled their masters and headed north to Philadelphia also used their husbands' status as free men to aid in their escapes. In May 1781 a "Negroe woman named SUE, about 45 years of age, [with] a down look, remarkable large breasts, and a wen upon the temple" was also advertised in the *Pennsylvania Gazette* as a runaway slave from Baltimore. The advertisement indicated that she had arrived in Philadelphia and was awaiting the return of her "free Mulattoe" husband, named Mark Stubbs, who had sailed from Baltimore on the ship *Enterprize*. The *Gazette* depicted Sue as a good cook and her husband as a butcher, and it predicted that "it is probable they may set up for themselves about the city."[18] Sue and Hannah were able to use their own skills as well as the freedom of their husbands to gain their own emancipation.

In some cases, enslaved women of the South sought the assistance of free husbands who had migrated to the cities of the North. Patty Gibson from Payuolank County, North Carolina, wrote to her husband in Philadelphia in 1797: "Dear Husban, I Know take this oppurtunity to inform you that I am w[e]ll at this time and hope this will find you the Same I Shold be vary Glad if you will com and fetch me some money by the first of January as I has put to be sold then and if you cold healp me to som Money you will much oblidge me."[19] Gibson explained to her husband that she had tried to escape, but "Got Ketch and Broat Back and put in Sale." Gibson ends her letter: "I hope you will try and do the best for me you can as I want to see you vary much Rimimber me to all my friends and I remain your [wife] and well wisher to this day Patty Gibson."[20]

Kinship networks remained extremely important for African American female servants, since their relationships with husbands and fathers could on occasion release them from servitude. Priscilla Waters was bound by contract to Robert Wharton of Gloucester County, New Jersey, along with her daughter, Charlotte. Her husband, Atlee Waters, a free man, purchased the remainder of his wife's and daughter's contracts by indenturing himself in their place. The cost of freedom for Priscilla and Charlotte Waters was thirty pounds, fifteen of which Atlee Waters paid in cash in May 1793. The remaining fifteen pounds was to be paid through service offered to Wharton by Waters himself. Waters agreed to "live with him as a hired servant for which he is to allow me two pounds per month."[21]

Across the North and even in the South, blacks used their free status to negotiate emancipation for family members. On occasion they purchased the freedom of their family members, at other times they supported underground networks to facilitate escape. In Philadelphia free blacks indentured their kinfolk. The experiences of Priscilla Waters, Sue, Hannah, and Patty Gibson did not represent conventional methods of attaining freedom during the late eighteenth century—emancipation conferred by the acts or the deaths of owners—but their lives illustrate the complexity of manumission for black women, as well as the advantages of kinship networks extending across geographic and free-status boundaries. But most women of African descent would spend many years of their lives as bound servants; Priscilla and Charlotte Waters, Patty Gibson, Sue, and Hannah represent only a small segment of Philadelphia's free black population who were able to take their own freedom with the assistance of their husbands.

The Gradual Abolition Act of 1780 forced many slaveholders to think about the eventual release of their slaves. Others considered immediate emancipation, and the Pennsylvania Abolition Society (PAS) was partially responsible for a wave of emancipations in late eighteenth-century Philadelphia.[22] In 1784 a group of eighteen men, mostly Quaker, met to reestablish the organization, proposing a plan of gradual abolition for the entire country, while working to better the conditions of free and enslaved men and women of color, as well as helping all black people held illegally in bondage.[23] The number of immediate manumissions skyrocketed between 1780 and 1800.[24]

Gary Nash and Jean Soderlund suggest that most members of the PAS were not among the economic elite and instead were established artisans, shopkeepers, and lesser merchants. We can assume that opposing slavery

would not further their class status or social position and that their abolitionist stance was somewhat altruistic.[25] It is impossible to know the inner-
most thoughts of PAS members, and "to diagnose group motivation is a
perilous enterprise."[26] It is clear that members invested a significant amount
of time and energy to win freedom for slaves, one case at a time, and did so
in a diplomatic fashion.

The Pennsylvania Abolition Society established itself as the primary advo-
cacy organization for both enslaved and free black men and women, and it
began its reorganization by carefully policing the enforcement of the 1780
act. Slaveholders who entered the state of Pennsylvania after March 1780 and
failed to release their slaves after six months found themselves the targets of the
society's punitive legal action. As word spread quickly through the city that the
society might be able to secure their freedom, black Philadelphians inundated
it with pleas for help. The PAS simultaneously assisted free and enslaved blacks
in immediate danger of being sold into slavery outside Pennsylvania.[27]

This was evident in the case of "Mary a Black Woman," who approached
the society in 1788. Mary and the society petitioned the Court of Common
Pleas in Delaware for her freedom from her owner, Mary McDowell.[28] Although the basis of her claim is a bit unclear from the court records, Mary
McDowell most likely had attempted to bypass Mary's manumission by moving to Delaware. With the assistance of the PAS, Mary was able to sue for her
freedom; according to the court, "the said petitioner is entitled to her Freedom,
[and] the said Mary a Black Woman [is] to be Free and at Liberty, and may enjoy all of the Benefits and Advantages that a free Negro may or can do within
this State."[29] The Pennsylvania Abolition Society assisted African American
women in Pennsylvania and neighboring states such as Delaware and New
Jersey, helping them use the Court of Common Pleas in securing their freedom,
an amazing realization for black women of the early republic.

The society also attempted to improve living conditions for free blacks by
creating employment opportunities, developing schools for children, and extending "friendly" moral advice to recently freed slaves. These activities fell
to the Committee to Improve the Condition of Free Blacks. This committee
of twenty-four men was divided into four subcommittees: the Committee
of Inspection, the Committee of Guardians, the Committee of Education,
and the Committee of Employ.[30] The Committee of Employ became quite
adept at finding work for recently freed slaves through the system of indentured servitude, and although many historians have portrayed the PAS as a
humanitarian society primarily concerned with the lives of black people, in
many respects their work propelled blacks into lengthy servitude at the turn
of the century. The society helped to revive the all-but-defunct system of

servitude by counseling recently freed blacks into servitude agreements, thus delaying their freedom.

Slavery did not come to a complete end in Pennsylvania until 1847, yet Philadelphia's free black community grew steadily and was significantly large for a northern city. The last decades of the eighteenth century witnessed a drastic reduction of the slave population within the city's limits. From 1763 to 1775 the slave population of Philadelphia reached its colonial peak at 1,481, and by 1770 there were between 200 and 300 free black men and women. In the five years before the war the number of free blacks doubled, and by 1783 more than 1,000 free black men and women called Philadelphia their home.[31] Following the enactment of the Gradual Abolition Act, the slave population of Philadelphia began to diminish. By 1800 there were only 55 slaves in the city, and the total free black population was just over 6,000 people.

The growth of the free black population in Philadelphia in the early decades of the nineteenth century was similar to that in other mid-Atlantic cities such as New York. By 1810 Philadelphia counted over 9,600 free men and women; only three slaves remained in the city.[32] Outpaced by Philadelphia, New York's free black population stood at over 7,400, yet more than 1,400 men and women still remained enslaved.[33] Gradual emancipation in New York came some nineteen years later than in Philadelphia, so that black men and women were left in bondage for a longer period. Yet, like Philadelphia's, New York's growing black population can be attributed both to African Americans who migrated from the nearby countryside and to those who were brought by their owners from Haiti.

From White to Black: Indentured Servitude in Philadelphia

As European immigration into the city accelerated during the early colonial period, indentured servants regularly signed four to seven years of their lives over to a master in return for passage to the colony, food, and lodging. The majority of these indentured servants were English and skilled in a trade. In many instances indentured servitude became a vehicle by which family members and friends could be brought over to the colony with an opportunity for success.[34]

By the mid-eighteenth century indentured servitude in Philadelphia changed along with the immigrating population. No longer were skilled English servants the majority of those who took on indenture contracts. Irish, German, and Scottish men and women quickly began to compose the majority of the servant population in the city. As Philadelphia became the commercial center of the

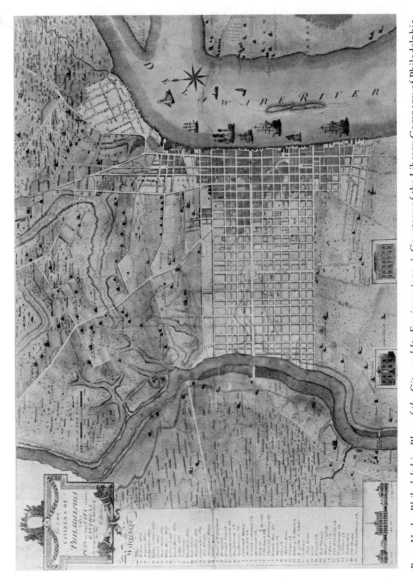

Peter Varle, *Philadelphia, Plan of the City and Its Environs* (1794). Courtesy of the Library Company of Philadelphia.

Delaware Valley, servants became valuable commodities. Established English immigrants simply stopped offering their family members the favor of passage to and indentureship in Pennsylvania. The cost of labor continued to increase and the bonds of family and friendship failed to trump financial gain.[35]

Following the Revolution, the British began to dismantle the servant trade in an attempt to fortify the labor pool at home in England. Fearing that the continuation of mass emigration to the United States would hurt the British labor force and leave parts of Ireland depopulated, the British passed two acts, in 1788 and 1803, severely limiting the number of indentured servants allowed to go from Britain to America. The emigration of the northern Irish was targeted in this movement, since they represented the largest block of indentured servants in the United States. The number of Irish indentured servants in Philadelphia was larger than the number of indentured servants from all other parts of Europe combined. Since Great Britain had served as Pennsylvania's primary source of servants, these acts brought about the end of white indentured servitude in Pennsylvania.[36]

The influx of Irish emigrants transformed labor scarcity into a labor surplus and prompted Philadelphia servant holders to rethink the indenture system. As it became much more cost-effective for masters to abandon the practice of supporting a servant and his or her family, wage labor became much more popular. Not only did masters prefer this transition, but it also became much more difficult to find European men and women willing to become indentured servants. Free wage labor became the preferred labor system; but as indentured servants were displaced, they were left vulnerable to a fluctuating labor market.

Yet as European emigrants were phased out of the indentured system toward the end of the eighteenth century, slaveholders used the system to hold on to their human property. After the Gradual Abolition Act passed, the system of bound labor was briefly revived by the inclusion of black men and women as indentured servants. As white slave masters attempted to maintain their property during the era of gradual emancipation, indentured servitude became a way in which masters could prolong their control and continue making profits. Black servitude had never been seriously considered or practiced before the Revolution; between 1754 and 1775 black indentures never totaled more than three per year.[37] Emancipation for African Americans in the 1780s most often entailed a period of servitude.

The indenture agreements of "Negro Judith" contained demands and provisions for servitude that were fairly common for both whites and blacks. In 1786 Judith was to serve the heirs of Elizabeth Lippincott for a period of thirteen years; she agreed to serve her mistress faithfully, keep her secrets, and "gladly obey" her. The indenture contract stated that Judith "shall not absent herself from her mistress day or night, without her leave but in all things behave herself as a good and faithful apprentice ought, during the said term of consideration."[38] Although Judith was bound out for thirteen years, she was entitled to a certain standard of living, a provision, in fact, that proved crucial for nineteenth-century black communities. In exchange for her service, "said mistress shall find and provide for said apprentice good and sufficient, Meat Drink Lodging, and apparel suitable for such an apprentice and shall teach or cause her to be instructed in all the branches of housewifery, she shall also give unto the said apprentice three months schooling within the said term and at the expiration thereof one good new sute of freedom cloaths together with her common apparel and the better to recommend her the said Judith, her said mistress shall than give unto her a certificate certifying how well she hath behaved during her apprenticeship."[39]

Indentured servitude could in no way compare to complete emancipation, but it did allow for the development of certain skills that would prove essential for black women after they completed their terms. The promised certificate or letter of recommendation from Judith's mistress would help in securing future employment as the domestic labor market grew more and more crowded. Judith was to be instructed in housewifery skills, which would assist her in the future as a domestic, and she would also have her three months of schooling. Some contracts offered as much as "six quarters half day schooling," which most likely amounted to eighteen months of half-day education.[40] This was quite generous for any indentured servant, for most agreements offered servants between three and six months' instruction.

Three months of schooling over thirteen years may not have been enough for functional literacy for Judith. The education offered to black indentured servants through the schools established by the Pennsylvania Abolition Society, however, began to lay the groundwork for widespread literacy in the nineteenth-century black community. It is possible that Judith could write her name at the end of her term of servitude; and at the very least, she likely recognized the letters of the alphabet and perhaps even a few small words.

Black women, who represented the majority of the indentured servant population, proved efficient at exacting control from their contractors. This is visible in the indenture documents. The records of the Pennsylvania Abolition Society note many if not most of the manumissions that took place in Philadelphia and surrounding regions during the early national period. The Manumission Book of the society illustrates the complexity of emancipation in Philadelphia, as the methods of manumission were both routine and rare. John Phillips, a merchant of Philadelphia, listed the manumission of his slave Lucy with the PAS: "I John Phillips Merchant of the City of Philadelphia Do hereby set free from bondage my Negro woman named Lucy, aged about twenty-six years and do for myself and my executors, Administrators release unto the said Negro Lucy, all my right and Claims whatsoever as to her person or to any estate she may acquire hereby declaring the said Negro Lucy absolutely free, without any interruption from me or my persons claiming under me. In Witness whereof I have hereunto set my Hand and Seal this fourteenth day of July in the year of our lord one thousand seven hundred and eighty four."[41]

Servitude, in purely practical ways, could be better than immediate emancipation, which often proved difficult for many young black women. Employment was difficult to come by; a recently freed woman of color, most likely lacking a skilled trade such as sewing or mantua making, and often unable to read or write, could easily be forced into an indenture, sometimes even to the old master.[42] Black women found themselves bound to domestic labor in both the city and the countryside, a situation that would persist well into the twentieth century.

Although the city did offer skilled jobs to a small number of recently freed slaves, men were more often the beneficiaries. Philadelphia valued artisan skills, and former male slaves were able to find work with master craftsmen and merchants. Both white and black women were kept out of craftwork, as they received very little, if any, formal training in the trades. If a freed slave was given the opportunity to work in a skilled trade, it was often as part of a task system that incorporated domestic crafts learned at home.[43] Black women were thus limited to domestic work.[44] But the influx of Irish and Scottish women during the early nineteenth century fueled fierce competition in that domestic labor market, and freed female slaves were at the bottom of the labor pool. As the majority of former slaves endured physical abuse and arduous labor, ex-slaves and black indentured servants spent the most productive years of their lives as bound laborers.[45] Many laborers experienced physical decline by their thirties and were fortunate to see their fortieth birthdays.

It was difficult for young black women to obtain work, but it proved almost impossible for elderly black women. In 1790 Isabella Robins, a widow of Philadelphia, "believing that freedom is just and right of all mankind," set free her seventy-seven-year-old mulatto slave Phillis.[46] Robins's manumission of an elderly slave was not rare: slaveholders routinely relieved themselves of the burdens attached to caring for aging slaves. Phillis's old age placed her in a difficult position, for the majority of the labor available to black urban women at the turn of the century was arduous manual work. Carrying large loads of laundry and hauling heaps of trash from the streets were typical tasks, and unless Phillis was skilled at sewing and could still see properly to thread her needle, she would most likely become a member of the desperately poor. Even so, sewing was intensely vulnerable work and women were often the victims of underpayment.[47]

Manumission occurred with specific rules and limitations: many slave-holders drafted documents that granted freedom only if the ex-slave followed certain provisions. In 1786 William McMurtrie agreed to set free his "Negro woman named Teeny." It was a standard agreement, with one exception. Teeny was to agree "that she shall have no more children [and] on failure of those considerations this agreement [will] be void."[48] Her manumission thus depended on her ability to prevent pregnancy. This component would have made a union with an enslaved or free man extremely difficult, as contraceptive methods were not dependable. Although the manumission documents for Teeny do not reflect the existence of a husband, the absence of a spouse from the documents does not automatically indicate that she was unmarried. Marriage would prove complex for Teeny; pregnancy could jeopardize her freedom and, therefore, the stability of her family.

Perhaps McMurtrie restricted Teeny's reproductive future as a way to keep her unmarried and therefore available to work for him, without the burdens or responsibilities of marriage and family. The disposition of her living children supports this interpretation. Two months later, Teeny's children were bound out to different masters. The toddler, two-year-old Scipio, was indentured for a period of twenty-six years, and Ishmael, age four, was to be set free on his twenty-eighth birthday. Such agreements show the draconian power that former owners and employers wielded in the indenture system.

But, on occasion, labor contracts exemplify the ways in which black women fought for their own freedom and the emancipation of their children. Take the deposition of Jane Fild, for example. Assisted by the Pennsylvania Abolition Society, she sought to release her son Peter from servitude to Thomas Egle. Although Jane Fild was indentured in Pennsylvania and did not live with her son, she recounted in great detail Peter's status, first in Delaware as a slave, and then as an indentured servant at age six in Pennsylvania. The outcome of this case is unknown. Yet Fild's testimony against a white man was no small act of resistance. Her poorly written "X" stood in the place of a signature on the court document that contested Egle's claim to her son as his own property.[49]

Mothers attempted sometimes to assert authority over their children in the terms of their indentures. They thus stood legally between child and employer, modifying the power of the latter. When "Negro Judith" was indentured to Elizabeth Lippincott, the indenture clearly stated that Judith, a minor, could indenture herself only "with the advice and consent of her mother Dinah and also the consent of Anthony Woodward formerly master of the said Dinah."[50] Dinah's inclusion in a legal contract regarding her daughter signified her responsibility and authority over her child.

Poor and abandoned black children found themselves without parental representation in the negotiating of contracts. Since 1780 the Philadelphia poorhouse had routinely hired out poor blacks to local farmers and merchants; many were children. Destitute parents unable to care for their children often handed them over to the poorhouse as a temporary recourse. This act almost always resulted in lengthy contracts of servitude for the children. The institution hired out Nancy Burns, for example, nine years old, to be trained as a domestic and to receive "eight quarters half day schooling."[51] Burns's contract did not include the consent of her parents, but it did not identify her as abandoned. And like private employers, the poorhouse indentured tiny children: "Sally a Negro aged two years," abandoned by her parents, was to serve Hester Eastburn for sixteen years. Sally was "to be taught to read if capable of being taught."[52] No one could predict that capability, since she could, presumably, barely talk. Sally was indentured until her eighteenth birthday, yet most black children were held for longer periods. Eighteen years was the standard term for black girls, whereas black boys were bound out until they were twenty-one.[53] But black children were typically indentured until they reached their twenty-eighth birthdays.

By the 1790s Philadelphia's black residents comprised a mixture of migrants from nearby states and the upper South, but they also consisted of indentured blacks from the Caribbean, especially from Santo Domingo (then known as Saint Domingue). During the mid-1790s, hundreds of French planters and their slaves made their way to the port city on the Delaware in search of refuge from the bloody political turmoil of their homeland. Having lost the majority of their property upon leaving the island, an estimated two hundred families relocated from the French West Indies to Philadelphia in 1792. White slaveholders took with them all their property that was mobile, including their slaves. By November of the following year, an additional four hundred refugees from Haiti arrived in Philadelphia.[54]

Throughout the 1790s, French planters brought upwards of five hundred slaves into the city of Philadelphia and quickly tried to circumvent the 1780 Abolition Act. Appealing to the Pennsylvania Legislature, French planters requested exemption from the law, which required the registration of all slaves brought into the state of Pennsylvania with the county clerk, followed by their release within six months of arrival. Although their requests were denied, French masters, like some Philadelphians, prolonged their claims to their slaves by emancipating and then immediately indenturing them.

The Pennsylvania Abolition Society attempted to halt this practice. Members of the PAS claimed that the actions of the French planters violated the spirit of the 1780 Abolition Act.[55] In 1794, however, the Pennsylvania Supreme Court upheld the planters' rights to indenture their former slaves, a decision that solidified the rise of black indentured servitude within the city.

The dramatic rise in the number of black indentured servants was directly connected to the influx of Haitian slaves brought into Philadelphia's city limits.[56] When this increase was coupled with a new population of native black servants, Philadelphia sustained a temporary momentum for the outdated system of servitude. The popularity of black servitude lasted a little more than a decade; the rate of indentures began to decline by 1802 and the practice virtually disappeared by 1820. Records indicate that the majority of the slaves brought from Santo Domingo were women and children, who were perhaps easier to relocate and less likely to escape during transport to Philadelphia.[57] Under Pennsylvania law, children would provide decades of service or income to their masters.

Philipe Michaut, a slaveholder, fled the slave rebellion of his island for Philadelphia. Like other French planters, he emancipated his two female slaves and immediately bound them: "Know all men by these presents that I Philipe Michaut late of St. Domingo now of the city of Philadelphia, of my own free will and accord and from the motives of humanity and benevolence have manumitted and set free from slavery my two female negress slaves, the first named Marie Claire aged about fifteen years and the last named Therese aged about thirteen years, reserving only to myself and my Asigns their services and labor until they shall have attained the age of twenty eight years for which purpose Indentures are to be executed."[58]

Virtually every slave brought from the island was indentured for the maximum number of years allowed by law; of the more than five hundred slaves brought to Philadelphia, only forty-five were granted complete manumission without contracts of indentured servitude. Two additional black Santo Domingans were allowed to purchase their freedom; the rest, more than four hundred slaves, remained as bound laborers.[59]

As the majority of black Santo Domingans created new lives for themselves in Philadelphia, a small number eventually returned to their homeland. In November 1798 the ship *Express* left Philadelphia for Cape Francois carrying 121 "refugees." Ship records indicate that the passengers were infirm

old men, women, and children returning to Santo Domingo. Children under the age of nine years were not recorded by name, so that the names of
only 100 passengers appear in the ship's records. More than half of these
returning refugees were women traveling with their children.[60] Listed only
by their first names, the returning passengers were likely all black Haitians
who had been given their freedom several years after arriving in Philadelphia. Their decision to return home is important, for it demonstrates
several possibilities. Unhappiness in America and the ability to return to
their home as free people were most likely the driving forces behind their
departure. It is possible, however, that white Americans, committed to the
philosophy of black colonization, also encouraged them. Their voluntary
reverse migration displays a longing for their homeland as well as the abandonment of a growing black community in Philadelphia.

On the other hand, many black Haitians opted to remain in America, and
the Pennsylvania Abolition Society found itself inundated with requests for
assistance from the newest additions to Philadelphia's black community. In
March 1805 Marie Louise, a slave born in Port-au-Prince, was brought up
on charges by her owner, Jean-Baptiste Lapointe, for having absconded with
her daughter Melanie. Marie Louise was transported from Port-au-Prince
by Lapointe and his sister, Madame Alivé, in May 1798. Lapointe and Alivé
must not have registered Marie Louise and her daughter appropriately, for
upon the court's review of the case, both mother and daughter were set free.[61]
Marie Louise planned her escape to coincide with her owner's travel abroad:
when Madame Alivé left for France, Marie Louise left the home of her owner
with her Philadelphia-born daughter. As word of the 1780 law had quickly
spread through the small streets and narrow alleys of Philadelphia, Marie
Louise used the absence of her mistress to gain her freedom. It is certain that
Marie Louise knew that she was free and simply took her freedom at the
most opportune moment.

In no way am I insinuating that indentured black women preferred this
system of bound labor, or that they chose this system of unfree labor to make
the transition from slavery to freedom. Black women understood their circumstances and the limits of their freedom, however, and they worked within
the confines of the institution to better their lives.

In 1800 "Negro Judith" completed her term of servitude. She, along with
thousands of other free black men and women in Philadelphia, made the
transition into a changing nineteenth century. Judith maneuvered her manumission and learned the skills of housewifery, familiarized herself with the
fundamentals of literacy, and secured several suits of clothing. Certainly, Judith would have preferred her freedom outright, but she made the best of

her period in servitude, looking forward to the promise of freedom in the future. During the nineteenth century many black women put their skills, patience, and freedom to work. They wrested what they could from their time as servants and set out on a path to reconstruct their identities: as African Americans, as women, and as free people.

Free Black Philadelphia:
Community Formation and Foundations

Freedom was full of possibilities and problems. As black women moved from indentured servitude to freedom, many found themselves trapped as unskilled domestics working in the homes of wealthy Philadelphians. Of the 1,897 free blacks who lived in Philadelphia in 1790, approximately half lived and worked in white households, and the majority of those live-in workers were women.[62] Black women who did not perform live-in services for white city residents found very little by way of diverse employment. The 1795 *Philadelphia City Directory* listed a total of 105 black residents; of those, 22 women were listed as heads of household. Although the majority of free black women listed in the directory were recorded as "washers," there were several exceptions. Tinee Cranshaw, who lived on North Front Street, was listed as a "Dealer in Fruit." Cranshaw was given the business upon the death of her husband in the early 1790s, and she maintained it through 1795, 1796, and 1797.[63]

Minia Brummage, who resided at Front and Arch Streets, was listed as a "Cake Seller," and she continued in her own business of cake baking and selling to both white and black Philadelphians well into the nineteenth century. Polly Haine was listed as a "Pepper Pot Maker," one of the other avenues of black female entrepreneurship during the era. Black female street vendors sold pepper pot, a soup, to black and white Philadelphians, and they were a noted addition to urban street life. Phoebe Anderson and Phoebe Seymor were listed as "Hucksters," most likely selling fruits and vegetables on the streets of Philadelphia.[64] Typically, poor women of both races worked in two or more forms of employment throughout the year. African American women who worked as street sellers turned to work as laundresses and seamstresses in cold weather.[65] Employment was always fragile.

There were several other examples of occupational options for black women in the late eighteenth century. Eleanor Harris, who resided at Sixth and Cherry Streets, was one of the few black female teachers listed in the directory. Her reputation as a respectable woman and instructor to the free black community was described in her obituary, printed in a Philadelphia newspaper.[66] Susanna Witcher, a widow, ran her own boardinghouse at Second and Pine in Stamper's Alley.[67]

Although the majority of black women worked as washers and domestics, there was in the 1790s a small yet developing class of free blacks who catered to the needs of other free blacks. As the free black population mushroomed during the first few decades of the nineteenth century, so did the need for independent black businesses. These businesses were patronized by the black community of Philadelphia, so that washerwomen, carters, laborers, and sawyers became extremely important to the embryonic class of black entrepreneurs.

Often finding it difficult to support themselves and their families with their meager earnings, African American women experienced the dilemma of freedom and poverty. Although they were no longer bound laborers, black women were still very much dependent on their employers for their wages. As black women toiled long hours in physically demanding jobs, they continued to find ways in which to resist and rebel within the workplace, most expressively through confrontational behavior with their employers. Deborah Norris Logan, a wealthy white Philadelphian, often noted how difficult it was to find "good servants" throughout the early decades of the nineteenth century. In one of her diary entries she recounted the dismissal of one of her servants: "I have had some domestic disquiets as of late with my servants and there seems a propriety in discharging Maggy Jones a coloured woman who has lived with us near three years. She has been of late (as the Irish say) too warm in her place and very impertinent in her remarks."[68] Elizabeth Drinker, another member of the Philadelphia elite, also noted in her diary similar methods of resistance exhibited by domestic employees: "Our black Jane is out now at near 11 o'clock. She is a Methodist, and this is Christmas Eve. If Jane don't come home by the time I have looked over the house, I shall lock her out."[69]

In addition to the complaint of impertinence exhibited by female domestics, white employers also began to remark upon the deterioration of domestic skills. Not only were employers frustrated with a growing sense of liberty demonstrated through the "back-talking" of their domestic help, but there also appeared to be dissatisfaction with the quality of their work. In July 1804 Elizabeth Drinker wrote in her diary: "Polly Summers, a black woman who has been with us 4 weeks tomorrow will be loath to leave us, but she knows so little of cooking that we cannot well make out with her, and she is so highly perfumed, that it is at times scarce bearable."[70]

Although white employers complained of the new liberties taken by free black employees, they continued to hire black women as their domestic

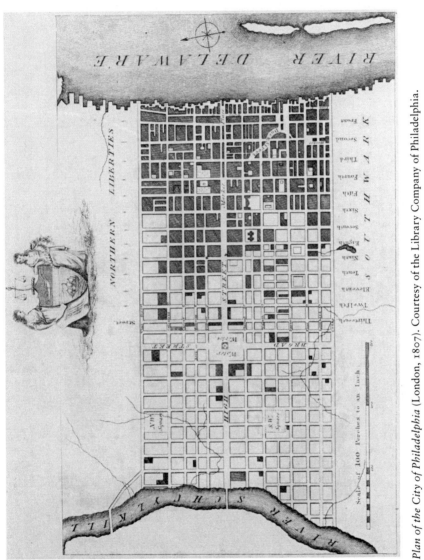

Plan of the City of Philadelphia (London, 1807). Courtesy of the Library Company of Philadelphia.

The Laundress. From *City Characters; or, Familiar Scenes in Town* (Philadelphia, 1851). Courtesy of the Library Company of Philadelphia.

servants and would continue to do so throughout the early decades of the nineteenth century.[71] The majority of black women in Philadelphia had no choice but to continue working as domestics for most of their natural lives, but they continued to bend and transform the rules of conduct. As black women maneuvered their manumission in contracts of indentured servitude, they also manipulated their working environment and employers, making better lives for themselves and for their families.

Creating Black Philadelphia
African American Women and Their Neighborhoods

The new century was the beginning of an important transition for African Americans in Philadelphia. Thousands worked in servitude well into the 1820s, but over several decades slavery became defunct. Philadelphia became a leading example of black freedom in the nation, and cities such as New York and Boston also extended liberty to African Americans. The times filled men and women with hope as well as disappointment. Emancipation, the first "rehearsal for Reconstruction," encompassed the end of indentured servitude, the beginnings of black activism, and the birth of a strident abolition movement.[1] African Americans worked in earnest to take advantage of freedom by constructing families, churches, and mutual aid societies. Optimism ran high, but free blacks also met white violence, hostility, and degradation in most aspects of their lives. They were also constantly reminded of their brothers and sisters still in bondage. Millions of enslaved blacks throughout the nation remained the personal property of others, and slavery jeopardized the emancipation of black northerners. As long as slavery remained intact, the future of free black men and women in Philadelphia and throughout the North remained fragile and uncertain. Free African Americans were forced to walk a difficult path, enjoying the early glimpses of freedom yet living with the reality of poverty, inequality, and violence.

As fugitive slaves and country people flocked to Philadelphia, they posed difficulties to free blacks who were already settled and building a diverse community. Free black Philadelphians received newcomers with respect and offered them assistance, yet they simultaneously expressed their weighty concerns about the reputation and stability of the fragile and free community. The political climate exacerbated social concerns. Free African Americans enjoyed their liberty only to have it challenged by the philosophy, goals, and aims of the American Colonization Society, an organization that promoted black migration to western Africa. The ACS was founded in 1816 in Washington, D.C., and supported the belief that blacks would never receive full citizenship in the United States. Some colonists blamed the racism of white Americans, which they claimed would never allow whites to see blacks as equals.[2]

Stating that blacks disproportionately filled prisons, almshouses, and asylums, the society targeted blacks in cities. The questionable statistics gathered by society members reinforced the belief that freed blacks would never be able to compete in a wage labor economy alongside whites. Repatriation to Africa would supposedly offer free blacks an opportunity to develop themselves both morally and economically.[3] A small number of blacks advocated the colonization movement and agreed that white racism would never allow free African Americans full access to equality and citizenship. White racism prevented blacks from achieving political and social success, and voluntary migration was the appropriate way to fight inequality. White colonists wanted blacks to be removed from the country, voluntarily or against their will. Racism was central to white colonization ideology; it was hostile at best.

The threat of colonization elicited anger and fear from most black Philadelphians, who were convinced that their removal was a very real possibility. In early January 1817, nearly three thousand blacks crowded into Mother Bethel Church to discuss and challenge the option of migration. The mood was tense, for "there was not one sole that was in favour of going to Africa."[4]

The threat of forced migration placed an even greater emphasis on community building for free African Americans. One response to this new threat was a concerted effort to rid the community of vice and ugly conduct such as public inebriation, the use of profanity, and physical disputes. Social support mechanisms, such as black schools and mutual aid societies, were created to ease the transition into freedom and self-sufficiency. Mutual aid societies and benevolent groups, however, reached but a small portion of the community. The large number of desperately poor African Americans searching for work, shelter, food, and other bare necessities must have overwhelmed early black mutual aid societies. Many societies asked their members to contribute meager membership dues to keep the organizations afloat. Although the dues were small in amount, their inability to pay them kept the poorest of the poor shut out of many private charitable organizations. These men and women were dependent on the Christian charity of local churches, the kindness of neighbors, and the assistance of extended kinfolk.

As African Americans of the North experienced a major shift in their social and political lives, so did American women. The nineteenth century witnessed the transformation of women's lives as new sentiments regarding domesticity, marriage, and motherhood redefined familial roles and altered the social landscape. Companionate marriage, the legitimization of women's education, and political activism would eventually change the American perception of wifely duties and motherhood as well as redefine the private and the public worlds. The acknowledgment of "separate spheres" soon defined the home and its surroundings as feminine, leaving all other matters to the charge of men.[5] Scholars have viewed this shift as a class- and race-based transition that served the interests of an emerging elite while bringing together a middle class.[6] The new mantle of republican motherhood imbued women with the civic responsibility for nurturing a new citizenry and brought women from political invisibility to marginality.[7] Prevailing attitudes regarding women's roles in the construction of a civil society, or "republican motherhood," were limiting, yet "female virtue" brought the worlds of domesticity and politics closer together.[8]

Most American women—poor, enslaved, laboring, and rural—were unable to secure the social respect accorded them by republican motherhood. It is evident, however, that by the 1820s many urban African American women did incorporate many of the related values and ideals—Christian piety, sobriety, and industry—into their private and public spheres. Faced with very different socioeconomic conditions, the constant threat of kidnapping and ensuing enslavement, and racial segregation, African American women developed understandings of womanhood that drew on domesticity but were shaped by race. For black women, motherhood and womanhood had to incorporate work outside the home, political consciousness (including consciousness of abolition), and the ability to deal politely with inhumane treatment. Although bondage and servitude had long prohibited black women from claiming full responsibility for their children, their marriages, and their communities, the early years of emancipation promised a great change. Ideas about the special role that women could play gave this promise a particular shape for them.

African American women's work as mothers encompassed nuclear and extended kinship relations, as well as entire black communities. Motherhood took on a different symbolic significance for black women involved in the work of building a new community. This extension of motherhood is most visible in the African American church. As the church became the nucleus for early black Philadelphia, it also became a complicated theater for the public and private lives of black men and women. It was within the walls of the church sanctuary and the homes of its members that the experiences of African American men and women were most closely examined, nurtured, and supervised. Black women "mothered" their fellow congregants, offering gentle support to those in need and strict discipline to those who strayed. For black churchwomen and the middle-class elite, it was their duty to raise children but also to lead an infant free black community to a mature and educated adulthood. A great deal was at stake; African American women nurtured, supported, and monitored this expanding community.

Motherhood, as conceptualized and practiced in church-run mutual aid societies, blurred the distinction between the public sphere and the private. As social hierarchies developed within the black church, a small group of women and men began to articulate standards of reputability and social protocol for black Philadelphia. The "mothers of the church," usually older, active in social uplift groups, and educated to some degree, protected themselves and embodied the stability of African American neighborhoods. Informal church law slowly codified, regulating marriage and the personal life. As African American church members found themselves interrogated and chastised by "mothers of the church" and male church officials, the private lives of black Philadelphians were made public in disciplinary trials and record books.

This does not mean that women took on formal positions of authority in the black church, for in fact men, not women, occupied the roles of deacon, elder, and minister. Led by Richard Allen and several other well-known and respected male church leaders of Mother Bethel Church, the disciplinary tribunal met regularly to hear the testimony of its members about domestic differences. The Minute and Trial Book of the church documented dozens of cases between 1822 and 1851, many of which were brought before the all-male committee by female members interested in protecting their own communities and, perhaps more important, the image of morality and stability affiliated with the church. The politics of respectability as well as the safeguarding of a new and fragile free black community stood as justification for the intrusion into the personal lives of free African Americans in the city of brotherly love.[9]

Minor infractions such as the use of profane language and unneighborly conduct, as well as more serious offenses such as adultery and murder, were investigated and tried in the African American church. As organizations such as the Female Benevolent Society of St. Thomas, the Daughters of Africa, and the African Female Band worked to promote social uplift through education and financial support, they simultaneously monitored their communities, ostracizing those who failed to follow ethical codes. Those who, by engaging in drinking, public brawls, or disagreements, chose not to live "pious" lives were not welcomed or supported.

African American women formed their own mutual aid societies and associations not only to assist the community, but also to chaperone it. A good wife, mother, friend, neighbor, educated person, and church member: these were all necessary components of black womanhood, and African American women enforced these ideas in their homes and in their associations.

By the early nineteenth century black religious affiliations began paving the road to education; black female churchgoers led the charge. Educational instruction by these women was not restricted to one-room classrooms or Sunday school meetings held in the basements of black churches. African American women not only instructed recently emancipated pupils in the basics of reading, writing, and arithmetic, but also trained black Philadelphians in personal conduct and social protocol. Through systematic education, religious instruction, and supervising private lives, black women attempted a large task: to transform the image of black Philadelphia, with the desire of attaining respectability and the rights of citizenship. Through the imposition of rigid codes of conduct, black women reconstructed a free community while developing notions of motherhood, womanhood, family life, and the personal domestic sphere.

Early Black Education in Philadelphia

Central to the formation of the free black community was education. As the 1790s ushered in a new spirit of self-help and autonomy among free people, black men and women began to mold and direct the education being afforded their children and, in many cases, the adult community. Philadelphia's story of formal black education began in the early 1750s with the Quaker activist Anthony Benezet. A Huguenot who migrated to Philadelphia in 1731, Benezet became one of the earliest outspoken antislavery agitators. Remembered most for his numerous antislavery pamphlets, Benezet became not only an agitator for the abolition of slavery but also an advocate for the rights of black men and women in America. Benezet, along with a handful of other members, was responsible for coaxing the Philadelphia Monthly Meeting to ban the institution of slavery among its members, coercing fellow Quakers to emancipate their slaves. Although many Quakers viewed Benezet as eccentric, he was held in high regard and appreciated by black men and women, for he was willing to participate in hands-on reform.[10]

According to Benezet's memoir, he began teaching black children in his Philadelphia home during the evenings. As he took on the role of "friend" to the black community, he argued against white assumptions of black inferiority and its connection to a "barbaric" Africa.[11] Benezet proclaimed that African societies had proven themselves to be extremely productive and notable cultures, and that Africa had been misrepresented as a "jungle of barbarianism." He suggested that a purposeful misrepresentation of the African continent served to justify the institution of slavery in America and the West Indies. Rather, Benezet taught his black students, the conditions fostered by slavery debased and degraded black Americans. The ability to learn was not specific to white people.[12]

Throughout the midcentury, other philanthropic individuals and organizations joined in the movement to educate black children. In 1758 the Bray Associates, an Anglican philanthropic society, opened a small school to educate both free and enslaved blacks within the city limits. The school was to enroll approximately thirty scholars per year; among the first students to be enrolled was one Othello, the house servant of Benjamin Franklin.[13] Male students were instructed in reading, while female students learned reading as well as the skills of sewing and knitting. In addition to academics both male and female students attended church services twice weekly.[14] The majority of small white philanthropic groups involved in African American education insisted on strict religious instruction, interpreting the Christian concept as an integral part of black education and of civilizing the entire black race. Poor white students were instructed in a similar manner in separate schools, where moral fiber and fierce piety served as the bedrocks of the curriculum.

In general, primary education for all classes remained elusive before the Revolution, which makes the inclusion of young black girls in these early colonial schools all the more notable. Unlike white schools throughout the North, black schools were coeducational from their inception. Young white girls, both servant and free, attended single-sex educational facilities.[15] Education for young black girls did not focus solely on the fundamentals of literacy, but also included skills such as sewing and knitting, which would undoubtedly assist them in a future of domestic service as well as in the care of their own families: in this regard the curriculum was similar to that taught to any poor girls.

The Quaker community of Philadelphia, and later the Pennsylvania Abolition Society, slowly began to support Benezet's goal of black education. Benezet worked to expand his efforts beyond his home, and in January of 1770 he approached the Philadelphia Monthly Meeting about its supporting an actual school for black children.[16] The Meeting agreed, and over the course of twenty years black education in Philadelphia moved from the home of Benezet to a new, freestanding schoolhouse. Like New York, Philadelphia would slowly produce a small cohort of educated black men and women, groomed to eventually adopt leadership roles within the free black community.[17]

There were many motives behind the construction of the school. Several members of the Quaker community expressed the desire to educate African American children as an immediate protest for equality; however, most Friends chose to support the school for different reasons. Believing that the existence of their school would gradually encourage slave masters to take greater responsibility for the education of their slaves, most Friends viewed their school as an example of the gradualist worldview.[18] As the school would be open to both enslaved and free children, members of the Quaker community hoped that slaveholders would educate their slaves to prepare them for freedom.

Other states such as New York also began to educate black men and women. The New York Manumission Society founded the African Free School in 1787. Like the Pennsylvania Abolition Society, the Manumission Society was interested in emancipation and convincing white New Yorkers of the benefits of a free society. They assisted enslaved and free men, women, and children in attending traditional schools; the Anglican Church of New York also educated slaves whose masters allowed them to attend school.

Philadelphia Quakers felt that education would uplift freed men and women from their enslaved pasts; it would also, supposedly, nurture the developing republic.[19] Quaker support allowed Benezet's small school to grow. In 1771 the one-story brick schoolhouse was built on Walnut Street, and over the next five years 250 children and adults received some form of elementary education at the small Walnut Street School. Although the war disrupted attendance in 1775, the Quaker school continued to educate black Philadelphians throughout the late eighteenth century.[20]

After Anthony Benezet died in 1784, a part of his estate was left to "hire and employ a religious minded person or persons to teach a number of Negro, Mulatto, or Indian children, to read, write, arithmetic, plain accounts, needle-work etc."[21] A section of his estate was designated for the establishment of the Rasberry Street School, which continued the process of educating free and enslaved blacks during traditional hours and at night at the turn of the nineteenth century.[22]

In 1793 the PAS opened another school for free blacks on Cherry Street in Philadelphia; for what appears to have been the first time, it employed an African-born schoolmistress to direct the school. Eleanor Harris, a respected member of the early black community in Philadelphia, taught and directed the school for four years, until her death in 1797.[23] Eleanor Harris's position of leadership in one of the PAS schools signaled a change in the understanding of black education. Though philanthropic leadership had charted the direction of instruction for both enslaved and free people of African descent, the turn of the century witnessed a transformation in the responsibility for and control over the education of black Philadelphians. Having received instruction in the small schools established by Benezet and other Quakers during the 1750s and 1760s, a new generation of black men and women wrested control of the schools away from white philanthropy. They set about on a new, autonomous path, constructing their own black schools.

The Black Church and Education

In the early years of the nineteenth century, black Philadelphians worked to create institutions that pushed for racial equality and assisted newly freed men and women. The most famed of these institutions were the churches: the First African Church, later renamed the African Episcopal Church of St. Thomas, led by Absalom Jones, and Mother Bethel, the first independent African Methodist Episcopal Church.[24] Both appeared in the early 1790s, ten years or more after enactment of the Gradual Abolition Act of Pennsylvania. The new spirit of autonomy and control among African American Philadelphians pushed them to mold and direct the education being afforded their children and the adult community. The rise of Sunday schools, beginning in the 1790s, played a significant role in the education of whites and blacks during the early republic, while an independent black church movement began working in tandem with independent black educators. The center of this black church movement lay within the walls of Mother Bethel African Methodist Episcopal Church, founded in 1794 by Richard Allen, a prominent black citizen.

Allen understood the need for the free black community to control its own church. Born a slave in 1760, Allen had been owned by Benjamin Chew, a lawyer and Philadelphia official. Although Chew lived in Philadelphia, he maintained a plantation in Delaware where Allen and his family resided. Allen experienced the breakup of his family as his parents and siblings were sold to different owners and he was left to make his own way. Following his conversion to Methodism, Allen was eventually offered the opportunity to purchase his own freedom, just before his twentieth birthday, in 1780. Allen adopted a new surname that signified his free status; he would lead black Philadelphians toward a path of religious autonomy.[25] By 1795 Richard Allen had established the first Sunday school for black children in America.[26] The next year Allen launched a night school for adults, a form of education extremely attractive to African Americans desirous of a formal education who had to work during normal business hours.

As African Americans worked to reform black education, they leaned on their friends in white philanthropic organizations. Unfortunately, black Philadelphians faced a succession of disappointments as organizations such as the PAS proved unprepared and unwilling to give significant control to blacks. In 1799 the PAS provided Absalom Jones of the African Episcopal Church with funds to open a preschool for black children in his home.[27] Jones's story was similar to Allen's. Jones was born a slave in southern Delaware in 1747. Separated from his family by a move to Philadelphia, Jones eventually purchased his freedom at the age of thirty-eight and spent the rest of his life building and promoting the free black community.[28]

The PAS also opened a school in the Northern Liberties section of the city operated by African American teachers for the instruction of young children.[29] Although the PAS allocated some control of their schools to black residents, they still reserved the right to determine the curriculum in their facilities. The PAS closed the Northern Liberties School and withdrew their support from Absalom Jones's preschool after the organization's inspecting committee claimed that Jones, like the teacher at the Northern Liberties School, was too "lenient" with his children. A committee report stated that "it is not practical at present to have black children properly taught by a black person."[30]

By the turn of the century, the Pennsylvania Abolition Society made their position on black education quite clear. Withdrawing all support from the three schools staffed and run by black Philadelphians, they created a new and larger school at Sixth and Walnut Streets, employing only white teachers to instruct black students. Absalom Jones and several other black teachers were all dismissed by the PAS, yet they continued to teach black children in their own homes or churches. Cyrus Bustil, an African American caterer and baker, opened a school in his home on Third Street in 1803, as a handful of black Philadelphians took on the responsibility of instructing the children of their community. In 1807 Richard Allen organized the Society of Free People of Color for Promoting the Instruction of School Education of Children of African Descent.[31] This organization committed itself to the collection of funds to enlarge and rejuvenate black education at Mother Bethel Church. Absalom Jones also enlarged his school at St. Thomas Episcopal Church and reopened the school for black children in the Northern Liberties section of the city that had been abandoned by the PAS.

According to the records of the Committee of Education established by the PAS, twice as many young black males attended school as did black females. In 1800 a "List of Girls in the Black School under the Care of the Committee of Education of the Abolition Society" recorded the names, ages, and academic information of all of their scholars. In July of that year only eleven black girls were enrolled in the school, whereas twenty-two black boys were in attendance.[32] Only small glimpses of young African American girls educated at the turn of the nineteenth century have been uncovered. Eight-year-old Jane Nash attended one of the PAS schools for whole-day sessions, where she was to master her "letters."[33] The records indicate that a John Folwell sponsored Nash's enrollment at the school, which indicates that she was most likely his indentured servant. As we saw in the servitude contracts, some white masters agreed to provide basic education to their servants, and John Folwell, John Richards, and Daniel Dupuy were listed on the student roster as having each sponsored one young girl in school. Sarah Lewis also attended the school, and at age fifteen, she had moved past the stage of "learning her letters" to that of spelling and reading. Her parents sent her to school for whole-day sessions, as they did seventeen-year-old Rebecca Lewis, most likely her sister. Three-year-old Patty Penington was also enrolled as a part-time scholar.[34] Young girls participated in formal education at the expense of both masters and parents.

Although earnest efforts were made to strengthen the education of black Philadelphia, only a fraction of black children attended school, either full- or part-time. According to the PAS, the problem began with the inability of many black families to release their children from work to attend school. The need to hire out children at an early age placed a tremendous obstacle in the path of education. In addition, the PAS noted that most whites who kept indentured servants were not willing to educate them, and they did not connect social improvement with the education of blacks. At a time when universal public education was unheard of, education beyond the rudiments of literacy was reserved for the wealthy. The expense of educating a servant could prove great, and it became more and more difficult for the PAS to convince white Philadelphia to help educate the free black community.[35] By 1804 the PAS had abandoned support for black school education, urging parents to bind out their children instead to masters who would teach them rudimentary literacy and a useful trade.[36] Although this alternative fell drastically short of the initial goals of the PAS, it was a way to offer at the very least a simple education to black children.

There is evidence that suggests white Philadelphians were not alone in their frustration and hesitation about educating African Americans. A small number of black Philadelphians themselves did not support formal education. A smattering of church sermons and memoirs suggests that black preachers were perhaps reluctant to encourage their parishioners to become literate, deeming a formal education an unrealistic demand. Some preachers saw blacks' lack of interest in night and charity schools as a testament of faith in the church as a tool for empowerment. It would be religion, not literacy, that would provide self-improvement and autonomy to the black community.[37]

Most African American preachers in the early nineteenth century were themselves illiterate. Many ministers, with the exceptions of Richard Allen and Absalom Jones, hesitated to comment on the issue. Making their way in the oral culture of the black church through their gifts for memorization, recitation, and exhortation, ministers would have uncomfortably felt the growing pressure to become educated themselves. Dodging the scrutiny of their congregations, they were cool to the school problem quite possibly in order to spare themselves embarrassment.[38]

But it is also important to note that African American preachers did not speak out against black education. Overall, scarce attendance at youth and adult day and evening schools should not be construed as blacks' apathy but as a consequence of arduous working hours. Men, women, and children often toiled twelve to fourteen hours a day, five to six days a week. The fledgling schools established by the black church continued to teach small numbers of the African American population throughout the first few decades of the nineteenth century. It would not be until 1822 that public school education was universally extended to black residents of the city.[39]

Providing Mutual Aid, Black Self-Help, and Philanthropy

African Americans continued to support the schools and the black churches. Religion and education, however, were but two components necessary for uplift and autonomy. Respectability and strict moral fiber would become central to developing communities. These values are most evident

in the construction of numerous mutual aid societies. Black beneficial benevolent societies in the city dated back to the Free African Society of Philadelphia, the first black mutual aid society created in America, founded in 1787.
This nondenominational organization welcomed men and women who led
"orderly and sober" lives.[40] In 1787 this would have implied piety, sobriety,
cleanliness, and some deference to the value of education.

Moral reform movements in the late eighteenth and early nineteenth centuries served as an impetus for black Philadelphians to lift others out of
their "irreligious and uncivilized state."[41] Northern communities witnessed
a great transformation in the years of the early republic: the end of servitude
and slavery and the beginning of the "market revolution."[42] This transition
provided a backdrop for the many reform movements that proliferated in
the 1820s, 1830s, and 1840s, including the work of the Free African Society,
which pioneered moral reform within the black community. Not only would
the organization monitor the personal lives of Philadelphia's African American residents; it would also observe individual society members. The Committee of Monitors conducted surprise visits at the homes of its members to
ensure morality and piety in the domestic sphere.

White women, too, throughout New England and the mid-Atlantic states
experienced the religious revival and reform of the Second Great Awakening, and they simultaneously organized societies designed to cure the evils of
society. Sometimes they worked in league with men, sometimes on their own.
Temperance groups, charitable and missionary organizations, and maternal
associations were intended to make them better mothers and wives and
thus contributors to the republic.[43] The historian Anne Boylan explains that
many postrevolutionary mutual aid organizations promoted self-empower-
ment among working-class women, who were perhaps the most vulnerable
to economic hard times. As laboring women in these mutual aid societies
helped themselves and their poorer neighbors gently challenge the hegemony
of wealthy white Protestant women's associations, they placed a great deal
of emphasis on improving the lives of members of their own religious and
ethnic groups.[44]

African American women's societies, preceding many of these better-
known white women's organizations, were created under a similar, yet more
intimate influence. African American women in the city knew personally
the effects of poverty; slavery was but a generation removed, and their extended kin benefited from black charitable assistance. White philanthropic
organizations, accustomed to assisting only poor whites, in many cases refused to aid black men and women. Thus, the black women's organizations helped to fill a void in the city's well-developed associational structure.

These associations allowed black women to feed their children, assist the sick, and bury the dead. Although extremely important, the societies were nevertheless able to assist only a fraction of the poor, usually those who were dues-paying members.

The existence of visible women's associations devoted to benevolence soon became the embodiment of the new nineteenth-century "true womanhood," expanded to include black women. Community members admired those who belonged to such organizations. These women incorporated democratic ideals in their societies and wove their relationships and friendships through community life. The organizations collectively "mothered" the black community of Philadelphia.

The Female Benevolent Society of St. Thomas, formed in 1793, is perhaps the oldest women's philanthropic organization on record. Organized two years before its male counterpart, the African Friendly Society of St. Thomas, this African American society appears to have remained active well into the 1820s.[45] Organizations such as the Daughters for the County Angola Beneficial Association, founded in 1808, grew in size and wealth; its forty members and annual income of one hundred dollars went to support impoverished black women and men.[46] During the first three decades of the nineteenth century, dozens of mutual aid societies began to offer a benevolent and recreational outlet for black women. Membership ranged from 240 women in the Female Shipley Association, which collected more than seven hundred dollars in dues and donations annually, to the small women's group the Daughters of Jerusalem, whose thirty-four members collected and distributed clothing to the sick and infirm.[47] Over sixty women's organizations existed in Philadelphia, and many women belonged to more than one at a time. Most provided food and clothing to downtrodden African American residents of Philadelphia.

The names of these societies evoked the members' faith, devotion to their churches, and abolitionist politics. Some of them during the first years of the nineteenth century were the Daughters of St. Paul, of St. Thomas, of St. James, and of St. Matthew, as well as the Daughters of Absalom and the Benevolent Daughters of Allen. Several organizations named themselves after more prominent white activists—for example, the Daughters of Garrison, the Female Benezet Society, the Female Arthur Tappan Society, and the Female Granville Society.[48] Many more organizations named themselves by religious affiliations. Others, interestingly, selected names connected to Africa or what was construed as African heritage: the Female African Benevolent Society, the African Female Band, the Daughters for the County Angola Beneficial Association, the African Female Union, and the Daughters of Africa. These women of the early nineteenth-century women's club movement were, in most cases, generations removed from the continent of Africa, yet they still recognized it as a central connection.

Few of the societies left records. The Daughters of Africa was one that did; their meticulous records allow a glimpse of the group's membership lists and finances. The Daughters of Africa helped poor African Americans with funeral expenses and aided the sick and unemployed. Their Order Book covering the years 1821–29 shows about two hundred African American women involved.[49] Occasionally working with other charities, the Daughters of Africa not only assisted the disadvantaged, but also formalized a black women's social sphere connected to reform and respectability.

Although the Daughters of Africa did assist nonmembers, their record books show that most contributions went to women affiliated with the society. This was fundamentally a mutual aid society, not a charity. Sidney Buck and Elizabeth Griffith appear to have been the financial liaisons between the officers and the members. The Order Book of the society noted frequent occasions when Buck and Griffith received money for sick members. In 1822, for example, the Order Book noted that "E. Griffith and Sidney Buck [be given] the sume of one dollar and fifty cents for Margaret Lynsey a sick member of the Daughters of Africa Society."[50] From the beginning, the minutes demonstrate a rudimentary grasp of writing skills, and with each year, as the Daughters of Africa helped their sisters in need, they educated themselves. Improved note taking, spelling, and grammar show the educational value of associational life.

Many requests for help came after the deaths of loved ones from those who were unable to gather the money necessary to bury the dead. The Daughters of Africa were particularly helpful to recent widows. The death of a husband could mean financial ruin, since so many black women were already teetering on the brink of destitution. The money allotted to members for funeral expenses varied. On May 1, 1822, E. Drummers received six dollars for the burial of her husband.[51] This amount was standard, but it defrayed only a portion of the cost of a burial. In a few instances the Daughters of Africa were asked to loan or donate larger sums, as in the case of one member, Rachel Corks: "To Mrs. Morris Treasurer of the Daughters of Africa Please to pay Sidney Buck one of the Committee the sume of Eighteen Dollars for the Funurall expense of Rachel Corks one of the members of the D."[52]

Membership in the organization thus ensured, at the very least, a decent burial. To many African American men and women—indeed, to all laboring people—a proper burial was of great importance. Throughout the nineteenth and twentieth centuries, African Americans worked hard to save money for a respectable burial. Poverty did not prevent many women from expecting an elaborate funeral, for death represented not only a solemn, sad occasion, but a jubilant event that marked an escape from the bonds of racism and poverty to a world of freedom in heaven.[53] Although the Daughters of Africa were free, most would have been indentured servants or enslaved in their earlier lives. Death meant sorrow, but also release, and it needed to be marked with care and love.

Membership in the early black philanthropic organizations provided an arena for self-help, stability, and socializing, while simultaneously ensuring those members with few or no kinfolk that they would be supported in their time of need. The minimal dues paid by the two hundred members were a form of affiliation, as well as social insurance. In providing a coffin for Mary Baxter or sick dues to Leah Gibson, the Daughters of Africa ensured that while supporting larger causes in the city the organization would also nurture its members. In an almost familial tone, African American women's mutual aid societies provided a social and financial support network for hundreds of black women living during the early years of the new republic.[54]

Social responsibility followed African Americans from their mutual aid societies into the streets and into their neighborhoods. Civil and appropriate neighborly relations were manifestations of a social decorum that by the 1820s had become sanctioned and protected by church law. In 1829, for example, the church tribunal of Mother Bethel Church met at a conference room on Spruce Street to discuss the case of one Ann Galdon. Galdon, a member of the church who was accused of a grievous public display of disrespectful behavior, had beaten her neighbor Anne Harris in the street.[55]

The brawl between two individuals became public controversy among the members of Mother Bethel, and the two women found themselves answering to a church tribunal. The victim, Harris, told the story of her assault in great detail. Neighborly relations had gone sour between the two when a rumor about Harris's drinking had circulated throughout the neighborhood. Concerned about her reputation, Harris confronted her accuser, demanding an explanation for the slander. According to Harris, Galdon met her questions with fierce anger and defensiveness, shouting obscenities and calling Harris "a black infurnall beach." Harris concluded her testimony, accusing Galdon of assault: "she struck me in the mouth."[56]

Galdon was given the opportunity to explain herself before the church tribunal, and her testimony differed greatly from her neighbor's. She claimed that the assault was a response to a previous incident involving her child.

The child had picked up an old piece of carpeting in the street and Harris had attacked the child because she wanted the rug. When Galdon approached her, Harris denied the allegation, calling her a "black hornery Negor." And so it went. Galdon warned Harris not to defame her: "I told her if she called me that againe I would strike her." Apparently, Harris did not heed her warning.[57]

There were several female witnesses called forth. Abigail Hamilton testified that the fight was fierce. She "saw them both fighting in the Publice Alley/ Blackbery Ally, [and] they tore each others H.Chifs [handkerchiefs] off there necks & there frocks were open behind & [Galdon] held fast of [Harris]. Mr. Hamilton parted them."[58] Mary Williams, a next-door neighbor, had never known Harris to drink or be imprudent in her behavior. After listening to the conflicting accounts, the disciplinary tribunal ruled: "We the Committee have taken the above case into Consideration & are of the opinion that Ann Galdon are guilty of a Breech of Discipline by striking her Sister A.H. & After being parted, [she] threat[ened] her againe to fight her—& is accordingly disowned. Ann Harris is sospended for 3 months from all privileges of close meeting for making use of improper Language to & fighting her Sister A. Galdon."[59]

It is clear from the tribunal's decision that improper conduct was unacceptable, and that no matter the reason, it would not be tolerated. Both Galdon and Harris not only had to endure suspension from the church, but also had to swallow public embarrassment.

The tribunal accounts demonstrate the immense control of the church regarding the lives of its members. Expulsion from the church was no small thing: black life was centered on religion and denominational affiliations. It meant social isolation and disconnection from any mutual aid or social associations, since those societies were so closely tied to the churches. Galdon was now ineligible for any assistance from the Daughters of Allen—or any other church society, for that matter. In a city that offered little in the way of public assistance to its residents of color, isolation from the church could lead to desperation and pauperism.

Appropriate language was also an issue. The use of obscenities—even imprudent language—was a breach of moral standards. A fit of rage or an altercation could provoke harsh and profane words, but swearing in the public streets, or even at home, could lead to dismissal from the church. Maria Bruston encountered this situation in 1829, when she was charged with immorality and profane swearing by the disciplinary committee. The accusation was coupled with a complaint of her refusal to pay back a loan to her neighbor, Mary Ann Roberts. Roberts reported to the committee that

Bruston often spoke poorly to the children in the neighborhood: "if she did not put a warrant on there backs she hope that Jesus Christ might come down and Dam her."[60] The invocation of Christ's name "in vain" was forbidden, and Bruston found herself in a serious situation when that charge was compounded by her inability to repay a five-dollar debt to the plaintiff. When the tribunal asked her for a response, she "confessed that she swares sometimes."[61] Although there is nothing in the records to indicate why Bruston could not pay back her loan, she made no excuses. Bruston was expelled from the church and ostracized because of her language and perhaps her inability to pay back a small loan.[62]

The close ties of black women had contradictory effects. Female neighbors approached their church elders with these cases, asking them to judge and punish those who committed infractions of the "moral law." We can understand their vigilance not only as an effort to shore up their own authority, but also as a practical response to disorder in their neighborhoods. Although major crimes were reported to the constables and watchmen who roamed the city, there was no formal police force. Neighborhood networks were a crucial means of self-regulation. The disciplinary committee was a formal mechanism to correct injustice and ensure vigilance. So "mothers of the church" nurtured fellow members through assistance and support in times of need, but they also disciplined each other. Petty domestic squabbles and altercations among church members were blemishes on the good reputation of the black community; in conjunction with traditional mechanisms of law enforcement, African American women monitored their neighborhoods to reinforce social order.[63] These women held no formal positions on the church disciplinary committee, yet they regulated social etiquette and behavior by informing the church of members' indiscretions. The church hierarchy was entirely male; but African American women used their positions as mothers, wives, neighbors, and obedient church members to bring their community members to trial.

The church also examined the private relationships between husbands and wives. In many instances, husbands and wives refused to take their personal business or arguments to the tribunal. In fact, it was peers and friends, mostly female, who pushed forth many of the cases. If the behavior of a husband or wife was suspect, even within the confines of the couple's own home, he or she was subject to the collective female gaze.

In 1823, for instance, Isaac and Jane Durham were brought before the tribunal for engaging in a domestic dispute that eventually led to physical violence. According to Jane's testimony, her employment outside the home was at the root of the argument. As a washerwoman (like thousands of other black women), she had to spend a great deal of time washing clothes for white families in the city. She was unable to spend all of her time at home, tending to the domestic duties expected of a "good wife," as her income was necessary to help support the family. Unhappy that her work kept her away from the house, Jane Durham's husband turned suspicious, subtly accusing her of improper behavior. One evening, as the couple prepared for bed, Isaac became enraged, questioning his wife's whereabouts; in Jane's words, "he asked me what I was doing there [a]nd why I did not go where I slept for these two nights."[64]

Jane Durham went on to explain to him that her washing kept her away from the home; her husband became angrier, however, and eventually kicked her out of the bed and began to abuse her physically. Jane Durham stated that "he struck me several times and hurt me very much. I hallowed murder and the watchman came."[65]

Isaac Durham's version was very different from the one recorded by his wife during the proceedings. His testimony stated that his wife came and awakened him "late at night [and] the candle was shining in my face. I told her to blow it out. I then asked where she slept last night. She [said] that was her bed and told me to go downstairs to my bed. I told her to hush and let me alone or I would put her out of the bed. She laid hold of the bed cloathes and then took a foul kick of me and then cryed murder until the watchman came."[66]

After both parties presented their testimony to the church elders, the tribunal found both Jane and Isaac Durham guilty of a "Breech of Discipline" and placed them on a six-month probation period. If any rules of decorum or piety were violated during their probation, both Jane and Isaac Durham would be permanently expelled from the church.[67]

Surveyed by one another, black men and women were constantly on display, so that the line between the worlds of the public and the private became blurred. Aware of the slight protections given them by the church, African American women used the disciplinary committee to control their own husbands. The threat of embarrassment or social ostracism could keep male church members in line. The church at times protected women from insult and injury, but it often proved very difficult for an African American woman to be a "good wife" in nineteenth-century Philadelphia.

Many cases were brought to disciplinary committees against a spouse, most often by a woman charging physical abuse or financial abandonment by her husband. Hannah Dublin brought her husband, Morris Dublin, an official of the church, up on charges that he was not able to support his family, and that he sold "the household goods and some of their belongings to other people, and [he took] his clothes and market[ed them] elsewhere."[68] Morris denied the charge; he claimed that he had to sell their household goods so that he could pay the rent. He countered with a charge against his wife: he took his clothes away from the house not to sell them, but because she refused to wash or mend them. Hannah would "take my cloathes and dash them on the floor." Dublin also charged that his wife had physically abused him by striking him on the head.[69]

Dublin was still found guilty of imprudent conduct, stripped of his formal office in the church, and placed on probation for six months. His suspension must have been extremely embarrassing for the once-respected official. Often the tribunal found in favor of the female plaintiff, especially in the case of physical abuse by a spouse. The committee would not tolerate physical abuse of any kind.

Adultery was central to many cases. It was frequently a charge brought by an outside party rather than a spouse. Perhaps because adultery was so extremely embarrassing, accusations of extramarital affairs or "immoral conduct" often came from church elders. The charge of adultery encompassed more than the act of infidelity: adults who had sex outside marriage were also charged and punished for inappropriate conduct.

In July 1829 a charge of adultery was brought against Hannah Sawden and Abraham Lunum. They had certainly cohabited: Lunum acknowledged "having lived in the same room" with Sawden, but he testified that he spent the nights on the floor until the winter came. Then it was the cold, not sex, that put the pair in the same bed. Sawden enticed him with the observation that "the weather was cold [and you] better come to bed." Lunum followed her suggestion and, according to his testimony, Sawden then "forced [him] to the Commission of the Act."[70]

Sawden refused to appear in front of the church tribunal: she "acknowledged that she was in the family way" and that the father of her child was indeed Abraham Lunum.[71] The outcome of this trial was not recorded, but we can assume that both Hannah Sawden and Abraham Lunum were disciplined, if not expelled from the church.

Church members publicly embarrassed at an open trial were also interrogated by church members in their households. Any member of the church community accused of an infraction of the discipline was visited at home and questioned before being summoned to court. A woman like Sawden, so clearly in the wrong by virtue of her pregnancy, most likely knew what the outcome of the trial would be, and she simply refused to appear. Perhaps embarrassment kept her away, or defiance of church authority, or dislike of meddlesome church elders. Like the adulterers

Sawden and Lunum, Robert Bell was summoned to trial on the same day for infidelity and "getting a woman with child." When asked by a member of the church if the accusation was true, Bell admitted that the child was his own but refused to attend the trial.[72] All three adulterers, Hannah Sawden, Abraham Lunum, and Robert Bell, were found guilty of "breech of discipline" and immoral conduct.

Sexual affairs created turmoil in the neighborhood. Abigail Robinson was charged with threatening physical assault on Dolly Thorn in 1823. Thorn had supposedly tried to seduce Robinson's husband and "from time to time decoyed [Robinson's] husband" into her home. According to the threatened wife, Thorn was involved with other married men, such as Morris Dublin, another member of the church brought up on charges of infidelity. Robinson made it clear to her adversary that "she should not part my husband and me."[73]

Robinson's reference to yet another case of adultery, which had already come before the committee, indicates the very public nature of these trials. They destroyed reputations and served as a showcase for communal hostility directed at anyone found guilty of immoral conduct. Robinson went on to state that her familial routine was often disturbed by Thorn, for "my husband had not time to eat his victuals for D.T. keeps sending him to pray for her 2 or 3 times during one meal." According to further testimony, Thorn was also given to profanity: she had called Abigail Robinson a "Devil" and hoped that she "would go to hell any how."[74] The committee ruled on the infraction without much explanation, simply noting a remarkable counterintuitive verdict. "The Committee are of the opinion that Abigail Robinson is guilty of a Breach of Discipline and is no more a member of the Society."[75] In this case the threat of public and physical violence trumped any accusations regarding possible infidelity.

Sometimes surveillance backfired on the aggrieved wives and virtuous neighbors. In 1830 Sarah Jones, a member of Mother Bethel Church, brought Robert G. Johnson and his wife in front of the disciplinary trial on the charge of "bedding together before they were married."[76] The Johnsons denied all charges. When Jones had to provide proof to support her accusation, she could only weakly state that when she had rented the couple a room, the woman's father had told her they were unmarried. Still, she rented them a place to live and "suffered them to sleep together 3 days or nights before she said anything to them."[77] The committee heard the accusations hurled at the Johnsons by Sarah Jones and "after mature reflection on the case we consider that Robt. & Wife [are] acquited of the Charge." The Johnsons were able to dodge condemnation, but Sarah Jones was not so fortunate. She was found "guilty of a Breach of the Discipline by suffering them to sleep there 3 nights before they were married nowlingly according to her own words in her house and is accordingly disowned from the Church."[78] Jones's attempt to use gossip and speculation as a way in which to embarrass and punish her renters proved to be self-incriminating—even though, as it turned out, she was right. Annoyed with what appeared to be a spiteful accusation, the committee found the plaintiff guilty instead of the defendants, an action that probably reduced the number of frivolous charges and accusations against church members and kept gossip-based charges at a minimum. The church disciplinary tribunal was a serious and important part of the free black community, and all its business was to be considered as such. If a charge came in front of the committee without substantial proof, not only would it be dismissed, but it could also be used against the plaintiff. Reputations were at stake and decorum and authority had to be protected. Men probably did not want to be seen as an extension of merely spiteful, gossip-mongering, meddling women—even though they worked mostly in tandem with them.

Among the many moral infractions that came before the committee, adultery was the most common. Crimes such as arson, robbery, and murder did not appear in the minutes; they were most certainly dealt with by city and state authorities. Another grievous infraction cited in the minutes of Mother Bethel was the "crime" of being illegitimate. For the members of Mother Bethel and the Philadelphia community, moral reform was deeply connected to the erasure of the abomination of slavery. The memory of the results of forced sexual encounters in slavery heightened black concern in the free community about the public image of African American men and women—especially women. Sex outside the confines of marriage was an individual sin, but it also damaged the image of the entire community. Among the respectable, single motherhood was a source of tremendous concern and anxiety.

Men and women were both punished for premarital sex. Male members were normally confronted with a short and succinct charge of immoral conduct, followed by expulsion. Women, however, were scrutinized and subjected to long, painful trials. In the 1829 case of Hannah Harris, for instance, Harris's neighbor Matilda Black charged her with pregnancy and infanticide. Harris was accused of delivering her illegitimate baby in the chamber pot of her uncle's privy—a classic place of birth for poor, frightened women—and of asking him to dispose of the baby after its birth.[79] According to Black's testimony, she learned of the situation after visiting Harris's home, where she noticed a change in Harris's appearance. Black stated in her testimony that she "had 4 children & that if she ever herself was with child that she believed Hannah Harris was with child."[80]

Harris denied that she had been pregnant at all and thus that she had murdered a child. She explained that her uncle emptied the privy for her on one occasion when her children were sick and she was not at home. Not only did Harris deny the accusations made against her, but she also brought forth several character witnesses. Bashley Chandler, a neighbor, insisted that "she never saw anything in or about her that looked like her being in the state of pregnancy."[81] Five other women also denied the legitimacy of the charges. The six women went before the church tribunal on behalf of their neighbor, telling the tribunal that she was a good neighbor, not "disrespectful" and not guilty. The church elders agreed and acquitted Hannah Harris.[82] Irregularities in personal routine such as Harris's uncle's disposing of the chamber pot's contents, or Harris's larger appearance, triggered an entire investigation. Her case makes clear that the private worlds of black men and women in early Philadelphia were easily penetrable and often made public.

Poised to expand their mutual aid societies, schools, and church organizations, African Americans in Philadelphia looked toward the coming years as a time of possibility. The building of a free black community was, for the most part, successful, and although African Americans were appreciative of the white philanthropy offered to them during the early years of nation building, many were ready to cut sponsorship ties. The doors to black education were opened during the eighteenth century, and black Philadelphians were more than ready to navigate the stewardship of black organizational and social life in the city. African American women mothered their neighborhoods and looked toward protecting their brothers and sisters still held in bondage. Abolition became the central political concern for most of the African American elite during the first half of the nineteenth century, and black women prepared themselves for one of the major national debates of that period.

4

Voices from the Margins
The Philadelphia Female Anti-Slavery Society
1833–1840

In 1840 Sarah Mapps Douglass, a well-respected African American teacher in Philadelphia, requested the formal separation of her small female academy from its parent organization, the Philadelphia Female Anti-Slavery Society (PFASS). Although the society is considered one of the first interracial women's antislavery groups, most of its members were white. As antislavery organizations appeared to be less interested in black education by the middle decades of the nineteenth century, Douglass decided to withdraw her female academy from the control of the society. In a letter written to the PFASS Douglass expressed her gratitude for the two years of financial support offered by the society; however, she, along with several other prominent African Americans, would take control of the school and manage its affairs without white support.[1]

Although dismayed by the request for withdrawal, the members of the PFASS agreed to consider the termination of support for the female academy. Tension between Douglass and the board of managers was increasing because of Douglass's administrative decisions concerning her students. The board of managers reprimanded Douglass for allowing students to make up school absences that were due to inclement weather or sickness. The board also refused to pay the salary of a student assistant hired by Douglass.[2] By 1840 Douglass, as well as many other African American women in the society, appeared ready to part company and to manage the school autonomously. The PFASS eventually agreed to terminate its supervision and maintenance of the school, though it continued to support the academy by token gestures of kindness. Little by little the women of the PFASS relinquished their concern regarding Douglass and her female academy; nine years later, in 1849, all financial support from the PFASS was withdrawn from the school.

Although it took close to a decade to break from the society, the incident symbolized a growing tension between a new generation of African American leaders and white Philadelphia. In this northern city, known for its powerful black leadership and community organizations, African Americans made the gradual transition from slave to servant to free, autonomous men and women by the 1830s. Although the PFASS would retain African American members throughout the decades preceding the Civil War, black women preferred their own organizations, in which racism and perceptions of inferiority were simply not present. Interracial networking did, however, prove extremely important during the years of antislavery agitation, and many African American men and women remained committed to interracial assistance as they nurtured a free and stable black community.

By the 1840s slavery had run its course in Pennsylvania and its mid-Atlantic neighbors New York and New Jersey. Indentured servitude was a memory, and in its place stood a free black community supported by autonomous religious and mutual aid organizations that were sustained by a mature leadership. As the antislavery movement began to change in the northern cities, African American men and women stood prepared and eager to participate in a new politics. Although black Philadelphians were no longer enslaved, their freedom was far from secure, which prompted African Americans to wage war against the peculiar institution. So in Boston, New York, and Philadelphia black men and women worked not only to loosen the shackles of slavery across the country, but also to protect the promise of civil liberties and newly found freedom for northern black communities.

Many historians see the beginnings of this new wave of antislavery agitation with the appearance of William Lloyd Garrison's publication the *Liberator* on January 1, 1831. The newspaper's insistence on immediate emancipation, without financial compensation to slave owners, and social equality for black Americans challenged colonizationist sentiment, which had monopolized white antislavery activism in the 1820s.

The break from a gradualist approach toward one promoting immediate emancipation, along with a complete rejection of colonization as a remedy for race relations in America, moved the antislavery debate in a bold, new direction.[3] Inflammatory writings, petitions, and political debate, filled with the rhetoric of enlightenment theory, began to characterize and shape the antislavery debate. Abolition moved from the political periphery to the center, transforming what had been a white gentlemen's political activity into a national reform movement for ordinary men and women, white and black.[4]

Developments such as the closing of the international African slave trade in 1808, gradual emancipation in the North, and the prohibition of slavery in the Northwest Territory undoubtedly moved the issue of slavery closer to the center of national political debate. American slaveholders were essentially forced to depend on the reproduction of their own slaves, which created a new and expansive domestic slave trade.[5] As the southern slave trade expanded, freedom found its way to many northern African Americans, the result being a rocky political terrain for both pro- and antislavery advocates. Simultaneously the religious revivalism of the Second Great Awakening during the 1820s and 1830s advocated a national need to reunite mankind with God. For many new converts, both black and white, slavery was indeed a sin against the Creator.

Perhaps the first arena in which black men and women worked for the antislavery cause was the church. By the 1830s African American churches found themselves at the center of the debate. A new generation of free black men and women filled the pews of Mother Bethel and surrounding churches, pushing for immediate abolition and black equality. African American church congregations found themselves more diverse than ever: some members had been born free; some had reached freedom through indenture; and some were fugitives. A tradition of social uplift, reform, and education was tied to the city's black churches: religious autonomy provided a new communal confidence.[6] This confidence, experience, and political maturity allowed African American churches and their members to move beyond local matters of self-help, philanthropy, and financial survival. As they continued to build educational programs and mutual aid organizations, African American church members became a part of the national debate regarding slavery. Black men and women engaged in what would become the political debate of the century: abolition.

Antislavery circles provided the first organized forums in which white and black men and women could come together as political activists, Christian brothers and sisters, neighbors, and, in some cases, friends. Although African American participation in antislavery activities was limited mostly to the middle and elite classes, those activities opened a door for cooperative interaction between white and black Philadelphians. The antebellum abolition movement would create a new, politically active black elite who would become the political link between white and black Philadelphians.[7]

Abolitionist reform work meant many different things to African Americans in the northern city at the time. Not only would immediate emancipation erase the constant threat of kidnapping and enslavement feared by northern blacks, but it would also accelerate the release of family members and friends still in bondage. This new era of antislavery work also paved the way to interracial coalition building and social reform; their activities strengthened the position of the black elite within their own communities and among white organizations. Although antislavery work served a much larger community, it specifically served the African American elite by enlarging their social networks and elevating their local and national reputations. For many of the black elite, political reform work bolstered the respectability that came only with freedom.

But as interracial cooperation changed the face of abolitionist reform, it was met with a wave of intense controversy. Interracial organizations dedicated to antislavery agitation often encountered the violent hostility of white northerners. The lives of antislavery activists were often in peril as mobs of urban whites attacked them in cities such as Philadelphia, Boston, and New York.[8] When black and white men and women addressed large crowds about the evils of slavery, white opponents responded with rioting, arson, looting, and personal violence. White female abolitionists who broke from traditional social codes by engaging in public speaking ignited the anger of men and women who stood firmly against women's political involvement. The gathering of "promiscuous" audiences and women's central role in the reform movement of the century elicited fury in city after northern city.[9] Similarly, the sensationalized image of racial "amalgamation" that was portrayed as abolition's natural consequence produced an exaggerated hostility from proslavery sympathizers.[10]

Several antislavery organizations led by example, creating space for both black and white reformers. The Philadelphia Female Anti-Slavery Society was one of the earliest women's organizations to permit African American participation. Many white women involved in abolition work came from the most venerable families along the northeastern seaboard, carrying with them the privileges and respectability connected with their status. African American female reformers, however, did not have access to the same kind of respectability that protected white female abolitionists. Constantly degraded and discriminated against because of their race, African American women found their virtue was always open to the scrutiny of others. Still, as black women in Philadelphia continued to redefine themselves as mothers, wives, and women, the 1830s expanded their opportunities to legitimize themselves as respectable people, regardless of their race and gender. Building on the experiences of their own autonomous mutual aid organizations and religious leadership, black women injected themselves into the political arena of the antebellum era, articulating their voices from the margins. Like their fathers, husbands, and brothers, African American women became deeply involved in the movement, not only to free their brothers and sisters in bondage, but also to dismantle the stereotypes of themselves.

Only elite African American women were able to bridge the gap between white and black abolitionists of Philadelphia. Undoubtedly, the white elite did not deem black women who washed clothing, scrubbed streets, and performed other forms of menial labor appropriate candidates for the PFASS. Financial obligations forced most black women to work outside the home, so there was little time left for antislavery activity. The majority of African American women in Philadelphia, then, assisted the antislavery crusade through small donations to their own churches or through personal assistance to fugitive slaves.

As black activists such as Charlotte Forten and Sarah Douglass navigated the politically charged atmosphere of antislavery circles, they did so as mothers, daughters, working women, and free women. The opportunity to work in autonomous black circles and interracial societies must have proven difficult and tiring during these years. The antislavery circles, however, would serve as another chance for elite black women to prove themselves respectable and honorable women, not only to their own communities but to white Philadelphia and eventually to the nation at large. Unfortunately, the optimism experienced by African American women on the antislavery stage would quickly dim by the 1840s. By the eve of the Civil War, interracial political cooperation would prove difficult to sustain, and black and white women were left to distance themselves from one another.

A New Wave of Abolition: The American Anti-Slavery Society

Three weeks before Christmas in 1833, sixty-eight abolitionists from ten of the free states convened in Philadelphia's Adelphi Building. They had come together to organize a national society that would have as its main tenet the total and immediate abolition of slavery in the United States and the expansion of civil and religious equality for African Americans. Philadelphia thus became the birthplace of the American Anti-Slavery Society.[11]

Its constitution, cobbled together by William Lloyd Garrison, editor of the Massachusetts paper the *Liberator* and first president of the society, detailed the radical goals of the organization: "We shall circulate, unsparingly and extensively, anti-slavery tracts and periodicals. We shall enlist the pulpit and the press in the cause of the suffering and the dumb. We shall aim at a purification of the churches from all participation in the guilt of slavery. We shall encourage the labor of freemen rather than that of slaves by giving a preference to their productions; and we shall spare no exertions nor means to bring the whole nation to speedy repentance."[12]

The goals and expectations pleased many of the participants of the convention, but four of the sixty-eight were frustrated with one aspect of the society's constitution. Lucretia Mott, Lydia White, Esther Moore, and Sidney Ann Lewis, all residents of Philadelphia and observers at the convention, were irritated by the society's one glaring omission: women were excluded from official membership. Although women's participation was not forbidden by the bylaws of the American Anti-Slavery Society, women were not officially associated with it except through what Mott and other female reformers saw as conciliatory female auxiliaries.[13] Women were permitted to form their own organizations, but they were marginal groups whose main purpose was to serve and support the father organization.

Women's society building was a common practice by the early nineteenth century. African American and white women had by the time of the American Revolution established a precedent for social and benevolent organizing.[14] It was not, however, until the period of the radical abolitionist movement that women found an open door to political organizing and activity at the national level. Nineteenth-century male reformers constructed ways in which women could enter the political arena through "spontaneous conventions." These conventions, such as the female antislavery conventions hosted by female abolitionists throughout the 1830s and 1840s, were seen as "efficient manufactories of public opinion" and were not connected to the state or party system. The constitutional rights to freedom of assembly and to petition the government provided female antislavery societies and conventions with opportunities originally created for men.[15]

The female auxiliary movement of the antebellum era served many purposes for both men and women. Women, both white and black, used the antislavery circles to gain a foothold in formal politics. Organizational structures such as minute taking, election of officers, formal correspondence, and the official recording of society finances were learned and perfected by black and white female reformers during this period.

The female auxiliary suited male reformers' political and personal agendas. Although single-sex organizations engaged female reformers in fundraising and petition work, there was a distinct barrier: women organized and participated in sewing circles and annual fairs, but male reformers attended their own meetings. African American abolitionist societies also participated in reform efforts that paralleled whites'. In the eyes of many white reformers, free elite and middle-class blacks were welcome to work against the institution of slavery, especially by gathering financial support from the African American community. Black abolitionists, however, remained largely segregated from white abolitionist circles.

It was not until the American Anti-Slavery Convention of 1840 that the issue of women's formal inclusion within male abolitionist circles came to a head. When Abby Kelley, a Massachusetts leader, ran for a position on the business committee in the national society, the antislavery circuit found itself divided beyond repair. As the organization splintered over the issue of women's formal participation, William Lloyd Garrison and other "radicals" protested the exclusion of women and supported Abby Kelley's nomination. Others—notably the New Yorkers Lewis and Arthur Tappan—disagreed with this departure from the past and left the American Anti-Slavery Society to form the American and Foreign Anti-Slavery Society.[16] As the American Anti-Slavery Society remained divided, white women were permitted to move from peripheral female auxiliaries into positions of shared organizational control among the radical abolitionists. While white women made some strides in the dismantling of traditional gender barriers in the antislavery movement, their success occurred as the importance of the society declined. Racism and attitudes regarding black inferiority never allowed African American men or women to secure the same privileges. Thus, the majority of African American female reformers remained at the margins.

The Philadelphia Female Anti-Slavery Society

The 1830s marked the heyday of ladies' societies, and it was at this time that the Philadelphia Female Anti-Slavery Society came to life. Ten days after the founding of the American Anti-Slavery Society, in 1833, a small group of women, mostly Quaker and very well known in Philadelphia's abolitionist circles, joined together to "effectively aid in the relieving of the oppression of our suffering fellow creatures" and established the Philadelphia Female Anti-Slavery Society.[17] Although female antislavery societies in England and Boston predated the Philadelphia organization, the PFASS soon gained tremendous popularity and respect among northern abolitionists. As many antislavery societies developed over the course of the 1830s across the northeast, the PFASS took on a leading role. The society's popularity was due in part to its members' hard work and political commitment, but also to their distinction: white women such as Lucretia Mott, Angelina Grimké, and Mary Grew were but a few of the members whose names and reputations gave validity to the small organization. The society also demonstrated a belief in interracial membership practices that proved to be a rare feature among the early female antislavery societies.[18]

Although the impressive membership roster bolstered the society's reputation, it was the biracial nature of the organization that helped lend credence to a society interested in the emancipation of men and women of African descent. African American participation was of great importance to the women of the PFASS, for it strengthened their stance on the position of equality. The inclusion of black women in their membership served as a powerful political symbol for white members. But black women always remained a controllable minority within the organization. Only the most elite and highly educated African American women joined the society. Yet African American membership did prove useful in constructing a political and social bridge between wealthy white reformers and the black elite.[19] Although short-lived, the political connections and friendships derived from antislavery work provided the first example of a shared political and social sphere among elite women of different races in the United States.

Of the fourteen women who came together to write the constitution of the PFASS, two drafters, Margaretta Forten and Sarah McCrummell, were African American.[20] Several others, such as Charlotte and Sarah Forten, Harriet Forten Purvis, Grace and Sarah Douglass, Hetty Burr, and Mary Wood, eventually joined and signed the constitution.[21] During 1834, the first year of the society's existence, twenty-nine women signed their names to the PFASS constitution. Of those original members, at least nine were black Philadelphians. Initially, the PFASS was dedicated to abolishing slavery and improving the lives of free African Americans.[22]

As we have seen, a rich history of antislavery activity dating back to the eighteenth century involved both black and white Philadelphians. When gradual emancipation in Pennsylvania was enacted into law, agitation by Philadelphia's black communities began to take on a different form. No longer did black men and women rely on the supposed goodwill of slave masters or the decline in the economic feasibility of African enslavement to end the peculiar institution. Black leaders such as Absalom Jones and Richard Allen moved the early black abolitionist campaign from the parochial boundaries of Philadelphia and Pennsylvania to the national level by petitioning the federal government to end the slave trade in 1799.[23]

Members of the black elite, including William White, James Forten, and William Gray, were heavily involved with early petitioning and collecting of signatures among free blacks throughout the Philadelphia community. The petition of 1799 sent to Congress expressed a sincere and deferential gratitude for the liberty acquired by free African Americans and promised that those freedmen would remain pious and industrious people. The black elite, however, understood that their own freedom did not completely remove them from the trauma experienced by the masses of African men and women held in bondage across the country. Petitioners wrote that "a sense of social duty" moved them to action on the slaves' behalf, "believing them to be the objects of your representation . . . in common with ourselves and every other class of citizens."[24]

The petition did not call for the immediate release of all enslaved men and women but relied on a gradualist push for emancipation. Petitioners asked Congress to "prepare the way for the oppressed to go free" and for the immediate repeal of the Fugitive Slave Act of 1793; it called as well for the termination of the transatlantic slave trade.[25] The petition was delivered to Congress in early 1800, only to be tabled; Philadelphia reformers moved forward, however, constructing a second petition in 1801 in which they asked President Jefferson to acknowledge their concerns and requests.[26]

Black Philadelphians pressed for emancipation not only at the national level but also in the state legislature of Pennsylvania. Although the Gradual Abolition Act of 1780 brought freedom to many in the state, it left close to two thousand blacks born before 1780 enslaved. In 1808 the black communities of Philadelphia openly celebrated, as Congress appeared to move in the direction of abolition: it banned the transatlantic slave trade on January 1 of that year.[27]

As male leaders within the African American communities of Philadelphia established a history of political activism through petition signing and society building, their wives, daughters, and sisters followed suit with the construction of their own organizations. The early battles to enact a gradual emancipation bill in Pennsylvania and the organizing around the improvement of living conditions for black Philadelphians groomed African American women in Philadelphia to enter the antislavery arena as political activists. Decades of struggle and activism, then, paved the way for interracial work. Black women had formed their own auxiliary abolition societies before the formation of the PFASS, and their experience in these organizations strengthened the work of the society. The women brought with them a tradition of leadership that was carefully balanced between activism and accommodation.[28]

The PFASS served both black and white women in many ways. It was an alternative for African American women, especially those of elite standing, to the earlier societies founded and managed by black Philadelphians. Just as white women of the PFASS struggled to be included in the membership of the all-male AASS, black women fought for inclusion among white female abolitionists in Philadelphia and across the northeast. The PFASS provided black women with the first opportunity for recognition and leadership in a political arena separate from the black church. As African American women moved beyond the scope of the black church, they found themselves cast into an interracial crusade against slavery. As their husbands and sons became involved in the national debate against slavery, African American women followed suit, using the PFASS as a vehicle for increased autonomy, uplift, and political networking.

Although membership was open to any woman subscribing to the social and political goals of the organization, it was clear that the society was a small, elite, and mostly Quaker group of white Philadelphia women. We know about several members because they would become extremely important in reform circles. Lucretia Coffin Mott, the first corresponding secretary of the PFASS, was often considered the driving force behind the creation of the organization. Born in 1793 to a Quaker family in Nantucket, she attended a Friends boarding school in Poughkeepsie, New York, and in 1811 married James Mott.[29] Lucretia, James, and their six children eventually settled in Philadelphia, where James halted his successful dealings in the cotton trade because of its connection to slave labor, eventually becoming a wool merchant.[30] As active members in the Society of Friends, the Motts found their place among the Hicksite Quakers, a faction that split from the denomination in 1827 and was known for its interest in social reform. Hicksite Quakers would become the heart of the abolitionist movement in Pennsylvania.[31]

South Carolina's soon-to-be-famous Grimké sisters, Sarah and Angelina, were also among the earliest members of the PFASS. Raised in the plantation South, both women were intimately acquainted with the horrors of slavery. As members of the wealthy elite, the Grimké sisters later testified to the sexual immorality of the slave system, emphasizing its effect on white women. Not only did both Sarah and Angelina eventually leave the South and move to the Northeast, but they also experienced a religious conversion before and during their move. Convinced of the sin and immorality of slavery and heavily influenced by Quaker antislavery activists, Angelina left the Episcopal

Church, of which she had been a member for many years. She first joined the Presbyterian Church, but she was still dissatisfied and eventually found her way to the Society of Friends.[32]

After Sarah Grimké arrived in Philadelphia in the early 1820s, she also converted to Quakerism. She began attending a Quaker Meeting that was led by Lucretia Mott, where there were also other future members of the PFASS.[33] Their decisions to reject the institution of slavery, to leave the South, and to become Quakers made the Grimkés subject to vilification. Consequently, they could never return to their home in South Carolina, and they would be rejected by the majority of their family and friends.

The Grimkés' introduction to the Society of Friends not only paved the way for their participation in antislavery agitation, but also prepared them to accept and participate in female political activism. Through the Society of Friends both sisters met and prayed with Quaker women in Philadelphia, New York, and Boston. Although religion played a fundamental role in bringing many white and black abolitionists together, for many white women a shared purpose was political networking. Contact between Quaker members of the PFASS and female abolitionists throughout New England strengthened the network of women activists across the northern states.

During the summer of 1836 the American Anti-Slavery Society in New York invited Angelina Grimké to speak at parlor meetings and women's sewing circles. Angelina and Sarah were the first women to serve as traveling agents for the organization. The sisters were the only two women of forty-two trainees at a convention held for new agents at which a unanimous vote allowed them to participate equally in discussions.[34] Eventually the sisters moved beyond the confines of sewing circles and parlors to the public spheres of church facilities and antislavery conventions of "mixed" (male and female) audiences, where their public speaking precipitated an enormous scandal.

Esther Moore, the first elected president of the PFASS, was also a Quaker and married to the prominent Philadelphian physician Dr. Robert Moore. Lydia White, the organization's librarian, owned a free-labor dry goods store; Anna Bunting was named the first treasurer of the society.[35] The recording secretary, Margaretta Forten, a daughter of the prominent sailmaker James Forten, was one of two African American women elected to an official position in the PFASS before 1840. The Forten family had a strong reputation throughout the city for achievement, abolitionism, and participation in the city's effort to aid fugitive slaves.[36]

The women of the PFASS and the women of the Boston auxiliary of the AASS considered themselves progressive, often boasting of their interracial memberships. Compared to such female auxiliaries as those in western New York, Fall River, Massachusetts, and New York City, whose memberships consisted only of white women, the PFASS and the Boston society were considered radical because of their inclusion of African American members and elected officers.[37] The PFASS was often compared to the Boston auxiliary antislavery society because of their interracialism and geographical connections: many of the women in the PFASS were born, raised, or educated in New England and eventually transplanted themselves to Philadelphia.

Members of the Boston society differed from the Philadelphia women in that they were predominantly Presbyterian, not Quaker, and represented diverse classes.[38] Many of the white and black women were not members of the elite and more than likely had to work outside the home as they tended to their families and participated in antislavery activities.[39] The historian Anne Boylan's work examines this mixed-class membership; she has noted members such as Maria Weston Chapman, a wealthy and aristocratic merchant's wife, Mary Parker, a boardinghouse owner, and Lucy and Martha Ball, sisters who were both teachers.[40]

Most of the women in the PFASS, both white and black, were Quakers who belonged to the merchant and artisan classes. Women from several of the wealthiest Philadelphian families were PFASS members, and most of the white women in the organization did not work outside the home. These elite women were unfettered by the burdens of wage earning and could devote large amounts of time to the Philadelphia society.[41]

Although interracial cooperation became a hallmark of antebellum abolitionist efforts, New York's female antislavery society was not able to overcome its own internal conflict and racism. Unlike the antislavery societies in Boston or Philadelphia, the Ladies' New York City Anti-Slavery Society refused to allow African American women to become members.[42] By 1840 the differences between the Boston and Philadelphia societies had become more pronounced. The PFASS chose to follow the call of William Lloyd Garrison and other radical abolitionists in the demand for immediate abolition and female participation in the national organization. The Boston auxiliary would eventually distance itself from the PFASS, as it did not agree with its Garrisonian tactics to end slavery or its position on the Abby Kelley question.[43]

The PFASS clearly positioned itself along the lines of radical abolitionism, as it offered financial support to Garrison's paper, the *Liberator,* and to the American Anti-Slavery Society's *Emancipator.* The society also created a library of antislavery pamphlets and books, all of which spoke to the society's goal of possessing and disseminating "correct" information about slavery. Perhaps one of the most important examples of antislavery literature owned by the society was Lydia Maria Child's *Appeal in Favor of That Class of Americans Called Africans.*[44] White members of the PFASS such as Lucretia Mott and the Grimké sisters shared the convictions of Child, who lobbied in person and in print to various legislatures on behalf of African American women and girls. The emblem of the kneeling and chained female slave became a powerful symbol that fostered support for abolition.[45]

The PFASS was a small group in which black and white women interacted in intense and momentarily fruitful ways. It is possible that the interracial contact meant more to the white women than to the black. What is important is that in the PFASS, as in a few other antislavery societies, the introduction of the enslaved black woman to the discourse of abolition took place in a context of self-discovery among white middle-class women. As Angelina Grimké wrote, "The investigation of the rights of the slave has led me to a better understanding of my own."[46] As Grimké, Mott, Lydia White, and other women of the PFASS worked toward their own inclusion in the American Anti-Slavery Society, they found the condition of enslaved women a useful metaphor when battling for equality with men. The abolitionist cause provided an avenue to expose the injustices of slavery, but it also allowed white women to express their dissatisfaction with their own subjugation both as women in the crusade against slavery and as women in America. Abolitionist women of the North had "cause to be grateful to the slave, [for] in striving to take his irons off we found most surely, that we were manacled ourselves."[47] For African American women abolition exposed racial and gender oppression, but it also provided a political platform to discuss the horrid conditions under which many blacks lived. Black women used abolitionist reform to address the trials of slavery and freedom.

African American Female Abolitionists

Free African American women were another source from which white female abolitionists could gain insights about black equality and the complexities of subjugation faced by all free women in American society. White women of the PFASS did not hesitate to call on their "darker sisters" for advice; the interracial nature of the organization, bolstered by personal testimony regarding the ugly nature of slavery and racial oppression, served as a badge of racial equality.

Philadelphians joined the women's auxiliary of the American Anti-Slavery Society for many reasons. Some joined because of an intense aversion to slavery and segregation, others because of religious conviction. Most of the African American women who joined the PFASS joined for these reasons but also from a feeling of racial obligation. The Forten and Douglass families are especially important in this regard; both were pillars of Philadelphia's black elite who between them were very much involved with the organization and represented more than half of its black membership.[48]

By the 1830s the Forten family had found significant financial and social success in Philadelphia. As reformers and abolitionists traveled throughout New England and the mid-Atlantic states, their itineraries almost always included Philadelphia, where they were always taken to 92 Lombard Street, the home of James and Charlotte Forten. The well-regarded James Forten had accumulated personal wealth in excess of $100,000 from his sailmaking business.[49] James Forten's great-grandfather had been enslaved and brought to Philadelphia by the Dutch; his grandfather was one of the first blacks to purchase his own freedom in the colony.[50]

James Forten was educated by the Quakers of Philadelphia and eventually served in the Revolutionary War. He was not involved with the creation of the Free African Society of Philadelphia, the first free black mutual aid society in the new nation, nor was he part of the movement that founded the first A.M.E. Church. But by 1799 he had become politically active by petitioning Congress to end the American slave trade.[51] The antebellum era marked a period of intense activism for the Philadelphia family: every member of the Forten family participated in the movement for abolition and for the social uplift of Philadelphia's free black communities.

Charlotte Vandine Forten, James Forten's second wife, was known as an "excellent motherly wife" and an active member in benevolent societies.[52] Aside from managing their three-story brick residence, she made certain that all of her children who lived to adulthood—James Jr., Robert B., William D., Margaretta, Sarah Louise, Mary I., and Harriet D.—received an education steeped in social and political activism.[53] The success of the Forten family was no small accomplishment. Not only had they placed themselves among the wealthiest of Philadelphians, but they also helped to create the beginnings of the black elite. Unlike most African American women who struggled to reach elite status by the middle of the nineteenth century, Charlotte Forten did not have to work outside the home. Forten became known as one of the first literate ladies of the black community in Philadelphia. She was recognized by both white and black Philadelphians and by abolitionists across the nation.

The Forten daughters were tutored at home, like young, upper-class white women, and spent their leisure time reading, visiting, doing charity work, and studying the ornamental subjects of art, music, French, and

German. All of the Forten women were founders of the PFASS. Although they benefited from the family's fortune, Margaretta and Sarah Forten nevertheless used their educations to work as teachers and as writers for antislavery newspapers.[54] Margaretta Forten taught at a small private school and served as the society's first recording secretary and as its treasurer in 1838.[55] Sarah Forten contributed many poems and essays to the *Liberator* and, along with her sister Harriet, participated in the sewing circles of the society.

Sarah and Grace Douglass, members of another prominent black family in the city, were also very active in the society. Like the Fortens, the Douglass family received visits from white abolitionists who ventured to the city of Philadelphia. Grace Bustill Douglass came from a distinguished African American Quaker family from Burlington, New Jersey. Her father, Cyrus Bustill, a baker and Quaker, was one of the early members of the Free African Society. Grace's mother, Elizabeth Morrey, was the daughter of an Englishman and a Delaware Native American woman.[56]

As a teacher, activist, wife, devoted Quaker, and mother, Grace Bustill Douglass operated a Quaker millinery store alongside the family bakery and was one of the charter members of the PFASS.[57] Her daughter, Sarah Mapps Douglass, became very much involved in the society and would eventually become one of the best-known African American women in Philadelphia. Born in Philadelphia in 1806, Sarah Douglass was an educational activist, crusading to better the lives of young black Philadelphians. Segregated public schools in the city were overpopulated, poorly equipped, and taught only by whites. Most African American families who could afford tuition sent their children to private schools or had them tutored at home.[58] Sarah Douglass herself received a sophisticated education and was privately tutored for several years. She eventually entered the "colored" school established in 1819 by her mother and James Forten.[59] Douglass and other elite African Americans benefited from the community-building efforts of the preceding generation.

After teaching for a brief period in New York, Sarah Douglass returned to Philadelphia to open an academy for African American girls. At the time it was the only school in the country that offered a high school education to young black women; the institution would eventually benefit from the society's financial contributions.[60] Although the school instructed forty students "selected from our best families, where their morals and manners [were] equally subjects of care, and deep interest,"[61] it fell into financial crisis in 1838. Because the school had insufficient revenue to maintain itself, the PFASS voted to "take over the school" and pay Douglass a salary of $300 a year and an additional $200 in rent and school supplies. This agreement lasted until 1840, when Douglass asked the society to relinquish its control.[62] The PFASS continued to support the school financially and paid from $90 to $120 annually to rent a classroom in which many of the society's meetings were held.[63] Sarah Douglass continued her career as an educator and in 1853 would oversee the girls' preparatory department of the Philadelphia Institute for Colored Youth.

Aims of the PFASS

Fourteen women came together to frame the constitution of the society, the first article of which declared that the society would collect and disseminate "correct information" on the condition of the slaves and "free people of colour."[64] A second aim of the society was to eliminate discrimination against free blacks and work toward "improving their lot in life."[65] The preamble of the constitution declared slavery and race prejudice as contrary to the laws of God and the principles of the Declaration of Independence. The women considered it their duty as Christians to demonstrate their objection to the "flagrant injustice and deep sin of slavery." All the charter members vowed to work toward the speedy removal of slavery and the restoration of "inalienable rights [to] people of colour."[66]

As the society expanded, abstention from buying and consuming the products of slave labor such as cotton and sugar, petitioning Congress to abolish slavery in the District of Columbia, and a project to open a school for black children were added to the agenda. The widespread distribution of petitions to Congress motivated women to walk through the streets of the city, knocking on doors to solicit signatures for the cause.[67] Although many Philadelphians refused to sign, one member, Mary Grew, wrote: "we do not regard those visits as lost labor, where our request was denied, or that time was wasted. The seed laboriously sown, falls into good ground, and after a little season springs up, bringing forth fruit, some thirty, some sixty, some hundred fold."[68] Collecting just a few signatures and perhaps enticing others to join in their struggle was well worth the time-consuming efforts.

In 1836 the PFASS published its *Address to the Women of Pennsylvania,* which asked for support in the campaign to bombard Congress with petitions to suppress the slave trade. Black and white members of the society also pushed Congress to abolish slavery in the District of Columbia and prohibit the interstate slave trade. The PFASS urged the Pennsylvania legislature to allow trial by jury for suspected fugitives and to grant certain rights to those African American men and women accused of escaping slavery and residing within the city limits.[69] Petition circulation became central to the Philadelphia society, since the right to petition was the only political tool that both men and women, black and white, could employ. By the mid 1830s petitioning became the abolitionists' weapon of choice. In a thriving Jacksonian political culture that emphasized public opinion, women across the North found their voice in the petition.[70]

Over the course of the late 1830s, however, enthusiasm for petitions declined tremendously. Women in Philadelphia and across the North were deterred by congressional gag rules created by southerners and northern democrats that prohibited their petitions from being reviewed and prevented the discussion of antislavery proposals in the House of Representatives.

Between 1836 and 1837 petitioning reached its peak for the women of the PFASS. In 1836, just three years after the founding of the society, members collected over thirty-three hundred signatures of Philadelphia's female residents. One year later the first Anti-Slavery Convention of American Women constructed a formal method by which to collect signatures in every town across the county, a method that placed two or three members in each district of the city.[71] The goal of the society was to visit every home and to convince every individual to sign his or her name. The belief was that if "all the maids and matrons of the land knock at the door of Congress, our Statesmen must legislate."[72] That year the PFASS collected approximately five thousand signatures on circulating petitions.

Female and male abolitionists were not the only groups to petition Congress. By the 1830s mass petitions from men on a variety of subjects flooded Congress. Although legislators in the House of Representatives grew accustomed to them, they were rarely dismissed with expedience. In many cases, the signatures represented large sections of the white male voting public, and their discontent could prove disastrous for upcoming elections.[73] Legislators looked seriously at many of the petitions, yet they failed to give equal attention to the demands put forth by antislavery women. Since women did not vote, their dissatisfaction with a specific congressman would not affect the outcome of an election. If their discontent spread to their fathers, husbands, and sons who were voting citizens, however, legislators could face extreme difficulties. Regardless of their views on slavery, male legislators found it difficult to view the petitions of women with the same seriousness that they accorded the demands of male voters. By the mid-1830s women's antislavery petitions were seen as more than just bothersome; they were political demands that were not going to disappear. The abolitionist William Lloyd Garrison wrote, "it is *now* objected that our power is so *great,* that it is dangerous to exercise it."[74]

The mob violence and physical danger that were the result of antislavery work halted the circulation of petitions by the late 1830s. In May 1838 the second national Anti-Slavery Convention of American Women convened in Philadelphia. After an evening session, an angry mob met PFASS members outside their convention hall and threatened bodily harm; the crowd eventually set fire to Pennsylvania Hall. This incident prompted several women in the PFASS to refuse to go door-to-door to solicit signatures. Although petitions to Congress continued to be written, the danger connected to the growing hostility in the city decreased the number of female members willing to collect signatures. In 1840 the society collected only 1,483 names on petitions to Congress, and in 1841 only 678 signatures appeared.[75] Violence, gag rules, and an eventual fracture in the American Anti-Slavery Society tempered the enthusiasm for petition writing.

Like many other white members of the PFASS, the stalwart Sarah Pugh refused to collect petition signatures for the society in 1838, and she wrote in her diary, "I never undertook anything that was so entirely distasteful to me; but, as it is in many things, the anticipation was more than the reality."[76] Pugh, along with many other reformers, began to consider their petition campaigns useless: she wrote, "in our aristocratic district we were generally civilly received and heard, and as civilly refused with words." For Pugh and others, constant rejection proved too much to handle. When antislavery activity became violent and genteel rejection was replaced by an angry mob outside Pennsylvania Hall, many female abolitionists began to rethink their commitments. By the mid-1840s, members of the PFASS and other abolitionists began to use short petitions, which did not contain the signatures of Philadelphia citizens. Only the presidents and secretaries of antislavery societies signed short petitions.[77]

By this time members focused their attention on annual fairs and fund-raising events for the state branch of the antislavery society. Reformers of the PFASS turned their attention to money after the attack at Pennsylvania Hall. Their successful fund-raising skills gave women a new sense of control that filled the political void created by the gag rule and mob violence. The annual fair also allowed members of the PFASS to align themselves closely with the men of the state society. From 1836 to 1853 members of the PFASS raised approximately $16,500 from their annual fairs. During the years from 1836 through 1844, Philadelphia antislavery fairs collected an average of $540 each year. From 1845 through 1852, the average amount soared to $1,170; in 1853 the total was $2,200. Approximately 85 percent of all revenue raised by the PFASS was donated to the Pennsylvania branch of the AASS.[78]

A tremendous amount of time and preparation went into these fairs. Each year from 1836 until 1861, members of the PFASS spent up to four months organizing the event, at which refreshments such as pound and orange cakes, fruits, and vegetables were sold.[79] Other "beautiful and fancy productions" were offered for sale: quilts, needlework, art pieces, and pottery. All materials sold at the fair supported the society's boycott of materials produced in conjunction with slave labor.[80] Fairs were usually conducted over a period of two to three days; the first was held in 1836 at the Fire Men's Hall, below Arch Street. It was a huge success: PFASS proceeds totaled more than three hundred dollars. In later years it became increasingly difficult to find halls or spaces where the PFASS could host their events.[81] By 1838 sentiment against the antislavery movement produced riots, arson, and looting, which often made it difficult for members to find secure and appropriate venues.[82]

From its contributions the PFASS was able to gain a small measure of leadership in the all-male organization. In October 1838 Mary Earle and Sarah Lewis, two white members of the PFASS, were appointed to the business committee of the Pennsylvania branch of the AASS, and in 1841, despite the split over Abby Kelley, Sarah Pugh and Lucretia Mott were elected to the state's antislavery executive committee. In 1843 Pugh became treasurer, and the following year Mary Grew became the corresponding secretary. By the mid-1840s PFASS members held four of the fifteen state offices.[83] But African American female members held none of these offices: the disappearance of work at the local level edged them out.

Aside from abolition, one of the original goals of PFASS was to assist free blacks in the city of Philadelphia. This goal excited African American members, who hoped the organization would move beyond simply demanding freedom for black Americans. In June 1834 the PFASS appointed a committee to assess the quality of the public school education for black students. By the end of the year the society created its own school for African American children. Rebecca Buffum, a white member, took charge of the project, combining the school with her own. After Buffum left the city in 1838, Sarah Douglass assumed total responsibility for the small school.[84]

The society's education committee dedicated itself to visiting various grammar schools for black children throughout the city. Members were to schedule visits and file formal reports with the society regarding the conditions of the schools. Other programs to "promote the moral and intellectual improvement of the people of color" included scientific lectures, sewing lessons, literary and religious instruction, and assistance in job placement in the trades for black men in Philadelphia. Although committees were appointed to oversee these projects, very little happened. By 1841 the PFASS had simply stopped visiting African American schools, and it failed to file any reports at all. Interest in the amelioration of conditions for free blacks all but disappeared, and by 1842 the society decided that outside philanthropic groups to which some of their members belonged were better equipped to help African American Philadelphians.[85] In short, as the political antislavery impulse strengthened in the 1840s, throughout the North almost complete attention was given to immediate abolition. Although evidence is lacking about black women's responses, surely they would have been disappointed with this departure from the original aims and goals of the society; they were left to better the lives of free blacks through their own separate organizations.

As part of the antislavery crusade, the women of the PFASS were also involved in aiding fugitive slaves. Although the organization did not devote large amounts of money or time to this effort, it did contribute to the Philadelphia Vigilance Committee, established in 1838 by an interracial group of men. Although the organization was interracial on paper, the majority of its active participants were black men. The Vigilance Committee policed and protected black communities in many ways, offering shelter, food, money, and legal assistance to runaways.[86] Although the black elites of Philadelphia were willing to aid their brothers and sisters in flight from previous slave masters, black Philadelphians became increasingly aware of the growing problems of fugitive and migrant blacks within their population. The Vigilance Committee was organized not only to protect the fugitive slave and the Philadelphia community, but also to help southern blacks make the transition to a northern and urban lifestyle.

The committee also helped patrol against the growing number of unlawful kidnappings of freeborn black Philadelphians. This concern was much more intimate and threatening to black abolitionists, but they were able to secure substantial support from the white philanthropic community. The PFASS usually supported the Vigilance Committee through annual donations that ranged from ten to twenty dollars. But over time it became increasingly clear that black citizenship and social parity were not priorities for the PFASS.[87] For some of its white members, this did not pose a problem. Many of them believed that the political goals of immediate abolition and female control and leadership in the parent American Anti-Slavery Society were enough. As white women reformers found themselves in positions of power outside the female auxiliary, their concerns and focus

Kidnapping. From Jesse Torrey, *A Portraiture of Domestic Slavery in the United States* (Philadelphia, 1817). Courtesy of the Library Company of Philadelphia.

began to change. But for African American members, this abandonment of assistance for free blacks and fugitive slaves signaled a change in the interracial cooperative.

Interracial Networking

Many of the records left behind by the women of the PFASS concern dry procedural and organizational business matters. Although the sentiments regarding antislavery were strongly enunciated in the constitution and petitions of the society, the interaction between the members of the organization went largely undocumented in the minutes. Tension and disagreement between specific members were for the most part unrecorded, and the Quaker tradition of consensus appears to have heavily influenced the problem-solving techniques of the society.

Personal documents, however, such as letters and diary entries written by members of the PFASS, give a more intimate understanding of the antislavery ladies of Philadelphia. They allow us to explore their relationships, both personal and professional, and the realities of the struggle for inclusiveness of both white and black women. Angelina Grimké used her personal relationships with African American PFASS members to better understand race prejudice, interpret her own subjugation, and comprehend the experiences of her friends. Shortly before the first Anti-Slavery Convention of American Women, in 1837, in a fascinating exchange, Angelina asked her friend Sarah Forten to write about her experiences, describing the effects of race prejudice on her life.

Sarah Forten replied to Grimké's letter as a friend, although she was "particularly sensitive on this point."[88] Forten's words were carefully selected and quite formal. She was able to convey to her friend and an anticipated audience (abolitionists often published their personal correspondence) examples of bigotry and discrimination she had encountered during her life and to reflect on the significance of white skin privilege. Forten wrote about the "mortification in my breast when I saw that many were preferred before me, who by education—birth—or worldly circumstances were no better than myself—their sole claim to notice depending on the superior advantage of being White."[89]

Forten made quite clear, however, that her experience as an African American woman in the urban North differed from the experiences of the vast majority of black men and women in Philadelphia. The Forten family's financial success placed her among the wealthiest of Philadelphians regardless of race, and she acknowledged the influence of wealth on her status as a free woman and its buffering effect against discrimination: "For our own family—we have to thank a kind Providence for placing us in a situation that has hitherto prevented us from falling under the weight of this evil. We feel it in a slight degree compared with many others. We are not much dependent upon the tender mercies of our enemies—always having resources within ourselves to which we can apply."[90]

She described how black men and women of an elevated class status were often able to avoid the degrading and humiliating experiences faced constantly by others. "We are not disturbed in our social relations—we never travel far from home and seldom go into public places unless quite sure that admission is free to all—therefore, we meet with none of these mortifications which might otherwise ensue."[91] Forten's letter not only explained the ways in which the black elite protected themselves from humiliation, but also recommended to "colored friends" that they follow her family's example in order to spare themselves unnecessary embarrassment.

Forten's recommendation sheds light on the ways in which African American men and women defended themselves against hostile behavior and racial intolerance. The strategy of social confinement certainly limited their lives; but it is also clear that social segregation helped to create a tightly knit black community along the northeast corridor. The black elite deemed it necessary to remain insular and exclusive to protect themselves from the indignities of racism. They segregated themselves not only from white Philadelphians but also from contact with the poor and uneducated masses. Although the wealthy and the poverty-stricken lived within blocks of each other, their social and religious arenas remained separate.[92]

Forten gave Grimké a window into her experience as a free African American woman in the antebellum North. She also spoke freely of her feelings about the abolitionist cause, criticizing the hypocrisy and racism practiced by "fellow abolitionists." Forten wrote: "To some of them it clings like a dark mantle obscuring their many virtues and choking up the avenues to higher and nobler sentiments. I recollect the words of the best and least prejudiced man in the Abolition ranks. Ah said he, 'I can recall the time when in walking with a Colored brother, the darker the night, the better Abolitionist was I.' '[H]ow much of this leaven still lingers in the hearts of our white brethren and sisters is oftentimes made manifest to us.' "[93]

Her letter illuminated the race prejudice felt and practiced by white abolitionists who often socially segregated themselves from black abolitionists. Sarah Forten was not the only black member of the PFASS to describe the racism in the abolitionist movement. As an educator, Sarah Douglass wrote to her friend Sarah Grimké of her own experiences not only as a free black in the antebellum North but also as a Quaker woman in Philadelphia. Douglass commented on the practices of the largest Quaker Meeting in Philadelphia, attended by many PFASS members, and other Quakers in the city. Douglass reminisced over past injustices: "I may say that there is a bench set apart at that meeting for our people, that my mother and myself were told to sit there, and that a friend sat at either end of the bench to prevent white persons from sitting there. And even as a child my soul was made sad with hearing five or six times during the course of one meeting this language of remonstrance addressed to those people who were willing to sit by us, 'This bench is for the black people. This bench is for the people of color.' "[94]

Women such as the Grimké sisters, Lucretia Mott, and Mary Grew used the experiences of their black female friends in their writings and lectures to express the fundamental problems not only of racism and race prejudice, but of discrimination in general. Sarah Grimké eventually left the Arch Street Meetinghouse in Philadelphia because of the segregated seating Douglass commented on. Forten, Douglass, and other black women discussed their personal combat with discrimination in antislavery newspapers and diaries intended for an abolitionist audience. These women also shared their experiences with their friends in the PFASS, which allowed white members to use their stories, continue an abolitionist crusade, and improve the position of white female abolitionists in the national movement. Thus, in this one place, the stories of the tortured, enslaved black woman and of the humiliated, free African American woman came together, pushing white women to think about women's rights.[95]

Walking in Different Paths: The Philadelphia Female Anti-Slavery Society after 1840

By the 1840s Pennsylvania abolitionists had adopted the goal of immediate emancipation as central to their political platform. Though commendable, this goal frustrated many and caused dissension among the members of the PFASS; in 1842 the society instituted new standards for membership. The PFASS's constitution firmly stated that members should work for immediate emancipation and the amelioration of circumstances for African American men and women. Yet in 1842 members were resolved that abolitionism required more: "we rely not on the efficacy of physical force, or political parties but on moral power, on the use of those weapons which operate on the heart & on the conscience."[96] Eventually the society chose to adopt the Garrisonian platform, one that prohibited abolitionists from voting in national elections and participating in mainstream political activity. According to the new philosophy of the PFASS, "abolitionists can consistently have no union with slave holders, by voting for officers who must swear to support the Constitution of the U.S."[97]

As the narrowed ideology of the PFASS created tension, many women simply abandoned the organization. Most did not resign, but instead gradually withdrew. White members such as Sarah Lewis, Susan Grew, and Mary and Phebe Earle were among the first supporters of the society in the early 1830s, yet they disagreed with the organization's new political philosophy. These women and many others left the PFASS, often joining less radical antislavery societies.

For many women in the society, the goal of women's inclusion in the mainstream organization was achieved with the election of Abby Kelley to the business committee of the AASS in 1840. What remains obscure are the tangible benefits for African American members of the PFASS. Black women never served as executive board members to the national organization, and although African American men sat on committees and as chairs of local branches, they were excluded from executive authority in the national body.[98] This fact, along with a decrease in attention paid to local issues, reminded African American women in the PFASS of the need to look for the advancement of civil rights and better circumstances elsewhere.

Similar concerns faced black New Yorkers involved in the antislavery movement. Increasing conservatism among white abolitionists complicated the belief in racial uplift and the improvement of conditions for black New Yorkers. Following the riots of 1834, many abolitionists, such as the Tappans, shifted their abolitionist goals to focus on the end of southern slavery. According to the historian Leslie Harris, there was a change for both black and white abolitionists, but "for white abolitionists, greater conservatism led to a retreat from funding practical reform efforts to address the material and educational needs of northern free blacks. . . . Black abolitionists continued to believe that the improvement of the condition of northern free blacks was as important as the abolition of slavery, and that the two goals were interrelated."[99] As a result, black and white abolitionists began to move in different directions.

Black membership in the PFASS declined during the 1840s, leaving only a handful of black members actively involved. From 1834 to 1848 there were never more than 24 black members in the organization, whereas white membership totaled 215 during the same time period.[100] The society's black membership was at its height during its early years. As the PFASS shifted its goals, African American women simply stopped joining the organization. Between 1836 and 1840, 86 new members joined the PFASS, only one of whom was African American. One more joined the PFASS in 1842, the last year in which the organization would add a new African American woman to its membership roster.[101]

Concentrating on moral suasion and immediate emancipation left little room for the betterment of free blacks' lives; although this appears to have been one of the founding principles on which the PFASS and other organizations were based, concerns for social equality disappeared. The most notable sign of the disenchantment experienced by black members appeared in 1840, when Sarah Douglass took control of her school and abandoned the support of the society. In 1848 Sarah Douglass was instrumental in the organization of the all-black Women's Association of Philadelphia, a group that supported Frederick Douglass's call for black nationalism.[102] Other African American women in the PFASS began to devote much of their attention to fugitive aid in the aftermath of the Fugitive Slave Act of 1850. African American women simply joined new organizations that continued in the crusade of antislavery but also pressed the issue of equal rights and citizenship for free blacks. In particular, black women rallied around issues concerning education for free black men, women, and children, continuing their previous work of improving their own education through the creation of literary societies and other educational organizations.

By the 1840s the society's goals no longer dovetailed with the needs of Philadelphia's free black communities. The idea of interracial cooperation had not vanished but was curbed by the split in Garrisonian politics and the fluctuating goals of white Philadelphian activists. The experiment of interracial collaboration between white and black female abolitionists was a unique moment in the antebellum era that served as an example for generations to come. Through the personal testimony of black members regarding oppression and discrimination, white women were able to solidify their own crusade for equality. At the same time, African American women created valuable contacts, locating themselves within the political debate of the century. They were painfully aware of all the work that was still undone, but they looked toward a future of autonomy and equality in which they would use their political activism, expand their education, and discover the power of the printed word.

Writing for Womanhood
African American Women and Print Culture

Print culture became a new and important vehicle in the fight to end slavery and in the development of free black communities throughout the North. The advent of black antislavery and religious newspapers such as the *Freedom's Journal,* the *Liberator,* the *North Star,* and a host of other periodicals gave African American reformers access to public forums of debate. By the middle decades of the nineteenth century a generation of free African Americans had been formally educated and were prepared to fight slavery and inequality on both the local and national levels. Published writings helped to move local Philadelphians into the national spotlight.

African American women found public writing to be most useful in their reform efforts and a wonderful opportunity to address the specific concerns and problems they experienced. A formal education and membership in elite literary societies bolstered African American participation in the national political arena. Most periodicals confined women's writings to editorials and the "poets' corner." But their contributions provide meaningful examples of antebellum political writing.[1] Often the black elite, including women, found their writings used by white and black antislavery agitators as shining examples of accomplishment and respectability.

Black women found themselves liberated and confined by the print world. While it supplied a forum for political debate, the nineteenth-century newspaper defined "woman's sphere" as inherently domestic, warning African American women that "a woman who would attempt to thunder with her tongue, would not find her eloquence to increase her domestic happiness."[2] Directed to be both silent creatures of virtue and active in building and improving the free black community, African American women navigated the tricky confines of domesticity, womanhood, and virtue while simultaneously becoming very public figures.

The antebellum newspaper was not the only arena in which African American women publicly expressed their political and private sentiments. Several women wrote about their experiences in the pages of spiritual autobiographies. Although the institution of southern slavery and its stubborn northern vestiges were major themes in the writings of black women, they were not the only issues addressed. Religion and religious reform provided additional fodder. During the Second Great Awakening, African American women in Philadelphia such as Jarena Lee and Zilpha Elaw used the genre of the spiritual autobiography to persuade Christian readers to obey the word of God, live pious lives, and challenge evils, especially slavery.[3] Thus, from the educated elite represented in national newspapers to the humble, pious women of the A.M.E. Church, black women used print culture to further define themselves and their personal and political goals. When we examine both national periodicals and spiritual narratives, the worlds of the spiritual and the secular intersect.

Literary societies were among the first sociopolitical organizations formed by and for African American women. Middle-class African Americans understood the tremendous importance of educating a new generation of free black men and women, but it was just as important for the black elite to improve themselves and prepare for the integrated public arena.[4] Literary societies allowed elite black women to socialize among themselves while they honed the political prose that would eventually appear in national periodicals. Within those societies, friendship and sorority met with the political. In the 1830s the generation of politically charged African American women who would play such an important role in abolition had indeed emerged from the arena of the literary society. The working poor and those of the "lower sort," however, were mostly absent. It would take decades for impoverished and undereducated black women to create a political voice for themselves.

As we have seen, presentation and public image became extremely important. The ability to present oneself in a respectable manner was practiced and perfected in the literary society. Mandatory public speaking and recitation were helpful to all, but especially to women unaccustomed to formal speaking. With a standard education, leadership skills, and a developed ease in public, African American women approached the middle decades of the nineteenth century with a new sense of self-confidence and social activism.

For most men and women in the early nineteenth century, education was a luxury. Before that time, elite women, both white and black, were often tutored at home and did not attend formal institutions of learning. For African Americans, whether they were ex-slaves or had never known slavery, education became an immediate goal. In 1822 Philadelphia began to offer public schooling to its black residents; universal public education had been made available to white children only four years earlier. Several racially segregated public schools opened their doors, but attendance among African American school-aged children remained low and inconsistent. The Bird School, later renamed the James Forten School, was the first public institution opened for blacks; a second segregated school opened its doors in 1830. In 1833 the Coates Street School, later renamed the Vaux School, began instructing African Americans, and several others followed suit during the ensuing years.[5] These schools were scattered across the city, allowing children who lived in the all-black Seventh Ward and beyond the opportunity for formal instruction. According to data compiled by W. E. B. Du Bois, who conducted a study in 1899 that resulted in the acclaimed *Philadelphia Negro,* there were twenty-five schools for African American children operating by 1838. Of these, only nine were free, and three additional schools were classified as "partly free."[6] Private schools remained an option for those blacks wealthy enough to afford the costly tuition. The remaining thirteen black schools were private. Of these, ten schools hired only black instructors.[7]

Although the number of black schools continued to increase throughout the antebellum years, attendance remained low. In 1838 approximately three thousand black school-aged children lived in the city, but only seventeen hundred were enrolled in school. Ten years later the population of school-aged children had increased to more than forty-five hundred, but only fifty-six additional students attended school.[8] This drastic decline in the rate of school attendance by black children was directly connected to the 1838 depression and the mounting racial tension following the violent attack on antislavery activists at Pennsylvania Hall.[9] The economic decline impinged on Philadelphia's residents, forcing many children to leave school in order to contribute to their household income.

Despite the problems of formal education, African American literacy rates increased as access widened, not only among children, but among adults as well. Older adults who had been enslaved became the subjects for new philanthropic attempts. Night schools were created by black institutions to serve African American adults who worked during the day. Several night schools remained open throughout the antebellum period, and most were supported and staffed by black church members. For black Philadelphians, formal instruction signified freedom and a great accomplishment. As late as 1856, a large proportion of African American residents remained uneducated: 45 percent of the black population was illiterate.[10] Only a small percentage of African American Philadelphians could read and write, and even fewer demonstrated the ability to "read, write and cipher."[11] For most blacks, education was tied directly to Philadelphia churches' night schools and Sunday schools.

In 1813 the city of Philadelphia counted six black churches: St. Thomas Episcopal, Mother Bethel A.M.E., Zoar Methodist Episcopal, Union A.M.E., Baptist Race and Vine Streets, and the Presbyterian Church. Just over two thousand men and women frequented these churches; approximately 50 percent attended Mother Bethel.[12]

Unlike St. Thomas, which was attended by many of Philadelphia's black elite, Mother Bethel had a congregation comprising, for the most part, poor, working African Americans. Domestics and manual laborers felt more at ease with the relaxed style of preaching associated with the Methodist denomination, and although Mother Bethel advocated formal education for its congregants, the church remained sensitive to the limitations and barriers to literacy faced by many black men and women.

The emotional nature of church services in the Methodist denomination attracted many of the city's recent southern migrants, who were accustomed to this specific style of preaching. During the Second Great Awakening of the 1820s–30s, Christian evangelicalism dominated almost every aspect of life. The North, in particular, saw a tremendous rise in the number of African Americans who belonged to a Methodist denomination, in particular the African Methodist Episcopal Church. The emotional conversion process connected to Methodism attracted black men and women who had previously been uncomfortable with other denominations that relied heavily on literacy.[13] The majority of Philadelphia's black elite found themselves attracted to churches such as St. Thomas, or to denominations such as Presbyterianism or the Society of Friends, in which "the message" was articulated in a more refined or even silent manner, but Mother Bethel and a handful of other black

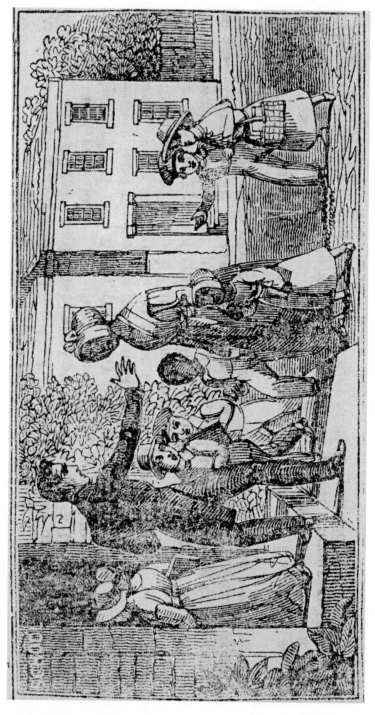

Colored Scholars Excluded from Schools. From American Anti-Slavery Society, *Anti-Slavery Almanac* (New York, 1838). Courtesy of the Library Company of Philadelphia.

churches adopted the stewardship of educating African American men and women, regardless of economic status.

The Literary Society

Churches were not the only institutions to promote formal education for African Americans. Literary societies arose in Philadelphia and across the Northeast. Barred from white literary organizations, a group of free black men came together on March 20, 1828, to organize a society that would promote the "mental improvement of the people of color in the neighborhood of Philadelphia."[14] Prominent black men of the city gathered that night and listened to an address delivered by William Whipper, a wealthy black Pennsylvanian. Whipper urged his audience not to "sit as idle spectators to the movement being carried on by nations to improve themselves." He added that black men should "feel bound to open an institution to which they may repair and qualify themselves for future usefulness."[15] Whipper's speech marked the founding of the Reading Room Society for young men in Philadelphia.

Many of the early societies expressed similar reasons for their organization: the stimulation of reading and the "spreading of useful knowledge." By providing libraries and reading rooms for black residents throughout the city, the black elite continued to emphasize education.[16] These literary societies constructed spaces for literary improvement and cultivated a generation of public orators and abolitionist politicians.

In 1831 African American women in Philadelphia formed the Female Literary Society of Philadelphia. A year later the society consisted of approximately twenty members, who congregated every Tuesday night for the purpose of "mental improvement." William Lloyd Garrison addressed the society that year, reporting in his newspaper, "if the traducers of the Negro race could be acquainted with the moral worth, just refinement, and large intelligence of this association, their mouths would be hereafter dumb."[17] Thus, literary societies and abolition were linked from the very beginning.

Between 1828 and 1841, nine literary societies appeared; at least three were women's. The Minerva Literary Association, formed in 1834 with thirty members, was typical; it organized a "school for the promotion of polite literature." Programs featured readings and recitations of original and selected published pieces, along with "other appropriate matters."[18]

The African American literary society appeared at a time when social graces and customs were extremely important to the black elite. The interracial abolitionist circles created an added incentive. As the black elite began their social and political networking among white Philadelphians through the politics of abolition, the literary society prepared and reinforced "the promotion of the polite."[19]

But respectability was not the only goal. The societies also served as examples for a reform-minded free community. In an 1837 address to the American Moral Reform Society, James Forten touched on this aspect of communal pride in the female literary societies. The diffusion of knowledge through reading and writing, he affirmed, reflected honorably on the community. The greater purpose, though, was to accomplish an intellectual and moral reformation.[20] Forten's comments stressed the societies' social importance. These were not just small book clubs; they were the bedrock of a social reformation.

In 1841 members of the African American elite moved beyond single-sex literary societies and organized the Gilbert Lyceum for "literary and scientific purposes." Lyceum groups of the antebellum era were concerned with the dissemination of information on the arts, sciences, and public affairs and became a powerful force in adult education and social reform. Members of the black elite such as Robert Douglass Jr., Joseph Cassey, John Bowers, Robert Purvis, Harriet Purvis, and Sarah Mapps Douglass, all well known for their ardent abolitionist sentiments, were among those listed as members of the Gilbert Lyceum. By the end of the year there were more than forty registered members of the society.[21]

African American literary clubs appeared first in Philadelphia, but the movement spread to cities such as New York, Boston, and Baltimore, and eventually to Albany, Rochester, Cincinnati, and Pittsburgh.[22] All of them, with the exception of the New York African Clarkson Society, were founded during the 1830s and 1840s.[23] Like the Philadelphia societies, the literary associations in cities such as New York and Baltimore encouraged the extension of education and moral reform and the promotion of the abolition of slavery.

The Printed Word: Black Women's Public Writings in Antebellum Philadelphia

Armed with a formal education, a generation of elite black activists continued to push for immediate emancipation. Racial hostility and violence directed toward free blacks became much more pronounced during the 1830s, and as the news of a major slave rebellion in Southampton County, Virginia, reached Philadelphia in August 1831, white Pennsylvanians feared a change in the demographics of the state. Free blacks in Virginia would most certainly be forced to relocate following the bloody Nat Turner rebellion, and many white Philadelphians expected that they would move north, settling within the city limits. Rumors that as many as five hundred southern freedmen had settled in the city in just two months during 1831 unnerved many white Philadelphians. Free blacks were blamed not only for inciting slave rebellions but also for luring fugitives to the urban cities of the North, elevating crime and poverty in the city streets.[24]

White Philadelphians began to petition the state legislature to enact restrictive laws. The proposed law of 1831 prohibited "ignorant, indolent, and depraved" free blacks from entering the state of Pennsylvania. The bill also attempted to regulate the lives of free blacks born in Pennsylvania. Local officials were to take a census of all blacks in their townships, noting the name, sex, age, and complexion of each person. Any African American man or woman attempting to move from one county to another would be forced to present proof of residency in the state.[25]

As the black abolitionists James Forten, Robert Purvis, and William Whipper drew up a memorial to be presented to the state legislature, the bill was lost in committee and never came to a final vote.[26] The derailment of the bill, however, was of no importance to the African American community, specifically the elite. The fact that such legislation could even be contemplated was threatening and spoke to the racial hostility of the 1830s. The next several decades proved more inhospitable and, in many cases, violent for black Philadelphians. As the country moved deeper and deeper into crisis, African Americans in northern cities became preoccupied with the status of their own freedom while southern slaveholders held on tightly to their property—even as the institution of slavery continued to expand across the country. Black Philadelphians remained steadfast in their efforts to abolish slavery and were perhaps more acutely aware of the fragility of their social status.

The Fugitive Slave Law of 1850 presented itself as one of the most troublesome measures passed by Congress, creating a storm of protest and fear among free black northerners. It was this law perhaps above all others that reminded free black northerners of their vulnerability. As the kidnapping of free blacks during the 1830s and 1840s prompted black men and women to live life cautiously, the Fugitive Slave Law heightened all fears, for it placed in even greater peril the lives of free blacks. Four years later Congress passed the Kansas-Nebraska Act, repealing the Missouri Compromise of 1820. The act opened the Northwest to slave trading and appeared to validate the expansion of slavery. For those who had assumed that slavery would eventually fade away, this act reinforced the fact that the institution of slavery would not simply disappear. In 1857 the Supreme Court handed down the Dred

Scott decision, which denied citizenship not only to enslaved black men and women but to all African Americans across the country.[27]

For black women in Philadelphia during this time, the struggle for abolition and the combating of racial stereotypes reinforced by newspaper articles and vicious cartoons, such as the "Life in Philadelphia" series, became an important and time-consuming process.[28] As they continued to work in mutual aid associations, antislavery societies, and benevolent organizations, black women also used the printed word as a form of agency, demonstrating their freedom and respectability. The interracial Philadelphia Female Anti-Slavery Society was not the only mechanism for social change and activism. African American women began to write for the protection of their womanhood and for freedom.

African American women used the black press and other public print forums to describe their life experiences and to create an imagery of African Americans in Philadelphia. Their opinions regarding motherhood, antislavery, and freedom appeared in local and national newspapers, as they took their private concerns and political debates to the public forum of the printed word. The *Liberator,* the *North Star,* and the *Pennsylvania Freeman* were but a few of the newspapers to which black women contributed poetry, short stories, and essays that expressed their feelings and their own experiences.

Challenging the contemporary codes of appropriate behavior for women through the act of public writing, black women often found themselves defending their right to self-expression. The simple act of writing challenged existing stereotypes regarding women's supposed intellectual inferiority in both African American and white political circles.

Sarah Forten, Margaretta Forten and Sarah Mapps Douglass all wrote in the spirit of protest. Others, such as Mary Ann Shadd Cary and Frances Harper, both of whom had strong ties to Philadelphia, joined the small cadre of writers. Although race prejudice made it difficult to publish, the abolitionist movement produced new contacts and avenues by which to have their works published. Prominent white female and male abolitionists such as Lydia Maria Child and William Lloyd Garrison assisted black women by publishing their poetry and essays in pamphlets and newspapers.[29]

Perhaps the earliest political writings by women appeared in the form of the petition.[30] Petition writing became a very popular method of political involvement for both white and black women during the antebellum era. Although many male reformers considered women's participation in petition-writing campaigns to be inappropriate, some abolitionists argued that the influence of women would help to purify the nation. Those who supported women's involvement in letter and petition writing viewed their activities as a continuation of patriotic traditions created during the American Revolution. Antislavery societies granted black women the first opportunity to participate in this early form of political writing, and during the early 1830s the Philadelphia Female Anti-Slavery Society sent several petitions both to the state legislature and to Congress demanding the termination of slavery.[31]

As black women began to diversify their political writings, moving from group petition writing to individual essays and poems, they stood as examples of educational progress and activism. Praised for their eloquent prose and sentimental poetry, black women political writers were often viewed as uplifters of their race. In his preface to a collection of Frances Harper's poetry, William Lloyd Garrison stated that her work stood as an example of progress, as it represented "intelligence, talent, genius, and piety." According to Garrison, Harper's representation of free black America would only "deepen the interest already so extensively felt in the liberation and enfranchisement of the entire colored race."[32]

Among the best-known newspaper contributors was Sarah Louise Forten, the daughter of James and Charlotte Forten and a leading member of the PFASS. Known by her pen names "Ada" and "Magawisca," Sarah Forten contributed over a dozen poems and essays to several different newspapers between 1831 and 1837.[33] Her poem "The Grave of the Slave" was set to music by the black bandleader Frank Johnson and was often sung at antislavery meetings. Frequently appearing in the poets' corner of antislavery newspapers, Forten stressed the hypocrisy of slavery while exhibiting her own writing talents. Forten's demonstration of her sophisticated education through her writings was another way to combat the racial hostility and white supremacist attitudes of the 1830s.

One of Forten's first published essays appeared in the *Liberator* in 1831, just as Garrison was beginning his venture. "The Abuse of Liberty" supplied a poignant discussion about the evils of slavery and its effect on the African in America: "I know no evil under the wide-spread canopy of Heaven, so great as the abuse of man's liberty; and no where has this vice a more extensive sway, than in the boasted land of Philanthropy, that offers to every white man the right to enjoy life, liberty and happiness. I say every white man, because those who cannot show a fair exterior, (no matter what be the noble qualities of the mind,) are to be robbed of the rights by which they were endowed by an all-wise and merciful Creator, who in his great wisdom, cast a sable hue over some of the 'lord's creation.' "[34] Denouncing the white slave master, Forten lamented the well-known horrors of slavery, beginning with the separation of family: "It is a lamentable fact that they [slave masters] can with remorseless hearts rush like fiends into the retirement of a happy unsuspecting family, and with unshaken hand tear the unconscious husband from his tender wife, and the helpless babe from its mother's breast."[35] She concluded her essay with a threat of unrest and rebellion, not merely from the slaves themselves, but, more important, from God, who, according to Forten, would eventually right the wrongs of slavery. Although her entry appeared some five months before the 1831 Southampton massacre, Americans, especially southern slave owners, worried about slave rebellion and violence. Forten's prophecy of violence would have resonated in the minds of many people. "He [God] is just, and his anger will not always slumber. He will wipe the tear from Ethiopia's eye; He will shake the tree of liberty, and its blossoms shall spread over the earth."[36]

A few weeks later Forten's "The Slave" appeared in the *Liberator.* It was a scathing criticism of slavery in the United States. She dwelled on the incompatibility of the war for independence with the enslavement of Africans:

> Our Sires who once in freedom's cause,
> Their boasted freedom sought and won,
> For deeds of glory gained applause,
> When patriot feelings led them on.
>
> And can their sons now speak with pride,
> Of rights for which they bled and died,
> Or while the captive is oppressed,
> Think of the wrongs they once regressed?[37]

Forten charged white America with obliterating the memories of the liberty and freedom for which the revolutionaries fought and now refused to the slave:

> Oh, surely they have quite forgot,
> That bondage once had been their lot;
> The sweets of freedom now they know,
> They care not for the captives wo.[38]

Forten contributed to several different newspapers in the 1830s, but much of her work appeared in the *Liberator.* Sarah Mapps Douglass, also known as "Zillah, a young lady of color," was another of Garrison's interests. Douglass contributed political essays addressing such issues as colonization, emancipation, and local Philadelphia issues. In 1832 Douglass wrote a letter to the editor of the *Liberator* about the Pennsylvania legislature's attempt to prohibit the migration of blacks to the state. Douglass connected the legislature's attempt at restriction to the growing racial hostility and social inequality experienced by all of Pennsylvania's citizens: "You ask me if I do not despair on account of the Bill now before our Legislature? I am cast down, but not in despair. I am aware that it will be our lot to suffer much persecution, and I have endeavored, for the last year, to fortify my mind against approaching trials."[39]

Like all black writers, Douglass was uneasy and angry about the heightened racism of the era. In her writings, however, were also expressions of hope for the future of race relations. She noted America's possibilities: "I see black and white mingle together in societal intercourse, without a shadow of disgust appearing on the countenance of either; no wailing heard, nor clanking chains, but the voice of peace and love and joy is wafted to my ears."[40] In another 1832 letter to the *Liberator*, she confronted the very serious debate regarding colonization among free blacks throughout the country. As this debate, which concerned the relocation of black Americans to Africa and Haiti, became a central political discussion in Philadelphia, Douglass expressed her resistance. She denounced colonization and reinforced a commitment and a desire on behalf of black Americans to maintain their residency in the United States: "Believe me, my friend, there is no spot in the known world where people are happier than in America. And bethink thee, dearest, it is our home. Think of this for one moment, and memory will call up so many fond and soothing reflections as will make thee loath to leave it."[41] Douglass's writings expressed gratitude for the principles on which America was founded, but her concerns regarding the social inequalities faced by enslaved and free black Americans were always central.

As the first black female newspaper editor, Mary Ann Shadd Cary created the *Provincial Freeman* (1853–57). Cary received tremendous praise from white abolitionist circles and free black communities for creating a political vehicle for the expression of black male and female voices. Born in Wilmington, Delaware, in 1823 to Harriet and Abraham Shadd, she was the oldest of thirteen children. It was a close-knit family of political activists; her father was a delegate to the annual Conventions of Free People of Color and served as the convention president in 1833.[42]

The Shadd family moved to the outskirts of Philadelphia and settled in West Chester, Pennsylvania. Abraham Shadd prospered with his boot and shoe store, and he was rumored to have served as a station on Philadelphia's Underground Railroad.[43] Having attended grammar school in Wilmington, Mary Ann Shadd completed her schooling in a private Quaker school just outside the city's limits.

Cary began her career, as did many other middle-class black abolitionists, as a teacher—first in Wilmington, Delaware, at the age of sixteen, and then in Pennsylvania. Throughout the 1840s she moved from one black school to another up and down the Northeast, spending a great deal of time in New

Jersey and New York. As she joined black abolitionist circles from Delaware to New York, Cary began to create a reputation as an activist herself.

In 1854 Cary became an editor of the *Provincial Freeman,* an antislavery newspaper in Ontario, Canada. Writing some twenty years after Sarah Forten, Cary had greater opportunity to address a wider range of issues than had her female predecessors. She used the newspaper as a vehicle to explore important questions that often divided black abolitionists of the 1850s.[44] With the woman suffrage movement under way and a greater acceptance of women as writers and public speakers, Cary could write and speak more freely, often condemning the paternalism of white abolitionism as well as assimilationist ideas promoted by many white men and women involved in the antislavery campaign. In one scathing editorial, Cary attacked "the disposition to make black appear white," and the desire to force "white standards" on blacks as the remedy for hostile race relations throughout the country. According to Cary, the adoption or assimilation of these standards stripped "the mis-called free colored man of all rights."[45]

Cary joined other black leaders who urged for migration to Canada, the West Indies, or Africa. Cary had lived in Canada for only a few months when she joined the migrationists, and her bold words and vehement stance regarding the emigration of black men and women to Canada often marginalized her within the black abolitionist community. Although she was respected by many, her abilities and her assertiveness often antagonized potential supporters and colleagues. As she attempted to move beyond the barriers of gender by participating in political forums, men, both black and white, often opposed her. In 1855 Cary traveled back to Philadelphia to attend the eleventh Colored National Convention, where she hoped to address all those present. No woman had ever been permitted to address the convention, and according to Frederick Douglass's newspaper, there was a great deal of discussion concerning Cary's participation: "There was much opposition manifested to her admission, on the part of some members, among them a rough, uncouth, semi-barbarous fellow who wished to know if 'we would admit Abby Kelley also?'" Although Cary was finally permitted to address the convention, her words were not well received. Her enthusiasm regarding emigration to Canada received little attention, for the majority of convention members were unhappy with having one of "the unfortunate sex" as their spokesperson.[46]

Like Mary Ann Shadd Cary, Frances Ellen Watkins Harper made a career for herself as a teacher, writer, and antislavery activist. Born in Baltimore in 1825, Harper was orphaned at an early age and raised by her aunt and uncle. As a free person in Baltimore, she attended her uncle's school until the age of thirteen, when she was forced to find employment as a servant in order to contribute to the family income. Her financial responsibility to her family temporarily superseded her educational goals, as was the case with many black men and women from modest households. As a seamstress and nurse for a white family in Baltimore, Harper still found time to cultivate her literary skills. Her employer, a bookseller, permitted her to read from his extensive library during her free time.[47]

As conditions for free blacks in Maryland began to deteriorate after the passage of the Fugitive Slave Act in 1850, Harper and her family left Baltimore and relocated in Ohio. Her educational background allowed her to move from domestic servant to respected educator when, at the age of twenty-six, Harper began her career as a schoolteacher there. As the first female teacher at the small school, Harper faced a great deal of resistance from male faculty members; she eventually moved back to the East Coast, to the outskirts of Philadelphia in York, Pennsylvania. There Harper continued in her struggle to uplift her race. Her statement that "the condition of our people, the wants of our children, and the welfare of our race, demand the aid of every helping hand" gave Harper the added incentive and needed strength to continue her teaching.[48]

Harper understood that her education allowed her to make the transition from domestic servitude. Unlike many other black female schoolteachers, however, Harper openly discussed the difficulties involved in teaching large numbers of uneducated black children with very few supplies. Black women who were given the opportunity to work outside the realm of domestic service were considered fortunate, and they were not often afforded the opportunity to discuss their occupational difficulties. For Harper, teaching became burdensome and an undesirable occupation. Limited because of her race and gender, she had few other opportunities, and she wrote to her friend William Still asking for his advice: "What would you do if you were in my place? Would you give up and go back to work at your trade [dressmaking]? There are no people that need all of the benefits resulting from a well-directed education more than we do. . . . It is a work of time, a labor of patience, to become an effective school teacher; and it should be a work of love in which they who engage should not abate heart or hope until it is done."[49]

It appeared to many black female teachers that their hard work was at times unnoticed. Compared to the backbreaking work of domestic labor, teaching was often considered somewhat luxurious. Only a few black women publicly expressed the difficulties of teaching. In 1832 Sarah Mapps Douglass wrote an essay in the *Liberator* in which she not only discussed the arduous work of the schoolteacher but also asked black schoolchildren to heed their instructors: "I hope the children who may read this tale, are very gentle and obedient to their teachers, because a teacher has many difficulties to encounter, and the good or bad conduct of children greatly increases or lessens difficulties."[50] Douglass ended her essay with the following: "I think, dear children, from what I have written, that you will understand that you have it in your power always to make the situation of your teachers pleasant. Will you not do so?"[51]

Having served as a teacher for many years, Harper nevertheless found a classroom of fifty-three children too much to handle. Her exposure to a community of free black abolitionists provided an entryway into a new career as an activist. Her transition to full-time antislavery agitator and writer allowed Harper to uplift her race in a different way; she concluded that "it may be that God himself has written upon both my heart and brain a commission to use time, talent and energy in the cause of freedom."[52] For the next few decades, Harper continued in the movement, lecturing throughout New England and the mid-Atlantic states; she supported herself through the sales of her poetry and books.

Harper lectured on many different topics during her antislavery tours, although her comments targeted the slave South and in particular the treatment of the enslaved woman and the dismantling of families. The North, however, was not spared from Harper's scathing commentary regarding race relations. In a letter written in 1858 she discussed the hazards faced by many black men and women, specifically those in Pennsylvania. "Now let me tell you about Pennsylvania. I have been in every New England state, in New York, Canada and Ohio, but of all these places this is about the meanest of all, as far as the treatment of colored people is concerned. . . . On the Carlisle road I was interrupted and insulted several times. Two men came after me in one day. I have met, of course, with kindness among individuals and families; all is not dark in Pennsylvania, but the shadow of slavery, oh, how drearily it hangs."[53] Harper used the platform of the press not only to express the injustice behind the institution of slavery but also to expose the problems of social inequality for black men and women in the North. Harper, Sarah Forten, Sarah Mapps Douglass, and Mary Ann Shadd Cary all used the vehicle of the press for their activism throughout the 1830s, 1840s, and 1850s, adding momentum to the abolitionist movement and pushing for equal rights for African Americans throughout the country.

African American Women and the Spiritual Narrative

As women of the black elite used newspaper articles, diary entries, and personal letters to speak out against the evils of slavery, they challenged societal norms that bound women to the silent sphere of the home. The

African American elite, however, were not the only women to confront and alter nineteenth-century tradition, for thousands of ordinary women supported political activism through small offerings of financial assistance and through individual work in local mutual aid societies. There was an even smaller group of women who dedicated themselves to lives of religious reform. As African American female church members monitored the private lives of black Philadelphians through church tribunals, women such as Jarena Lee and Zilpha Elaw attempted to uplift the African American community through evangelization, spreading the Gospel to all who would hear it. Consumed with the business of saving souls, Lee and Elaw broke from traditional roles to become female itinerant preachers and religious reformers. Their spiritual narratives of the antebellum era contribute another layer to the multifaceted political writings of African American women, offering a different perspective on the public and private lives of antebellum black women.

Beginning with the formation of the African Methodist Episcopal Church, black congregations created a unique religious culture that was based heavily on populist ideology. During the early nineteenth century, many African American men and women considered themselves qualified to preach the Gospel after experiencing conversion, discounting formal training as a necessity. It mattered not if a person was poor or uneducated, for the religious culture of black Philadelphia was much more accepting of a lay ministry.[54] A relaxed Methodist denomination allowed African American women to enter the field of private exhorting in prayer meetings and small gatherings. The black Methodist church did, however, hold to traditional gender roles, which made the advancement of women such as Lee and Elaw from the prayer group to the pulpit a difficult and often dangerous journey.

The majority of nineteenth-century African American spiritual autobiographies begin with the story of slavery. So does the *Religious Experience and Journal of Mrs. Jarena Lee, Giving an Account of Her Call to Preach the Gospel.* Jarena Lee, born in 1783 in Cape May, New Jersey, was separated from her parents at the age of seven when she was indentured as a servant girl some sixty miles away from her family. She endured the psychological hardships that would have afflicted any small child removed from her parents' home; she admitted to depression and fleeting thoughts of suicide. In 1849 a conversion experience intervened during an episode of emotional anguish. Lee credited it as saving her life both spiritually and physically: "by some means, of which I can give no account, my thoughts were taken entirely from this purpose. It was the unseen arm of God which kept me from self-murder."[55]

Lee's conversion took place during a sermon delivered by the Reverend Richard Allen and prompted her to join the African Methodist Episcopal Church. Although put off by what appeared to be the rigid rules of the Methodist Society, Lee wrote: "That moment, though hundreds were present, I did leap to my feet and declare that God, for Christ's sake, had pardoned the sins of my soul. Great was the ecstasy of my mind, for I felt that not only the sin of malice was pardoned, but all other sins were swept away together."[56] Lee's renewed commitment to religion led her to follow a life that was unconventional for an African American woman: she moved from new convert to pious church member and eventually to itinerant preacher.[57]

Zilpha Elaw, born in Pennsylvania around 1790, experienced many of the same life challenges as Lee. Elaw was also separated from her parents as a young child; when she was twelve, her mother died while giving birth to her twenty-second child. Elaw was then consigned to Pierson and Rebecca Mitchel, working as an indentured servant until her eighteenth birthday.[58] Like many other black Philadelphians then, both Elaw and Lee experienced servitude and became free in the early 1800s.[59]

Elaw converted as a teenager. Finding herself completely alone, she began her first intimate conversations with God, a great help amid the difficulties of servitude and loneliness. Following her conversion, she wrote that all the hardships and unfortunate circumstances that she had experienced before her conversion vanished, allowing her rebirth with a new temper, disposition, and heart: "After this wonderful manifestation of my condescending Saviour, the peace of God which passeth understanding was communicated to my heart; and joy in the Holy Ghost, to a degree, at the least, unutterable by my tongue and indescribable by my pen; it was beyond my comprehension; but from that happy hour, my soul was set at glorious liberty; and like the Ethiopic eunuch, I went on my way rejoicing in the blooming prospects of a better inheritance with the saints in light. This, my dear reader, was the manner of my soul's conversion to God."[60]

Both Lee and Elaw continued to study the Bible and to speak at small gatherings, and eventually they began calling themselves preachers. The response to female exhorting by the members and officials of Mother Bethel was far from warm. Although they attempted to nurture the spirits of their community members, they saw these women as attacking the role of the male minister. It mattered not that they worked to spread the word of God. What mattered was their gender: women were not to preach. Although many female members of Mother Bethel led prayer groups at home and at church, few were brave enough to move beyond.

There were, however, some who refused to scorn the women of the word. According to the autobiographical sketches written by Lee and Elaw, both women drew large crowds of black and white men and women who assembled to hear them preach or to hold prayer meetings in every city and state to which they traveled. Across the country, people journeyed long distances to hear the female preachers, and although the A.M.E. Church did not formally recognize these women, they were viewed by many members as instruments of God, and they attained the folksy image of wandering women preachers.

Navigating between the Worlds of Womanhood and the Ministry

The majority of African American female itinerant preachers of the nineteenth century wrote extensively about religious and spiritual matters. Absent from their autobiographies is the personal experience of marriage and motherhood. Although the personal is briefly discussed in their writings, it often appears as peripheral to their lives. Both Elaw and Lee wrote about the impediments to religious work that arose from family obligations, in particular the problems of marriage. With the responsibility of raising families and the hurdles of disagreeable husbands, both women were unable to begin their preaching careers until later in their lives. Both Lee and Elaw were widowed and eventually relieved of the duty of rearing their own children.

Zilpha Elaw's memoir explores the difficulties of young women preparing to enter into marriage. In Elaw's 1846 spiritual memoir, she mentions nothing about courtship or love; she writes instead of marriage as a duty to which she had to submit. "In the year 1810, I surrendered myself in marriage to Joseph Elaw, a very respectable young man, in the general acception of the term, but he was not a Christian,—that is, a sincere and devoted disciple of Christ, though nominally bearing His name."[61]

Elaw's use of the term *surrendered* is revealing, for although it was a common way to describe the act of marriage for a woman, Elaw described her union as a failure. Constantly complaining of her husband's irreligious ways, Elaw noted its effect on her own spiritual well-being. Although she experienced conversion, the role of wife took priority over her religious calling. For single young women in servitude, marriage often provided a way by which to liberate oneself from a white master. African American women used servitude to gain access to freedom; marriage was another vehicle used to gain stability. Although authority concerning the lives of black women was transferred from employer to husband, it nevertheless allowed for a more autonomous family life, filled with possibilities.

Companionate marriages became increasingly acceptable among the elite by the middle of the nineteenth century, but the romance involved in choosing one's partner was often absent in the writings of ordinary women such as Elaw.[62] There was no mention of love or mutual admiration in her narrative; instead, she compared her marriage to a "millstone" hung about her neck. Troubled by her husband's lack of deference to religion, Elaw warned young female readers about the seriousness of marriage, especially to a nonbeliever: "Oh! let me affectionately warn my dear unmarried sisters in Christ against being thus unequally yoked with unbelievers. In general your lot would be better, if a millstone were hung about your necks, and you were drowned in the depths of the sea, than you should disobey the law of Jesus, and plunge yourselves into all the sorrows, sins, and anomalies involved in a matrimonial alliance with an unbeliever."[63] Elaw's warning hinged on the problems of marriage to a man who lacked piety, but her words represented a more general message about the institution of marriage. Her husband had been expelled from the church society; instead of denouncing him, however, Elaw found it within her heart to pity him: "I could not regard him as a backslider from religion, for I am of opinion that he had never tasted of the pardoning love of God through the atonement of Jesus Christ."[64] Joseph Elaw promised his wife that he would cleanse his soul and mend his ways by reuniting with the church, but this never happened. He moved farther away from the church and attempted to bring his wife into the "world of sin" by taking her to ballrooms and other social spaces filled with spiritual temptation. Elaw remained steady in her faith and confident that her marriage to a nonbeliever was a mistake, but divorce was an impossibility for any ordinary woman, black or white, in early nineteenth-century America.

Still, Elaw made certain to make clear to her reading public that she respected the bonds of matrimony and thought it the respectable way to form a family. Elaw tested the waters of "the marriage question" in early nineteenth-century feminism; however, she remained publicly committed to traditional ideas. Following her statement regarding the problematic nature of marriage to a nonbeliever, Elaw strategically expressed a very traditional viewpoint in which she blamed youth, foolishness, and haughtiness as the causes of troubled marriages:

> This mischief frequently emanates from the delusive sentiments in which the female portion of the Christian community is steeped. Young ladies imagine themselves their own mistresses before they are able to shift for themselves; and especially when they attain the legal maturity fixed by civil law. Pride, consequential haughtiness, and independent arrogance in females, are the worst vices of humanity, and are denounced in the Scriptures

as insuring the severest retributions of God. Isaiah iii. 16–24. The laws of the Scripture invest parents with the trust and control of their daughter, until the time, be it early or late in life, when the father surrenders her in marriage to the care and government of a husband: then, and not till then, the guardianship and government of her father over her ceases; and then, formed as she is by nature for subordination, she becomes the endowment and is subject to the authority of her husband.[65]

Elaw also labeled women who spoke against the wishes of their parents or their husbands as indecent, impious, and disrespecting the scriptures. Ironically, this female minister denounced independent women as unnatural, stating that "the fancied independence and self-control in which they indulge, has no foundation either in nature or Scripture, and is prolific with the worst results both to religion and society."[66] Elaw proclaimed that a father should be the steward of a young woman until she married, when her husband would assume a governing role. But this practice of transferring paternalistic control proved extremely problematic for women like Elaw. She was in essence an orphan and an indentured servant: who took on the authority of stewardship for young black women like her? Although white masters attempted to control many aspects of their servants' lives, they were far from acting as surrogate parents. As slavery and indentured servitude had separated families from one another, who was to pick up the mantle of governor? Many African American women took seriously the idea that they had "none but God to look to" and therefore governed themselves with the hope of divine guidance.

Jarena Lee approached the subject of marriage in a manner similar to Elaw's. Her memoir recounted an uncomfortable story of marriage to a pastor outside Philadelphia. "In the year 1811, I changed my situation in life, having married Mr. Joseph Lee, pastor of a Society at Snow Hill, about six miles from the city of Philadelphia. It became necessary therefore for me to remove."[67] Although Lee was not faced with the difficulties of marriage to a nonbeliever, she was forced to move out of the city, "a great trial at first," since she left her network of Christian friends behind. While in Snow Hill, New Jersey, Lee continued to practice her faith with diligence, but she noted that she never found in her new home state the closeness that she had experienced with her Philadelphia band of followers.

Within the course of a year, Lee attempted to persuade her husband to move back to Philadelphia. Unwilling to leave behind his congregation, Joseph Lee refused, leaving his wife with no option but to remain, unhappy, in New Jersey. Lee received a divine message while she slept that convinced her that her husband's duty was to remain: "Joseph Lee must take care of these sheep, or the wolf will come and devour them."[68] She expressed her discontent in a different manner: she became ill.

Illness in the early nineteenth century plagued many people frequently and for long periods. Throughout the century, diaries and memoirs written by women depicted various health afflictions that were often of unknown cause and difficult to treat. A malady or debility forced many women to take to their beds, particularly after the birth of a child.[69] Lee's illness was never given a specific name or cure. She spiraled downward: "After this, I fell into a state of general debility, and in an ill state of health so much so, that I could not sit up. . . . From this sickness I did not expect to recover, and there was but one thing that bound me to this earth, and this was that I had not as yet preached the gospel to the fallen sons and daughters of Adam's race to the satisfaction of my mind."[70] Neither her husband nor her two infants gave Lee the will to live. It was her desire for fellowship and her dream eventually to spread the Gospel that kept her from death. Lee remained ill for six years, a time in which five family members lost their lives, including her husband.

Lee never discussed her marriage or her husband's death in detail. She simply stated that, among the fatalities of her family members, her husband's "was the greatest affliction of all"; she was left alone with two small children, with none but "the promise of Him" to depend upon. She did note that she became an older, more mature woman. Joseph Lee's death would free her not simply from unhappiness in Snow Hill, but also from the confines of coverture and submission.[71] Lee was at last in the position to make her own decisions.

Both Elaw's marriage of thirteen years and Lee's of six ended with the deaths of men who prevented them from doing the Lord's work. Once their husbands were gone, both Elaw and Lee were free to live the lives of preacher women; widowhood had its privileges. Their unorthodox desire to preach in public often incited anger and hostility and on occasion jeopardized their physical safety. Although many African American women were accustomed to a lack of protection from violence, black women preachers were especially at risk. Traveling from city to city, alone and in strange environments, women such as Lee and Elaw had to provide for themselves, which proved particularly difficult in small towns throughout the South. Denouncing slavery as un-Christian, African American women preachers placed their lives in danger as they spread the word of God.

Although Jarena Lee and Zilpha Elaw have been labeled biblical feminists for their contested and sometimes dangerous stand as ministers, these two women, as well as many other African American women of the nineteenth century, found it extremely difficult to balance the demands of the private and the public world. In many cases, the private and public worlds of African American communities appeared to be seamless. Under the gaze of white Philadelphians, or the vigilance of independent black communities, the private world designated as "woman's sphere" at that time was in many instances open to public scrutiny. For women such as Lee and Elaw, the act of becoming a wife or mother provided additional difficulties to an already unconventional lifestyle.

Motherhood and the Ministry

Lee and Elaw were wives and mothers, yet these very personal relationships are nearly absent from their spiritual narratives. Perhaps the absence of family in the narratives of these women served as a way to protect their private lives. This, however, appears odd for nineteenth-century African Americans, since recently emancipated Philadelphians worked so hard to locate and nurture their families in the aftermath of slavery. For most, family and, in particular, motherhood represented a treasured declaration of freedom. This, however, was not declared by Elaw and Lee.

For women of the postrevolutionary era, the concepts of feminine virtue were deeply rooted to the status of motherhood.[72] For African American women, the privilege of motherhood was twofold: it allowed for a semi-autonomous role within the family, and it allowed them to participate in the shaping of a virtuous black community, as the family became extremely important as a measure of progress. Many African Americans believed that if virtuous republicanism could be displayed in the black community, then perhaps the recognition and benefits attached to citizenship would eventually be extended to them. For African American women, there was much more at stake than one's own reputation if one failed at motherhood.

In Elaw's writing, her daughter is never mentioned by name, nor is there any discussion of her or the relationship they shared. Like many widows, Elaw was unable to support her family independently. Forced to hire out both her daughter and herself, Elaw reentered the world of employment outside the home, but her illness prevented her from working steadily. As an alternative, Elaw was able to open a small school for African American students. Her previous education, most likely gained while she was an indentured servant, allowed her to move beyond the scope of domestic service, a privilege enjoyed by very few black women.[73]

Still, she was extremely unhappy, for the responsibilities of motherhood prohibited her from concentrating on the call to preach. Invited to travel to Philadelphia to preach with several other church members, Elaw found herself desperately wanting to abandon her role as mother and join her brothers and sisters of the faith in their travels. Unable to arrange her affairs or collect sufficient financial support to depart with her neighbors, Elaw noted that her initial decision not to begin her career as a traveling preacher hinged on the responsibility attached to motherhood. It was only after her young daughter noticed her mother's depression that she convinced Elaw to begin her travels: "I returned home, and my little daughter seeing the tears flow from my cheeks, said to me, 'Now, mother, what is the matter?' for she was aware of the great anxiety of mind I had so long been labouring under, and said all she could to comfort me; and added, 'If I were you, I should not mind what any person said, but I should go just as I had arranged to go, and do not think anything about me, for I shall do very well.' "[74]

After receiving her daughter's permission to abandon her familial responsibilities, Elaw announced that all of her "tears were dried away" and God allowed her to take leave. Elaw put her daughter in the care of a relative, moved on to Philadelphia, and "commenced in her Master's business." The call to preach the Gospel trumped all other responsibilities. She would have relied on the charity of black mutual aid societies. Organizations like the Daughters of Allen provided assistance to women, specifically those who were ill or widowed, so that Elaw could continue her preaching. "Everyone appeared to be acquainted with my situation. I preached in a great many chapels, and every congregation voluntarily made a collection for my aid; and every person whose house I visited gave me something for my journey."[75] Thus, church members came to Elaw's aid. Often ambivalent about the role of the female preacher, they still maintained their commitment to feed, clothe, and house the needy.

Like Zilpha Elaw, Jarena Lee never mentioned the birth of her two children in her spiritual autobiography, nor did she discuss her personal relationship with them. Only after the death of her husband did Lee write that she was left alone with two infants, "one of the age of about two years, the other six months."[76] The section of her narrative following the death of her spouse is entitled "The Subject of My Call to Preach Renewed," in which she focused on her mission to preach. The Reverend Richard Allen gave approval for Lee to minister to members of the African Methodist Episcopal Church while she "kept house" with her "little son who was very sickly."[77]

Throughout the remainder of her narrative, Lee described her family as consisting of two people, herself and her son, James. The death of one of her children never appears in the text. Her son remained ill and was continually left in the care of friends and family. Although the death of her husband was discussed in brief detail, the death of the child was completely omitted. The status of widowhood gained by her husband's death was necessary in the construction of her identity as a wise and older woman capable of preaching the Gospel. Yet the death of a child, rather than evoking respect or sympathy, could easily bring blame on a mother who refused to stay at home. Because of her frequent absences, Lee may very well have been held accountable for her child's death by the community to which she preached.

As for small and sickly James, he spent a great deal of time separated from his mother. Although she occasionally took him with her on missions to New Jersey and Delaware, James remained mostly in the care of friends. Employing the assistance of her mother, who lived in Cape May, New Jersey, Lee often left her son with family, even when he was seriously ill. Lee left her son in the care of friends and relatives, although her narrative states that she gave her son over to the Reverend Richard Allen for a little more than two years, making the Allens James's main caregivers. Upon returning to Philadelphia from a trip to Baltimore in 1830, Lee commented on the parental responsibility Allen had assumed for her son: "Next I left Baltimore for Philadelphia, my home, and found my friends all well; and my only son also, was well, and remained with Rev. Bishop Allen, where I left him before I went away. After being absent for two years and six months, I found Bishop Allen in very ill health, but he ever had continued on with unwearied interest in my son's welfare, by sending him to school, and otherwise improving him in education; by which he has made considerable improvements therefrom; which gave me great reconciliation of mind; one thing lacking, which was a trade."[78] In 1831 Richard Allen died, leaving behind a huge congregation and a national network of friends and followers. For Lee, not only was Allen's death sorrowful, but it also created a need for a new source of child care. Noting that she was troubled by her son's limited formal schooling and his lack of a trade, Lee placed the boy with a "French gentleman." James, then approximately fifteen years old, would begin to learn the cabinetmaking business as an apprentice.[79]

The writings of African American women, both elite and ordinary, demonstrate the difficulties of racism, sexism, motherhood, and familial obligations during the nineteenth century. As women such as the Fortens expressed these challenges in the pages of national periodicals, their focus often centered on the political issues of the era: slavery, temperance, and reform. Women such as Jarena Lee and Zilpha Elaw, who were not members of the black elite, focused on the importance of religion and the difficulty of familial obligations. Both genres of writing allow us to see into the personal worlds and intimate difficulties of African American women: for what the writers say, and for what they do not say.

6

A Mental and Moral Feast
Reading, Writing, and Sentimentality in Black Philadelphia

> *Readers! Within these folds you'll find*
> *Effusions various as the mind.*
> *From numerous prolific brains,*
> *In sorrowful and merry strains.*
> *This little book in prose or rhyme,*
> *Is meant to cheat old father Time,*
> *And so a delicious hour beguiled,*
> *With poetry in every style.*

The mid-nineteenth century was perhaps one of the most complicated eras for African American men and women of the urban North. Although constantly faced with mounting inequalities and the persistent struggle to end the institution of slavery, African American men and women continued to redefine themselves as free people living in America.[1] A foundation of free African American religious organizations and educational facilities dating back to the late eighteenth century gave rise to a politically active black elite in cities such as Philadelphia. Not only did African American men and women struggle to free themselves from the vestiges of slavery, but they also experienced a dynamic socioeconomic transition as the nineteenth century unfolded. As they moved from slavery to indentured servitude to wage labor, men and women of African descent found themselves confronted with a changing urban and rural landscape, and the black elite balanced the precarious nature of their freedom with a developing bourgeois culture.[2]

African American elite women saw themselves, their families, and their communities in a state of perpetual motion. As wives and mothers, black women juggled their domestic duties in their own households with work outside the home. Unlike white elite women in Philadelphia, African American women were forced to earn additional income in an effort to support their families, often finding jobs as teachers, nurses, and caterers.[3] For African Americans, middle-class status was often elusive and, if attained, always precarious. The weight of racism and disfranchisement as well as the concern for millions of blacks held in bondage compounded fears regarding the stability of their own financial and social status. As kidnappers scanned the small streets and alleys of Philadelphia's black community, members of the black middle class worried not only about their social positions but also about the security of their freedom.

The lives of African American women were filled not only with work in and outside the home, but with additional charity work, political activism, and religious devotion, all of which they believed would both benefit the black community of Philadelphia and transform the negative stereotypes of African American women. As these women constructed their personal and public spheres, respectability as well as sentimentalism became central in their nineteenth-century social circles. The world of friendship and sisterly love helped to strengthen political networks and extended kinship ties across the urban epicenters of the mid-Atlantic and New England regions.

Sentimentalism was a central component of nineteenth-century American culture, especially among the middle class. As the scholar Shirley Samuels suggests, sentimentalism became a "set of cultural practices designed to evoke a certain form of emotional response, usually empathy."[4] Sentimentalism worked across race, class, and gender boundaries, creating guidelines for the expression of feelings adopted by most female reformers, particularly those involved in the work of abolition. The plight of the black slave, the horrors of rape and sale on the auction block, as well as the corruption of the white family were central to the antislavery literature of the century, within which sentimentalism became an effective tool for reform. Scholars have given much attention to the work of sentimentalism in the nineteenth-century novel, as it was the genre most often used by male and female writers. The modern critique of the sentimental novel has shifted several times as scholars have moved from declaring the novel "a lesser genre" to a feminist rejection of the absolute binary of separate spheres.[5] Sentimental literature was a method by which women achieved significant cultural gains. The sentimental novel introduced a popular feminine aesthetic that transformed traditional print culture and created a new space for women's writings, somewhere between the public and the private spheres.[6]

Although the culture of sentimentalism has been thoroughly examined with respect to published literature, there is still room for a critique of personal or private writings of nineteenth-century women, specifically the writings of African American women. The personal and semipublic arena of the friendship album allows us to examine the public and personal worlds of African American women who used the same methods of expression as did their white female counterparts. One of the most beautifully written and intriguing ways of creating community and friendship among women of the nineteenth century was the maintenance of friendship albums. As friendship albums were passed from friend to friend along the East Coast, the display of immaculate penmanship, proper grammar and spelling, and respectable prose regarding the private and the political allowed African Americans to reinforce their respectability within their own social circles. As the albums traveled from Baltimore to Philadelphia and as far north as Boston, educated African Americans established a protocol regarding discussions pertaining to womanhood, motherhood, and emancipation.

The friendship albums of African American women clearly echo the nineteenth-century sentimental albums of white women as well as novels, though the use of sentimentalism is far more complex than simple mimicry. As the scholar Claudia Tate suggests in her work on postreconstruction black female novelists, black women in their writings focused on sentimentality and respectability.[7] Elite African American women participated in the same discourse in antebellum Philadelphia as they wrote about their own lives and the possibilities for the future, providing a rare glimpse of their public and personal concerns. Tate writes that African American women used sentimental writing as an entry point to discuss the social and political issues of the era; she argues that idealized domesticity and sentimentalism represented "a fundamental cultural symbol of the Victorian era for representing civil ambition and prosperity."[8]

Despite the disappointments of the postreconstruction era, the genre of sentimentalism promoted the social advancement of African Americans, and for women of the antebellum North, the same held true. Moments of hope and possibility attached to gradual abolition of the 1780s were followed by decades of violence and hostility toward the free black community. Although the dreams of recently emancipated black men and women were probably much more tenuous than those of their successors during the Reconstruction Era, the antebellum black elite wrote for the promise of the future, using sentimentalism in their friendship albums as a tool for reform. African American women shared their writings, both demonstrating learned social etiquette and simultaneously expressing the dream of complete freedom and equality.

On occasion, African American women shared their albums with white friends, asking them to enter their thoughts or good wishes. The writings contributed by white acquaintances to the albums were frequently political in nature, denouncing the evils of slavery and bolstering the burgeoning women's rights movement. The writings of white acquaintances lacked the intimacy and sensitivity demonstrated by African Americans who penned their thoughts in the albums. Whites failed to sympathize with the personal joys or tragedies of black men and women, nor did they comment on the personal life of the album's owner. Although their contributions were made with the best of intentions, the entries were clearly political.

Only four friendship albums belonging to nineteenth century African American women remain intact.[9] These albums serve as unique historical treasures, for they reveal the personal writings and feelings of the black elite, not only in Philadelphia but also throughout the urban North. Historians of antebellum African American women are often confronted with a scarcity of sources, as time and time again they are forced to reinterpret primary sources written and maintained by people who were not of African descent. Additional historical sources for African American women come from their public writings, usually in the form of newspaper articles and pamphlets, as well as minutes from local and national organizations. The recent discovery of these albums is of extreme importance: they have helped to define the intimate relationships and community-building practices among privileged African American men and women and have provided new insight into the private worlds of kinship and friendship.

The album stands as a midpoint between the public and private arena among the African American elite. As self-proclaimed representatives of their race, black men and women of Philadelphia were under the watchful eye of white residents. The words and actions of an African American individual would more than likely be seen as a representation of an entire community, so that the private sphere of the black elite was constrained. Album contributions provide an entry into the guarded, intimate lives of African American women. Within the pages of the friendship album, black women were provided an opportunity to write to and about one another; they brought sentimentality and very public debates such as abolition and women's rights into a protected space. Not only did the album serve as a badge of respectability, but it also provided elite black women with an additional platform on which to reconstruct their image and expand their private relationships.

Words between Friends: Expressions of Female Friendship

In stark contrast to instruments such as public newspapers, the friendship album provided a more personal forum in which ideas and emotions could be exchanged. Nineteenth-century albums included poetry, short stories, personal letters, and watercolors, providing women with an unrestricted arena in which to express their admiration and affection to their friends.[10] Although these albums were the private possessions of their owners, the contents were not, simply by the way in which friendship albums were exchanged. The owner of the friendship album passed her keepsake to a friend, often allowing her to possess the album for days at a time.

Most nineteenth-century middle-class white women lived in a world defined by the domestic sphere, spending their time caring for the home, participating in religious activities, and visiting one another on a regular basis.[11] They helped one another with chores and the raising of families during times of illness, economic strife, and the deaths of loved ones. Female friends who resided in cities such as Philadelphia were able to visit one another with more frequency than those who lived in the hinterland, often traveling with one another in the absence of a husband or male relative. When women spent intimate and extended periods together without the daily constraints of family or housework, friendship became an escape from the confines of the domestic sphere.

Race and class redrew the confines of domesticity for middle-class black women, placing them in both the private and the public spheres. Bound to the traditional duties of wife, mother, and good Christian, they simultaneously participated in the very public work of antislavery and black mutual aid. Their work inside and outside the home influenced black female friendship and the worlds of love and sentimentality. Much of the extremely insightful scholarship regarding women's lives of the early nineteenth century focuses on the friendships between white women. The issues of slavery and racial discrimination did not find their way into the central discussion of those women's friendships, yet they were crucial to the lives of African American female friends.[12] As race and class constructed a multifaceted and complex domestic sphere for African American women, the communication between black female friends reflected emotional support as well as a political agenda. The precarious position of middle-class black women during the early decades of the century did not always allow for a harmonious life, "free of emotional tension, enclosing within it secret sources of power and joy."[13] African American women of the middle class worked constantly at bolstering the black image and, more specifically, the reputations of African American women. Friendships between black women were extremely important for many of the same reasons they were important to antebellum white women, but African American women found in their friendships much more than an emotional crutch or an escape from the domestic sphere. Their friends became an extended kinship network, which would not only assist them in times of illness and despair, but also form a political alliance that would work to bring an end to the system of slavery. For African American women, friendship combined sentimentality with practicality.

The friendship album served as a symbol of sentimentality and popularity for African American women in Philadelphia and across the urban North. Most nineteenth-century sentimental literature was produced for and by white women, but scholars such as Jocelyn Moody have examined African American women and their connection to the genre. Moody argues that antebellum sentimentalism consisted of a basic set of core values used differently by women, both black and white. Early uses of sentimentalism appeared not only in the literary form of the novel, but in autobiographies as well.[14] Friendship albums used sentimentality as a vehicle to engage invited contributors while demonstrating common cultural assumptions about piety and virtue, at the same time deepening emotional and ethical ties between friends and colleagues.

As the content of the album was of sentimental importance to the owner, the reputation of those who penned their good wishes was also of great significance. Amy Matilda Cassey's friendship album, filled with beautiful calligraphy and genteel watercolors and bound in black morocco, provides historians with a window into album culture. Cassey was born in 1809 to a family of well-established African Americans in New York. The daughter of the Reverend Peter Williams, a leader in the black community, she married a member of Philadelphia's black elite in 1828. Joseph Cassey, a wealthy hairdresser and importer of perfumes, was a generation older than Amy and already entrenched in early antislavery activity and black improvement societies.[15] He aided in the creation of the first African

American newspaper, *Freedom's Journal,* was a founding member of the American Anti-Slavery Society, and was a sales agent for William Lloyd Garrison's *Liberator.*[16]

Following their marriage, Amy Cassey became involved in many reform movements and women's organizations. In 1833 she became a member of the Philadelphia Female Anti-Slavery Society, and in 1836 she helped to launch the Moral Reform Association, a national African American temperance and uplift organization.[17] In addition to national movements, the Casseys were involved with local black improvement efforts such as the Gilbert Lyceum. Although Cassey's friendship album was a private journal, she understood that it would be read by all its contributors. Cassey wrote a preface to the album in which she invited her friends and colleagues to enjoy each other's contributions:

> Now reader as you find delight,
> In scanning o'er what others write,
> 'Tis hoped in gratitude alone,
> You'll add a tribute of your own.
> And thus with one choice piece at least
> enrich this mental pic-nic feast.[18]

Cassey's invitation made clear that although she selected the friends and acquaintances who were to write in her album, it was still a semipublic forum of expression among the black elite of Philadelphia.

Many of the entries recorded in nineteenth-century friendship albums represent the written expression of love between female friends. Appreciation of friends and positive depictions of acquaintances were scattered about the albums' pages and expressed in various styles. In many cases, the sentimental expression appeared in the form of a poem such as the one written in May 1833 by Sarah Louise Forten in Cassey's album. The original poem may very well have been shared in the public setting of the Gilbert Lyceum, of which they were both members. Although this specific poem was never printed in a newspaper of the time, it was representative of the type of poetry written between female friends and for the public:

> My prayer for thee dearest, is warm from the heart,
> Unmingled with flattery—unsullied by art,
> 'Tis the first fervent wishes I've traced on this page
> May they ever attend thee, in youth and in age.
> I pray that thy pathway on earth may be bright.[19]

As Sarah Forten expressed her good wishes to her friend Amy Cassey, she touched on several very common themes in the writings of nineteenth-century women. In addition to wishing happiness to her friend, Forten extended the hope for a healthy and harmonious marriage for Cassey. She wished them well through the good and difficult times, but she specifically wished that Cassey's husband would have the ability to endure the trials of marriage and that "from the love he then pledged may he never depart."[20]

The importance of marriage among nineteenth-century women, in particular black women, recurred as a central theme throughout many friendship albums of the era. As the institution of slavery had prohibited or at the very least limited the option of marriage, free African American women of the antebellum era took very seriously the ability and the perceived need to be married. Victorian respectability hinged on the formation of a nuclear family and the importance of marriage. As Forten's entry wished Cassey and her husband well, it also served as a reminder of the significance as well as the respectability attached to the institution of marriage.

As the African American elite wrote to one another and for one another in the friendship album, their displays of sentimentality differed according to the individual writer. Mary Forten showed her feelings of admiration and love for Amy Cassey through the contribution of a poem entitled "Friendship."

> Friendship! to thee unsullied joys belong;
> Joys that bless e'en Heaven's immortal throng.
> In those bright realms so rich in every joy;
> That hope herself would but the bliss annoy.[21]

Themes of motherhood and womanhood were constants in the poetry written in the album, though issues such as religion and piety were also included.

An invitation to write in a friendship album was not only an honor but also a way to be identified as a member of, or connected to, the African American elite. To enter one's prose and poetry in an album was a privilege respected by many, but at times it appears to have been difficult for women and men to find the appropriate words for a friend. Such was the case with Susan Wright, who was asked by Amy Cassey in November 1833 to contribute to her album. Wright titled her entry "My Friend" and wrote a five-line poem.

> My Friend,
> You ask me on this page to write
> A *copy* of my heart for you,
> But thoughts and words have fled tonight,
> Be sure the original is true.[22]

Friends took home each other's albums and found on occasion that words did not come with ease. It appears, however, as though it was better to be honest about the inability to write with ease than to risk offending a good friend or important acquaintance.

Expressions of Love: African American Men's and Women's Writings

The friendship album was shared not only with female friends; male friends and acquaintances were also asked to add their writings and thoughts to the album. Although the overwhelming majority of writers appear to have been women, male members of the African American elite did contribute their sentiments, and the difference in their writing style, as well as in their sentimentality, sets them apart from their female counterparts. Although men's contributions were sentimental, they often lacked the degree of intimacy that appeared in the poetry and prose written by African American women. Often men simply copied short stories and poems written by others instead of contributing original pieces, and many of the entries had very little if anything to do with friendship; instead, they revolved around political issues of the moment. In the friendship album of Mary Virginia Wood Forten, James Forten Jr., her brother-in-law, entered a poem entitled "On Time":

> All powerful Time! thy potency we own,
> Countless the trophies that adorn thy throne
> At thy rebuke the elements decay,
> Man's boasted hope, before thee melts away
> His proud memorials too soon are thine
> His pomp and glory but adorn thy shrine
> Yet mighty king! though ancient is thy reign,
> In terrors clad thy potency is vain;
> Thou too shalt fail when on thy yielding shore
> The final trump proclaims that time shall be no more![23]

Forten's entry to his own relative was fairly devoid of emotion as well as sentimentality. He failed to mention any of the noble attributes or personal characteristics of his own family member, nor did he wish her health, happiness, or success, as did the many women writers. His entry did share several philosophical commonalities with the entries penned by women, however, the most obvious being a reference to the power and potency of time. As the friendship album was a way by which to "cheat old father time," Forten was able to immortalize his thoughts within its pages.

Other well-known African American men contributed to the culture of album writing. Patrick Henry Reason, a commercial engraver from New York, inscribed Washington Irving's poem "The Wife" in Amy Cassey's album, and James McCune Smith and John Chew contributed several writings as well.[24] Chew's entry, "To the Lost One," was written following the death of Joseph Cassey in 1848. The twenty-year marriage between Amy and Joseph Cassey had ended, and Amy Cassey's close friends dedicated several sonnets to her husband's memory.

In a number of cases, men who chose to write in the albums explained their lack of sentimentality. In January 1850 Frederick Douglass contributed to Cassey's album. Unlike Forten, Douglass explained his awkwardness and inability to write in a sentimental fashion: "I never feel more entirely out of my sphere, than when presuming to write in an Album. This suggestion of beauty elegance and refinement—whilst my habit of life passed history—& present occupation—have called into exercise all the sterner qualities of my head and heart."[25] Douglass's explanation for his inability to write with sentimentality rested on his experience as an enslaved man and his abolitionist activity. The brutality he had experienced as an enslaved person, as well as his challenging and often dangerous life as an agent of antislavery activity, proved for him incompatible with expressing sentimentality. Douglass completed his entry by asking forgiveness "for not writing something becoming the pages of your precious album."[26]

Accompanying Douglass on his visit to Philadelphia was Charles Lenox Redmond of Salem, Massachusetts. As a wealthy black businessman, he was the first African American lecturer for the Massachusetts Anti-Slavery Society and popular in many circles among the black elite. In 1850 Amy Cassey married the articulate antislavery lecturer, becoming Mrs. Charles Lenox Redmond and relocating to Salem.[27]

Reflections on Womanhood and Motherhood

Not only were the friendship albums of the nineteenth century used to express feelings between friends, but they also served as emblems of etiquette among the African American elite. Friends and family shared poems and short stories with one another that contained moral messages and reminders about respectability and the appropriate role of wife and mother. Discussion regarding the proper dependency and submissiveness of women was often found in the writings of the black elite. As these women generally worked outside the home to help support their families or as philanthropists, they found it necessary to remind each other of the appropriateness of strength and dependency. Across the country women such as Sarah Mapps Douglass and Frances Ellen Watkins Harper served as schoolteachers for black children. Mary Ann Shadd Cary became editor of the *Provincial Freeman,* and both Margaretta and Sarah Forten were regular contributors to the *Liberator* and the *North Star.*[28] Although elite status and the desire for respectability reinforced the label of the "weaker sex" among the black elite, the actions of these women worked to dismantle the stereotype.

An unsigned poem in the Cassey album entitled "The Fair Sex" described in a somewhat humorous manner the weakness of women:

> When Eve brought woe to all Mankind,
> Old Adam called her wo-man;
> But when she woo'd with love so kind,
> He then pronounced her woo-man.
> But now with folly and with pride,
> Their husbands keenly trimming,
> The ladies are so full of whims,
> That people call them whim-men.[29]

The gender of the poem's author is unknown, but its central conviction is quite clear. The stereotype of the whimsical and evil woman was not an inappropriate or uncommon subject for the friendship album. The religious condemnation of Eve and her centrality to earthly problems reinforced the degraded position of women in nineteenth-century thought. As African American men and women found their nucleus for community formation within the church, the immorality of woman, generated from the biblical story of Adam and Eve, placed them in a submissive position. Women's inability to think reasonably or act appropriately designated their position in life, and in many ways antebellum black women understood and reinforced their own social subjugation.

Although many black women found themselves in positions of shared authority in their own households, they nevertheless often subscribed to many of the same beliefs and customs of wealthier white women of the antebellum era. The majority of African American women were forced to work outside the home for economic survival, but they promoted the idea of the centrality of the home as well as the duties of a good wife.[30] As a civil institution, religious vow, and intimate personal relationship, marriage is an important social construction to examine, specifically among African Americans of the early nineteenth century. Still forbidden to most African Americans of the South, marriage became a symbol of freedom and possibility for free blacks throughout the North. Marriage, family, and home ownership during the era of slavery were understood as privileged, precious, and precarious for most African Americans in the northern antebellum city. The understood duties of

the "good wife" were not simply imitated by black women; they were practiced with the hopes and expectation of eventual social equality. The writings
of Mary Forten to Amy Cassey express the duties of a good wife through
poetry. Her poem "Good Wives" made clear the duties and expectations of
a married woman:

> Good wives to snails should be akin—
> Always their houses keep within
> But not to carry Fashion's hacks,
> All they are worth upon their back
> Good wives like city clocks should chime
> Be regular and keep in time
> But not like the city clocks aloud
> Be heard by all the vulgar crowd
> Good Wives like echoes still should do
> Speak but when they are spoken to;
> But not like echoes most absurd
> Have forever the last word.[31]

Forten's words not only indicate the importance of wifely duties within
the household, but also reinforce the subjugated role of a wife. Forten's
poem advised women to follow the example of the snail and "always their
houses keep within," reiterating the centrality of the home in the lives of
African American women. It is also quite possible that this line referred
to confining personal business to the home. Not only were good wives to
keep themselves in the household, but they also were to follow the lead of
their spouses, "echoing" their husbands' words, speaking only "when they
are spoken to."[32] "Good Wives" served as a reminder of the importance of
respectability to the black female elite. Women such as Forten and Cassey
worked hard to reshape the image of blacks in Philadelphia and elsewhere
from the verbose, aggressive, and independent African American woman
to the modest and respectable Victorian lady. Victorian ladyship, as can
be seen through public and private writings of the period, was more than
an imitation of white society. African American women celebrated and
critiqued the institution of marriage, using the trope of the "marriage
convention" to explore "race, racism, and racial identity" and "complex
questions of sexuality and female subjectivity."[33]

In addition to her poem on the role of the good wife, Forten addressed
issues of freedom and representation. The antebellum years marked a period of heightened racial hostility in Philadelphia, and as African Americans in that city began to experience and assert their freedom, one way in
which they demonstrated their new status was through their appearance.[34]

The acquisition of new clothing and the adoption of European speech patterns and mannerisms were often viewed as offensive by many whites. The majority of white America simply ridiculed black men and women for their expressions of freedom.[35] Their ridicule was sometimes expressed in the popular nineteenth-century art form of the politically satirical cartoon. Derogatory images were frequently reproduced in newspapers and prints, mocking the supposedly lavish style of dress exhibited by newly free men and women.[36] Most often targeting the poorest of free African Americans, these disparaging portraits showed apelike women dressed in gaudy clothing with abundant accessories such as jewelry, hats, and gloves.

The first racist caricatures appeared in Philadelphia in 1819 and became extremely popular by the middle decades of the nineteenth century.[37] William Thackera, a well-known artist and engraver for the city of Philadelphia, created the first series of prints mocking the dress, speech, and appearance of black Philadelphians. Edward W. Clay, a Philadelphia sketch artist of some repute, became one of the first artists to exploit the image of the overdressed and newly freed black Philadelphian.[38] His infamous sketches entitled "Life in Philadelphia," and his disparaging comedic references to African American men and women in pamphlets sold across the country and eventually overseas, became popular icons of the era.[39]

Although Clay's caricatures targeted both black men and women, his depiction of the emerging black middle-class female was particularly hostile. Much more vicious than the cartoons drawn by Thackera, his images repeatedly portrayed black women as ridiculous creatures, overdressed and inappropriate. In one particular image from the series, Clay depicted an African American man and woman dressed in overly ornate clothing. The female protagonist has donned a large hoopskirt, fancy lace gloves, garish jewelry, and a headpiece. As in all of his sketches, the black woman is heavyset, dwarfing her male counterpart. Her thick neck, buckteeth, large hands and feet, and short-cropped hair reinforce the animal-like image of African American women commonly reproduced at the time.[40]

It wasn't only physical appearance that was ridiculed in these cartoons, but speech patterns as well, specifically black vernacular. In Clay's sketch entitled "Miss Minta," a gentleman of African descent inquires of his female friend, "Shall I hab de honour to dance de next quadrille wid you?" Miss Minta replies, "Tank you, Mr. Cato,—wid much pleasure, only I'm engaged for de nine next set!"[41] The hostile depiction of black women not only scorned black dialect and a supposed lack of education, but also reinforced the image of the hypersexual black female. Miss Minta's eager response to the dance request of her male suitor, along with her acceptance of nine other dance partners, fortified the racist imagery of the sexually impure black woman.

Clay produced many more sketches in his series, all of which poked fun at newly freed African Americans. In addition to using an apelike image of the African American woman, he paid much attention to her supposed inability to dress appropriately. White Philadelphians commented on the attention blacks gave to expensive clothing, and Clay's sketches reflected their hostile ridicule. In another sketch, also titled "Miss Minta," Clay poked fun at a black woman shopping for a new bonnet. As the large woman peers into a mirror, her entire face is hidden by a ludicrously oversized hat. Her large feet and hands defeminize her appearance as she asks her male friend his opinion of her new chapeau: "What you tink of my new poke bonnet Frederick Augustus?" Augustus replies, "I dont like him no how, 'case dey hide you lubly face, so you can't tell one she nigger from anoder."[42]

Faced with what appeared to be a campaign to disparage the image of African American men and women, middle-class women of African descent not only contested these images through public writings, but also reminded one another of the importance of appearance. Mary Forten's entry in Cassey's album spoke directly to the issue of the representation of freedom. For the African American elite, an understated and modest manner of living was emblematic of respectability, and it would simultaneously attempt to dismantle the disparaging images of free men and women.

Poetry and short stories designed to temper the fashions of African American women often blended notions of Christianity and piety with social commentary, and the Dickerson albums represent much of this. The Dickerson family lived on Locust Street in Philadelphia and was involved in many of the same activities as Amy Cassey and her husband. Martin Dickerson, patriarch of the family, released himself from bondage and worked as a male nurse. His wife, Adelia, ran a tavern in the Walnut Street Theatre and outlived her husband by nearly forty years, dying in 1877.[43] The couple was representative of the nineteenth-century black middle class, having two wage-earning adults in the household. The Dickersons raised five children, two sons, Charles and William, and three daughters, Amelia, Martina, and Mary Anne.

Both Martina and Mary Anne maintained friendship albums similar in appearance to Amy Cassey's album. Mary Anne Dickerson's album recorded her birth around 1822; she was eleven years old at the time she began collecting the prose and poetry of her friends. She married John Jones of Baltimore in 1846, enhancing an already long-standing network between the black elite

"Shall I hab de honour to dance . . ." From Edward Clay, "Life in Philadelphia" (Philadelphia, 1829). Courtesy of the Library Company of Philadelphia.

"What you tink of my new poke bonnet . . ." From Edward Clay, "Life in Philadelphia" (Philadelphia, 1830). Courtesy of the Library Company of Philadelphia.

"Have you any *flesh* coloured silk stockings . . ." From Edward Clay, "Life in Philadelphia" (Philadelphia, ca. 1830). Courtesy of the Library Company of Philadelphia.

of the two cities. Her sister Martina Dickerson began her album in 1840.[44] Both Mary Anne and Martina Dickerson attended Sarah M. Douglass's school, like others of the black middle class.

In July 1840 Rebecca F. Peterson of New York wrote to her friend Martina Dickerson a simple poem entitled "A Lady's Dress":

> Let your earings be Assension encircled
> by the pearls of Refinement: the diamond
> of your necklace be Truth and the chain
> Christianity, your breast pin be Modesty set
> With Compassion, your bracelets be Chairity orna-

mented with the tassals of Good Humour. Your
finger rings be Assension set round with the
pearls of Gentleness, let your shoes be Wisdom
secured by the buckles of Perserverance.[45]

Peterson's poem, although centered on the topic of fashion and appropriate apparel, more clearly focused on the morality and refinement of "A Lady." Peterson's poem gently emphasized Christianity and compassion and, unlike Mary Forten's "Good Wife," did not promote submissiveness. For Peterson, refinement, truth, Christianity, modesty, compassion, charity, good humor, gentleness, and perseverance were prescriptions for ladyship, a category not easily attained by African American women, even those of the middle class.

As the bonds of friendship crossed state lines, friendship albums traveled from friend to friend across the entire Northeast. African American women in Philadelphia were concerned about the image of respectability, as were their female friends in Baltimore and New York. Martina Dickerson asked her friend Rebecca Peterson to make a contribution to her friendship album. Peterson's entry reflects the heightened desire for respectability, though Peterson's writing was directed to her literate friends and acquaintances. Her poem "On a Lady's Writing" contributed to the rules of decorum for these women, besides reinforcing the concept of "woman's place":

Her even lines her even temper show
Neat as her dress, and polished as her brow;
Strong as her judgement, easy as her air
Correct though free, and regular though fair.
And the same graces o'er her preside,
That form her manners and her footsteps guide.[46]

Peterson's words, such as "even lines," connected respectability to literacy and penmanship, which for many early nineteenth-century African American men and women were still highly inaccessible. For African Americans living under a social microscope, even one individual's successful writing served as a badge of respectability. Proper penmanship and correct spelling were acquired from formal instruction and equated with appropriate manners. Supposedly, "On a Lady's Writing" served as an example of general decorum. For women such as Martina Dickerson, however, who most likely benefited from the best education available to her at the time, the poem served as a reminder of her responsibility as an educated African American woman. Not only were Dickerson and her female friends and companions who shared the book obligated to continue the pursuit of education and literacy, they were to do so with an even temper. The polished graces and social etiquette assumed by elite African American women were to be practiced and adhered to in all forums, from the privacy of their own homes to the words of their personal writings.

The rearing of children and the importance of motherhood were also explored through poetry and prose. In 1834 Mary Anne Dickerson Jones asked her friends to submit entries to her album, but she herself chronicled the major happenings in her life in its pages. The first entry in the album was a print of a small child entitled "The Mother's Joy." The poem that followed the print was an original work written most likely by Charlotte Forten.[47]

> Thine is a happy lot sweet boy
> Oh! that mine were the same,
> Like thee, to my mother's joy
> Like thee to lisp her name[48]

There were many references to motherhood throughout Mary Anne Dickerson's album, some written by her friends and others by her own pen. It appears as though her album was not only a place in which to collect the writings and the admiration of her friends, but also a way in which to help her deal with the death of her own son. In January 1851 one-year-old William Dickerson Jones, the son of Mary Anne Dickerson Jones and John Jones of Baltimore, died, leaving behind distressed parents. As Dickerson Jones had entered all the marriages, births, and deaths of her immediate family in her album, she included the death of her own son, affectionately called Willie. Shortly after his death, Dickerson Jones wrote about the pain of losing a child.

> To my dear Willie
> Slumber sweet infant
> Thy spirit is free,
> The portals of Heaven
> Are open to thee
> The hopes of fond parents
> Lie burried in gloom,
> For the pride of their hearts
> Is cold in the tomb.[49]

Although many contributions to the friendship albums of the nineteenth century discussed motherhood, Mary Anne Dickerson Jones's album had many more entries concerning children, parental relationships, and death than did the albums of her friends. It is quite probable that her friends understood the loss of her infant son as a traumatic experience in her life, and they therefore wrote to encourage and uplift the spirit of the bereaved mother. John Jones, her husband, wrote an entry in which he attempted to describe the pain and anguish felt by family members in mourning the death of a loved one. His poem "The Night of Death" captured the depression and sorrow brought about by such loss.

> The Night of Death
> There's beauty in the hues that paint
> The sunset skies;
> The beauty fades, and soon grows faint
> The brilliant dyes
> Night from her dim and dusky skies
> Her gloom doth shed
> And darkness seems o'er all the zone
> A mantle spread
> So when the lights of life may fade,
> And all that's bright;
> We shall repose amid the shade
> Of death's dark night.[50]

Husbands and wives occasionally used the friendship album to express love and gratitude to one another, but their writings most often appeared after the death of a spouse. D. Alexander Payne of Baltimore expressed his grief over the loss of his wife and daughter in the friendship album of Amy Cassey. His first poem, "Lines Occasioned by the Death of my Sainted Wife Julia Ann Payne," not only revealed a deep longing for his partner, but also reinforced the image and reputation of his wife. Through his eulogizing poem, Payne wrote of his wife's strong faith and the good deeds she accomplished throughout her lifetime. She left her existence with her worldly family as a pious Christian, mother, and wife to be embraced by the arms of God in heaven:

> Thou art gone! to the land of the blest,
> Thou art gone! to the home of the pure,
> Thou art gone! to thy heavenly rest,
> Thy Saviour and God to adore.
> Thou art gone! from the region of death,
> Whose sorrow and suffering use rife;
> To the clime, whose ethereal breath,
> *From my arms—to the bosom of God!*[51]

Payne's poem about his wife expressed to the Philadelphia, Baltimore, New York, and Boston African American elite his sincere admiration of his wife.

The mention of her works while on earth implied that not only was she a loved wife and mother, but also that she provided for and nurtured the entire community. According to Payne's poem, the work of motherhood brought about her early departure; Julia Payne's death occurred during childbirth, proving how dangerous motherhood could be:

> Like the silk-worm that weaves its own shroud,
> And dies to give birth to its fly
> So didst thou! Then upon a bright cloud
> Thou art gone to the mansions on high![52]

Payne also discussed in Cassey's album the death of his daughter, which occurred some two years following the death of his wife. Payne described this death as "another painful blow"; he acknowledged, however, that his daughter, as a child of God, did not belong solely to him but to the Lord:

> There she blooms in a brighter clime,
> Where all is pure, and sweet, and green,
> Where fell disease, and storms of time,
> Are neither felt, nor heard, nor seen.
> I'll mourn not for thee my sweet one
> Thou wast loan'd never given,
> *bright gem, from the land of the Sun!*
> *Go shine midst the jewels of heav'n!*[53]

Payne acknowledged his daughter's transition into heaven through the title of his poem, "To My Daughter in Heaven." In its text Payne depicted his pure and sweet infant daughter as going "away to the home in the sky! away to the bosom of God!"

Payne wrote of his double loss shortly after the death of his child. His entry in Cassey's friendship album made no reference to its owner or her relationship with the Payne family. The album was simply used as a forum in which to express the grief following the death of a loved one and a vehicle by which to praise members of the black elite. Thus, the friendship album was a place in which both elite women and men expressed their feelings about family, grief, and love.

Not only was the friendship album a space in which African American men and women could engage in personal writings about private matters, but it also served as a forum in which to discuss and publicly debate the politics of the mid-nineteenth century. Topics such as slavery, moral reform, and the removal of Native Americans from their homeland found their way into the pages of the friendship album. Political commentary from men and women both world renowned and obscure demonstrated

Sarah Mapps Douglass, "A token of my love from me, to thee": butterfly watercolor. From the Amy Matilda Cassey Friendship Album, 1839. Courtesy of the Library Company of Philadelphia.

Margaretta Forten, poem and watercolor of a vase of flowers. From the Amy Matilda Cassey Friendship Album. Courtesy of the Library Company of Philadelphia.

the vast political and social networks established by both the African American and white elite of Philadelphia. In the Cassey album the writings of women such as Anna Warren Weston articulated the central political debate of the century. Weston's abolitionist writings, of which this untitled poem is but one example, made clear her opinion of the injustice associated with slavery:

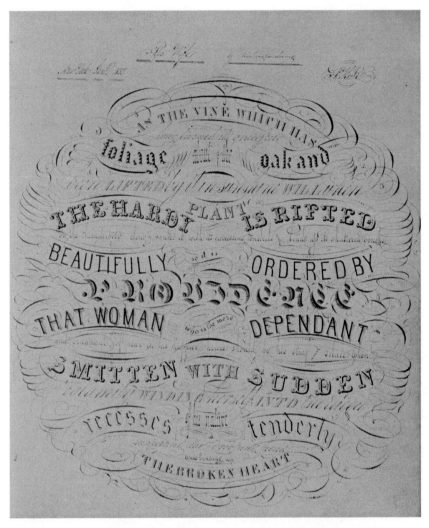

Patrick Henry Reason, "The Wife, by Washington Irving." From the Amy Matilda Cassey Friendship Album, 1839. Courtesy of the Library Company of Philadelphia.

> Three million men of God release free
> In this America of ours are slaves
> Lives dark with suffering, unremembered graves,—[54]

Weston's entry demonstrated her abolitionist sentiment, but it also gave her a semipublic forum in which she criticized the policies and social customs of the country. In her poem Weston chastised America as a strong and

Sarah Mapps Douglass, poem and watercolor of a rose. From the Amy Matilda Cassey Friendship Album. Courtesy of the Library Company of Philadelphia.

powerful nation that enslaved the "weak & poor." Weston also charged America with a hypocritical expression of Christianity through its institution of slavery:

> The bitterer shame and anguish is that we
> The eighteen millions strong, & rich, & great,

Proud of the memories those from Plymouth date;
In Christ's own Gospel swift are parts to claim,
Are yet the enslavers of the weak & poor,
Or worse the jailers at the prison door.
This is the cause for anguish, *this* the shame![55]

Weston's contribution most likely represented the feelings of many if not all of Cassey's friends and acquaintances who contributed to the pages of the album. It was William Lloyd Garrison who wrote perhaps one of the longest entries in Cassey's friendship album. "The Abolition Cause" elaborated on many of the ideas expressed by Weston. But unlike Weston, Garrison focused in the first section of his writing much more on the plight of the abolitionist than on that of the enslaved:

> They knew that slander would blacken their characters with infamy; that their rebukes and entreaties would be received with ridicule, anger and reproach; that persecution would assail them on the right hand and on the left; that the dungeon would yawn for their bodies; that the dagger of the assasin would gleam behind them; that the arm of power would be raised to crush them to the earth; that they would be branded as disturbers of the peace, as fanatics, madmen and incendiaries; that the heal of friendship would be lifted against them, and love be turned into hatred, and confidence into suspicion, and respect into division; that their worldly interests would be jeoparded and the honors and envolvements of office be withheld from their enjoyment. Knowing all this, still they dared all things, in order to save their country, and abolish the bloody system of slavery.[56]

Garrison's words targeted those most likely to read and write in the Cassey album: African American abolitionists. His friendship with many of the African American elite in Philadelphia allowed him entry into the semiprivate and public world of black Philadelphians through the friendship album. Although his writing supported abolition, his entry was aimed at the African American elite as a group of political and social activists, and through it he strengthened his ties to friends and colleagues in abolitionist circles.

Abolitionism was not the only political commentary to present itself in the friendship album. The subject of women's rights appeared in Mary Anne Dickerson Jones's album. William C. Nell of New York copied a well-known poem as his entry, "The Rights of Woman." As the 1840s provided a developing public forum in which women and men could discuss the social and political inclusion of women, the friendship album reflected the attitudes of African Americans on the subject. Nell did not write about the need to grant suffrage or political rights to women, but instead he encouraged a traditionally paternalistic viewpoint. While Nell acknowledged that the rights of women "merit some attention," he went on to state that an "earned right of Woman is—protection" a clear suggestion that women should maintain their dependency on fathers, husbands, brothers and the like. [57]

As elite African American women created a space for themselves to begin political dialogue concerning issues such as slavery and women's rights, they still sought to embody an elite understanding of womanhood and motherhood. The semiprivate sphere of the friendship album allowed black men and women to share ideas, concerns, and political ideology with one another, extending the social and political networks of black Philadelphia throughout the northern states. Unlike the friendship albums maintained by white women, blacks' sentimental albums and diaries maintained African American friendships over long distances and time. Catherine Kelly's work on rural women in New England demonstrates that white women wrote in sentimental albums for very different reasons. Although many albums focused on the importance and fragility of friendship, as well as documentation of sentimental memory, the white woman's friendship album served simply as a way by which to curate memory, not as a method by which to maintain networks. There were certainly thematic similarities between the albums of white and black women, particularly with regard to gentility and offers of warm wishes. Adaliza Cutter Phelps of New Hampshire contributed to her cousin's album words that were very similar to those found in Amy Cassey's album:

> on this page, so purely white
> I'll trill a simple, heartfelt lay,
> With other friends my name I'll write,
> And bind in Friendship's sweet boquet.[58]

Friendship was elusive to many white antebellum women who studied at the female academies of New England, for although they cultivated strong relationships with women from different geographical regions, they found themselves unable to maintain their friendships over extended periods. Hard work and the care of family replaced the importance of friendship, and Kelly notes that "in the countryside, the culture of friendship rarely survived the transition from girlhood to adulthood."[59]

This was not the case for African American women of the same time period, however. Friendship albums served as a vehicle to draw communities of elite black women together throughout the Northeast. Although African American women were separated by geographical space, they expected to see one another at social gatherings and political functions. Albums maintained by these women represent a network of friends and acquaintances that would be nurtured, not dismantled. Although Amy Cassey lived in Philadelphia, she had spent a great deal of her childhood in New York; she often provided friends in Philadelphia with contacts and connections in her hometown. When a group of young African American women traveled to New York to attend a women's antislavery convention in 1837, Cassey made arrangements for the group to board with her parents.[60]

The sentimentalism of friendship was but one aspect of the relationships between women of the black elite. Friends constantly visited and often wrote letters of introduction for one another, at times easing what could be a difficult journey into a racially hostile environment. Friendship was not a luxury; it was for many a necessity. For African American women, friendship albums assisted in the maintenance of long-distance relationships; they expected that friendship would survive across time and space. The albums simultaneously reinforced nineteenth-century notions of womanhood, motherhood, and reform. They stood as symbols of work that was yet to be completed in the African American communities of the North as well as the promise of emancipation and citizenship not yet achieved.

Conclusion

The antebellum struggle for autonomy and equal treatment in black Philadelphia would continue throughout the 1850s up to the eve of the Civil War. The work and goals of abolition remained central to the lives of African American men and women. For the most part, black Philadelphians struggled to survive on their meager earnings as laundresses, hucksters, stevedores, and other types of laborers. Freedom was a reality for African Americans in Philadelphia, though civil rights and the benefits of citizenship were yet to be attained. In May 1854 Charlotte L. Forten began a journal that chronicled her life as a young black Philadelphian in search of an exemplary education. Forten left Philadelphia to attend school in Salem, Massachusetts, where she received a stellar education that she would later share with freedmen and freedwomen on St. Helena Island in South Carolina. Charlotte Forten took the northern struggle for black equality to the South during the Civil War.[1]

Forten's experience as a member of the African American elite allowed her entrance into the world of education and activism. Her social status granted her the opportunity to help herself, to help others, and to speak her mind. In a journal entry dated June 18, 1857, Forten wrote, "Went to Independence Hall.—The old bell with its famous inscription, the mottoes, the relics, the pictures of the heroes of the Revolution—the *saviours* of their country,—

what a *mockery* they all seemed,—here where there breathes not a freeman, black or white."[2]

Nearly half a century of progress, exemplified by African American institutions, expansive education, and political activism, stood poised for the ultimate victory: the dismantlement of the institution of slavery in the United States. On the eve of the Civil War, African American men and women in Philadelphia were free from the bonds of slavery. Yet they remained dedicated to the abolitionist struggle that would eventually prove victorious in emancipating over four million African American men and women.

In 1860 African Americans living in Philadelphia witnessed a change in the political and social landscape of their city and the nation as a whole. While the excitement and hope spurred by change enveloped most of black Philadelphia, African Americans continued to experience many of the same indignities as their mothers and fathers. For the majority of black Philadelphians, life was challenging: African American men attempted to find work in a growing industrial center, while their wives, mothers, and sisters remained trapped in the low-paying domestic service industry. The population of the city numbered slightly over a half a million people, twenty thousand of whom were black. The majority of the city's black population was female.[3]

Feelings ran high in the black neighborhoods, and African American men left behind their businesses and families to enlist in the Union army. Although black men were at first not permitted to join the armed forces, a lack of manpower due to a lengthy war forced Abraham Lincoln's administration to reconsider the policy. Black men from the region traveled as far as Massachusetts to enlist in the famous 54th Massachusetts. The need for further troops resulted in the establishment of Camp William Penn outside Philadelphia.[4] All the men who were trained at Camp William Penn were volunteers. On June 26, 1863, regiments with over 8,600 African American men from Philadelphia and other regions began their training at the camp, several of whom participated in intense combat. In spite of discriminatory practices, extremely low pay, and disproportionately high death rates, African American men willingly gave their lives and their livelihoods to a war that would eventually lead to freedom.[5]

Once their husbands and sons were permitted in the army, African American women immediately began to support their troops by raising money, rolling bandages, and preparing care packages. Members of the PFASS continued to participate in fund-raising activities, and others began the work of assisting refugees who had made their way to Philadelphia.[6] For years black members of the community had offered assistance to runaways through Philadelphia's Vigilance Committee. Fugitives who made their way to Philadelphia met

William and Letitia Still, who interviewed fugitives and offered them shelter until arrangements could be made to transport them farther north or to Canada.[7] The stream of fugitives who made their way to cities such as Philadelphia, New York, and Boston grew thick by the early years of the war, and African American women did their best to help acclimate their new neighbors to freedom and the opportunities available in the cities.

The war brought great hopes to the majority of black men and women living within the city limits of Philadelphia. The black elite moved forward in their struggle for social equality; they "had lived down the most intense and bitter race feud and had gained the respect of the better class of whites."[8] Although the 1850s brought about significant advancements for African Americans in education, real estate ownership, and employment opportunities, the end of the Civil War and the following years would prove stormy for most.

Elite African American women experienced a sense of political uncertainty, but the majority of black women in Philadelphia were concerned primarily with matters of everyday life. Most of black Philadelphia remained poor, undereducated, and in search of secure employment. African American women continued to work as domestics, although the majority of them did not live with their white employers; instead, they became a part of the growing Seventh Ward, which by the end of the century housed the majority of Philadelphia's black population.[9] As Philadelphia became more segregated, African Americans were faced with new concerns. Slavery was dead, but in its place stood a virulent racism that would continue to treat African Americans as second-class citizens.

The Civil War era ushered in a new generation of African American leaders, both male and female. Awaiting them was a new political landscape, a fractured Union in need of intense care, a presidential assassination, and a decade of possibilities. African American women of Philadelphia once again stood prepared to continue in their struggle for equality, respect, and the opportunity to better the lives of men and women who were sure to follow in their footsteps.

Notes

Introduction

1. Julie Winch, *The Elite of Our People: Joseph Willson's Sketches of Black Upper-Class Life in Antebellum Philadelphia* (University Park: Pennsylvania State University Press, 2000), 10.

2. Amy Matilda Cassey, Friendship Album of Amy Matilda Cassey, 1833–56 (Library Company of Philadelphia), 3.

3. Dorothy Sterling has greatly contributed to the historiography of African American women from the colonial era through the nineteenth century. Her work *We Are Your Sisters: Black Women in the Nineteenth Century* (New York: W. W. Norton, 1983) was one of the first collections of primary documents relating to African Americans to emerge during the 1980s.

4. See Gary Nash, *Forging Freedom: The Formation of Philadelphia's Black Community, 1720–1840* (Cambridge: Harvard University Press, 1988), 62–63.

5. Ibid., 246–79. Also see Leonard P. Curry, *The Free Black in Urban America, 1800–1850: The Shadow of a Dream* (Chicago: University of Chicago Press, 1981).

6. The number of white indentured servants in Philadelphia declined drastically by 1775, but the number of black servants rose steadily. See Sharon V. Salinger, *"To Serve Well and Faithfully": Labor and Indentured Servants in Pennsylvania, 1682–1800* (New York: Cambridge University Press, 1987).

7. See Gary Nash and Jean R. Soderlund, *Freedom by Degrees: Emancipation in Pennsylvania and Its Aftermath* (New York: Oxford University Press, 1991), xv.

8. Ibid.

9. Curry, *The Free Black in Urban America*, 245–57. Also see Roger Lane, *Roots of Violence in Black Philadelphia, 1860–1900* (Cambridge: Harvard University Press, 1986), 7.

10. Nash, *Forging Freedom*, 167–69.

11. Ibid.

12. Leslie Harris, *In the Shadow of Slavery: African-Americans in New York City, 1626–1863* (Chicago: University of Chicago Press, 2003), 74.

13. Winch, *The Elite of Our People*, 2–4.

Chapter 1. Slavery and the "Holy Experiment"

1. Isaiah Thomas Jr., *Eccentric Biography, or Memoirs of Remarkable Female Characters, Ancient and Modern* (Worcester, Mass., 1803), 9–11.

2. Edward Raymond Turner, *Slavery in Pennsylvania* (Baltimore: Lord Baltimore Press, 1911), 1–2; Jean R. Soderlund et al., eds., *William Penn and the Founding of Pennsylvania, 1680–1684: A Documentary History* (Philadelphia: University of Pennsylvania Press, 1983), 144.

3. There are various reports regarding the number of slaves in the colony of Pennsylvania in 1770. Estimates range from 2,000 to 10,000 regarding the numbers of blacks in the colony. The most recent estimate of 6,000 slaves comes from the U.S. Census Bureau, *Historical Statistics of the United States: Colonial Times to 1957* (Washington, D.C., 1960). Also see Gary Nash, "Slaves and Slaveowners in Colonial Philadelphia," *William and Mary Quarterly* 30, no. 2 (April 1973): 223–56.

4. See Jean R. Soderlund, "Black Women in Colonial Pennsylvania," in *African-Americans in Pennsylvania: Shifting Historical Perspectives*, ed. Joe William Trotter Jr. and Eric Ledell Smith (University Park: Pennsylvania State University Press, 1997), 43–45.

5. Nash, *Forging Freedom*, 8–9.

6. Richard S. Dunn, "Penny Wise and Pound Foolish: Penn as a Businessman," in *The World of William Penn*, ed. Richard S. Dunn and Mary Maples Dunn (Philadelphia: University of Pennsylvania Press, 1986), 37.

7. Ibid.

8. Edwin Bronner, *William Penn's "Holy Experiment": The Founding of Pennsylvania, 1681–1701* (Westport, Conn.: Greenwood, 1978), 24.

9. Ibid., 25

10. Ibid.

11. Gary Nash, *Red, White, and Black: The Peoples of Early North America* (Englewood Cliffs, N.J.: Prentice-Hall, 1991), 120–45.

12. Francis Jennings, "Brother Miquon: Good Lord," in *The World of William Penn*, ed. Richard S. Dunn and Mary Maples Dunn (Philadelphia: University of Pennsylvania Press, 1986), 196.

13. Nash, *Red, White, and Black*, 120–45.

14. Ibid.

15. Ibid.

16. Gary B. Nash, *Race, Class, and Politics: Essays on American Colonial and Revolutionary Society* (Urbana: University of Illinois Press, 1986), 94.

17. Nash and Soderlund, *Freedom by Degrees,* 21.

18. Turner, *Slavery in Pennsylvania,* 144. Also see Julie Winch, *A Gentleman of Color: The Life of James Forten* (Oxford: Oxford University Press, 2002), 10.

19. Nash and Soderlund, *Freedom by Degrees,* 42.

20. Winch, *Gentleman of Color,* 10. Also see Soderlund, "Black Women in Colonial Pennsylvania."

21. Winch, *Gentleman of Color,* 10.

22. Nash and Soderlund, *Freedom by Degrees,* 16.

23. Ibid.

24. The end of the French and Indian War brought about a rapid decrease in the number of slave imports, since white labor was once again available. In 1767 there were close to 1,500 slaves living in the city of Philadelphia and its suburbs of Southwark and Northern Liberties. By 1775 the number of slaves in the city hovered around 700, a decrease of about 50 percent. Over the course of those eight years, the slave population dropped from 5.6 percent to 2.2 percent of the total.

25. Benjamin Franklin, *The Papers of Benjamin Franklin,* ed. Leonard W. Labaree, 38 vols. (New Haven: Yale University Press, 1959–), 4:230.

26. Salinger, *"To Serve Well and Faithfully,"* 73.

27. Ibid., 74. Also see Cheesman A. Herrick, *White Servitude in Pennsylvania: Indentured and Redemption Labor in Colony and Commonwealth* (Philadelphia: J. J. McVey, 1926), 204.

28. Salinger, *"To Serve Well and Faithfully,"* 75.

29. *Pennsylvania Gazette,* April 23, 1747.

30. Ibid., March 9, 1758.

31. Nash and Soderlund, *Freedom by Degrees,* 67.

32. Soderlund, "Black Women in Colonial Pennsylvania," 76.

33. Ibid.

34. Ibid., 81. These statistics are based on Chester County records from the colonial period.

35. Soderland, "Black Women in Colonial Pennsylvania," 81.

36. *Pennsylvania Gazette,* February 9, 1764.

37. On a trip to Barbados in 1671, George Fox spoke against the lifelong enslavement of Africans, suggesting that gradual abolition release each slave after thirty years of service. See Sydney James, *A People among Peoples: Quaker Benevolence in Eighteenth-Century America* (Cambridge: Harvard University Press, 1963), 104–5.

38. Nash, *Forging Freedom,* 26–27.

39. Nash and Soderlund, *Freedom by Degrees,* 51–52.

40. Nash, *Forging Freedom,* 26–27.

41. Milton C. Sernett, *Black Religion and American Evangelicalism: White Protestants, Plantation Missions, and the Flowering of Negro Christianity, 1787–1865* (Metuchen, N.J.: Scarecrow Press, 1975), chap. 1.

42. Ira Berlin, *Many Thousands Gone: The First Two Centuries of Slavery in North America* (Cambridge: Belknap Press of Harvard University Press, 1998), 137–39.

43. Nash, *Forging Freedom,* 19; also see Franklin, *Papers of Benjamin Franklin,* 2:257–58.

44. See Benjamin Quarles, *The Negro in the American Revolution* (Chapel Hill: University of North Carolina Press, 1961), chap. 2.

45. John W. Jackson, *With the British Army in Philadelphia, 1777–1778* (San Rafael, Calif.: Presidio Press, 1979).

46. Winch, *Gentleman of Color*, 30–33.

47. Berlin, *Many Thousands Gone*, 230.

48. Winch, *Gentleman of Color*, 30.

49. Quarles, *The Negro in the American Revolution*, 9–18, 50–63.

50. Harris, *In the Shadow of Slavery*, 55.

51. Ibid.

52. See Nash and Soderlund, *Freedom by Degrees*, 85–95.

53. M. V. Brewington, "The State Ship *General Greene*," *Pennsylvania Magazine of History and Biography* 60 (1936): 233. Also see Nash and Soderlund, *Freedom by Degrees*, 95.

54. Nash and Soderlund, *Freedom by Degrees*, 92–93.

55. See ibid., chap. 4, and Nash, *Forging Freedom*, chap. 3, for a detailed discussion of emancipation and gradual abolition in Pennsylvania.

56. Anne M. Boylan, *The Origins of Women's Activism: New York and Boston, 1797–1840* (Chapel Hill: University of North Carolina Press, 2002), 6–7. Also see Linda K. Kerber, *Women of the Republic: Intellect and Ideology in Revolutionary America* (1980; rept., New York: W. W. Norton, 1986), 269, 285; Nancy F. Cott, *The Bonds of Womanhood: "Woman's Sphere" in New England, 1780–1835* (New Haven: Yale University Press, 1977), 146–48.

57. Nancy Woloch, *Women and the American Experience*, 2nd ed. (New York: McGraw-Hill, 1994), 90.

58. Nash, *Forging Freedom*, 72–73.

Chapter 2. Maneuvering Manumission in Philadelphia

1. Indenture of Mary Kerr to Mary Lewis, recorded in Indentures Book D, folio 92, Historical Society of Pennsylvania.

2. Ibid.

3. Mary Lewis appears to have been a literate woman, who signed her name on the indenture agreement instead of inscribing the traditional "X" in place of her name.

4. This information comes from Gary Nash and Jean Soderlund's work in *Freedom by Degrees*, 149. A listing of Philadelphia manumissions by occupation from 1780 to 1800 was collected from manumission records and Philadelphia city directories.

5. Nash and Soderlund, *Freedom by Degrees*, 150. It is important to note that Nash and Soderlund state that by 1800, 57 percent of the 421 blacks who were manumitted were women, girls, and boys under the age of sixteen. This figure is a bit misleading, for it implies that more women were becoming free than men. These numbers, however, represent only the recorded manumissions of blacks whose sex was known. And, of course, it does not include the number of men who freed themselves by escape, or those manumissions not reported at all.

6. *Journals of the House of Representatives of the Commonwealth of Pennsylvania, 1776–1781* (Philadelphia, 1782). There are many names associated with the authorship of the Gradual Abolition Act of Pennsylvania—Benjamin Franklin, Thomas Paine, and William Lewis among them. George Bryan, however, is most often referred to as its author. See Nash and Soderlund, *Freedom by Degrees*, 101.

7. Thomas D. Morris, *Free Men All: The Personal Liberty Laws of the North,* 1780–1861 (Baltimore: Johns Hopkins University Press, 1974); and Nash and Soderlund, *Freedom by Degrees,* 101–3.

8. Nash, *Forging Freedom,* 62–63. Also see Edward R. Turner, *The Negro in Pennsylvania: Slavery, Servitude, Freedom,* 1639–1861 (1911; rept., New York: Arno Press, 1969), 77–79.

9. Nash, *Forging Freedom,* 61. Over one hundred male and female slaves from Philadelphia escaped during the American Revolution.

10. Ibid., 63. Also see the *Pennsylvania Packet,* March 13, 1779, and January 1, 1780.

11. Joanne Pope Melish, *Disowning Slavery: Gradual Emancipation and "Race" in New England,* 1780–1860 (Ithaca: Cornell University Press, 1998), 64–65. Also see Harris, *In the Shadow of Slavery,* 11.

12. Claude Levy, *Emancipation, Sugar, and Federalism: Barbados and the West Indies,* 1833–1876 (Gainesville: University Presses of Florida, 1980), 33. Also see Kathleen Mary Butler, *The Economics of Emancipation: Jamaica and Barbados,* 1823–1843 (Chapel Hill: University of North Carolina Press, 1995), 30–33. In Jamaica apprenticeship appears to have lasted longer for those slaves involved in agricultural work, specifically those involved in the production of sugar. Unlike those in Pennsylvania, domestics were more likely to serve shorter periods of apprenticeship.

13. Howard Johnson, *The Bahamas from Slavery to Servitude,* 1783–1933 (Gainesville: University Press of Florida, 1996), 25. Johnson concludes that it is difficult to gauge the level of interest in indentured servitude throughout the Bahamas. Most of the references to servitude appear in the colony's newspaper advertisements regarding runaways.

14. Ibid., 34–35.

15. The data concerning runaway slaves comes from Billy Smith and Richard Wojtowicz, comps., *Blacks Who Stole Themselves: Advertisements for Runaways in the "Pennsylvania Gazette,"* 1728–1790 (Philadelphia: University of Pennsylvania Press, 1989), as well as from a survey of nineteen other Pennsylvania newspapers by Gary Nash and Jean Soderlund. The number of runaway slaves was probably higher than the 122 counted in the surveys. There are probably omissions due to a lack of reporting by some slave masters.

16. Smith and Wojtowicz, *Blacks Who Stole Themselves.*

17. *Pennsylvania Gazette,* July 13, 1785.

18. *Pennsylvania Gazette,* May 16, 1781.

19. Patty Gibson in North Carolina to her husband in Philadelphia, November 10, 1797, Cox-Parrish-Wharton Papers, vol. 14, Historical Society of Pennsylvania.

20. Ibid. It is unknown if Gibson received the money from her husband and avoided being sold to a different master as punishment for her previous attempt at escape.

21. Indenture of Atlee Waters to Robert Wharton, May 1793, Pennsylvania Abolition Society, microfilm, series IV, reel 23, Historical Society of Pennsylvania. Wharton resided in New Jersey, but the Pennsylvania Abolition Society kept records of black servants in neighboring counties and states. It is quite possible that Atlee Waters resided in Philadelphia, for the negotiations between Wharton and the Waters family were signed and dated in Philadelphia.

22. For information regarding the founding of the Pennsylvania Abolition Society as well as its involvement in the life of black Philadelphians, see Edward Needle, *History of the Pennsylvania Abolition Society* (Philadelphia, 1848).

23. The original organization was named the Society for the Relief of Free Negroes Unlawfully Held in Bondage and was founded in 1775. It was not until 1787 that the organization re-created itself and adopted the name Pennsylvania Society for Promoting the Abolition of Slavery (PAS). The constitution of the Pennsylvania Abolition Society, which was adopted in 1787, explains the goals and purpose of the society; a reprint of it can be found in Roger Bruns, ed., *Am I Not a Man and a Brother: The Antislavery Crusade of Revolutionary America, 1688–1788* (New York: Chelsea House, 1977).

24. According to census records for the state of Pennsylvania, the number of enslaved black men and women dropped dramatically between 1790 and 1810. The total slave population of Pennsylvania in 1790 reached 3,737 of a total 10,274 black inhabitants. By 1800 the total slave population of Pennsylvania had decreased by more than 50 percent: there were 1,706 black men and women enslaved of a total black population of 16,270. Of this number, 4,000 black men and women lived in Philadelphia. For more information regarding census information, see Alice D. Adams, *The Neglected Period of Anti-Slavery in America (1808–1831)* (Boston: Ginn, 1908), 3–7.

25. Nash and Soderlund, *Freedom by Degrees*, 115–17.

26. Ibid., 118.

27. After the 1780 Abolition Act was passed, many slaveholders in Philadelphia attempted to avoid losing their investments by quickly selling their slaves out of state. Although the act prohibited this behavior, many tried to sell their slaves to nearby states such as New Jersey, Delaware, and Maryland. Enslaved men and women from Philadelphia requested the help of the society, most often through personal appearances at their meetings or at the homes of influential PAS members.

28. See the case of "Mary a Black Woman against Mary McDowell," Pennsylvania Abolition Society Manumission Book A, 1780–1793, PAS, microfilm, series IV, reel 20, Historical Society of Pennsylvania.

29. Ibid.

30. Pennsylvania Abolition Society, Committee to Improve the Condition of Free Blacks Minute Book, 1790–1803, reel 6, Historical Society of Pennsylvania.

31. I have drawn from several sources to calculate the enslaved and free black populations of Philadelphia. Gary Nash and Jean Soderlund have accumulated what appear to be the most accurate statistics for the city in their *Freedom by Degrees*, 58, 59; see also Nash, *Forging Freedom*, 36–37. I have drawn only from records concerning black men and women in the city.

32. Nash, *Forging Freedom*, 136–38.

33. Shane White, *Somewhat More Independent: The End of Slavery in New York City, 1770–1810* (Athens: University of Georgia Press, 1991), 26–27, 155–57.

34. Salinger, *"To Serve Well and Faithfully,"* 2–4.

35. Ibid. Salinger discusses the history of indentured servitude in Philadelphia as falling into three distinct periods: 1690–1720, 1720–80, and 1780–1820.

36. See Marcus Lee Hansen, *The Atlantic Migration, 1607–1860* (Cambridge: Harvard University Press, 1940). Also see Maldwyn Allen Jones, *American Immigration*, 2nd ed. (Chicago: University of Chicago Press, 1992), 65–68.

37. Jones, *American Immigration*, 65–68. Also see *Records of the Guardians of the Poor*, Historical Society of Pennsylvania, in Nash, *Forging Freedom*.

38. Indenture of Negro Judith, August 31, 1786, recorded in Indentures Book D, folio 92, Historical Society of Pennsylvania.

39. Ibid.

40. Indenture of Polly Lacount to William Lewis, March 16, 1801, recorded in Indentures Book D, folio 92, Historical Society of Pennsylvania.

41. Pennsylvania Abolition Society Manumission Book A, 1780–1793, microfilm reel 20.

42. The art of mantua making appears to have been one of the more skilled trades for black women of Philadelphia in the late eighteenth and early nineteenth centuries. Mantua makers were not simply sewers; they specialized in the making of loose-fitting gowns worn by women over petticoats or a separate skirt. By 1840 mantua makers were called dressmakers. In all the census information from nineteenth-century Philadelphia, "sewer" was always distinguished from "mantua maker."

43. Christine Stansell, *City of Women: Sex and Class in New York, 1789–1860* (1986; rept., Urbana: University of Illinois Press, 1987), 14–15.

44. The exception to this was employment as a teacher. Opportunities for black women to teach black children, however, did not really exist until the nineteenth century.

45. The mortality rate for black Philadelphians in the late eighteenth and early nineteenth centuries was extremely high. Many blacks did not live past their thirties. The Gradual Abolition Act kept men and women enslaved until their twenty-eighth birthdays.

46. Indenture of mulatto Phillis to Isabella Robins, 1790, recorded in Indentures Book D, folio 92, Historical Society of Pennsylvania.

47. See Stansell, *City of Women*, chap. 6, for an explanation of women and the sewing trades in the nineteenth-century urban North. Much of this chapter focuses on the exploitation of the sewing trade and the appalling conditions of "outwork" in midcentury New York.

48. See Indenture of Negro Woman Teeny to William McMurtrie, August 16, 1786, Pennsylvania Abolition Society Manumission Book A, 1780–1793, PAS, reel 20.

49. See Sworn Deposition from Jane Fild to Free her Son Peter, October 30, 1804, in Pennsylvania Abolition Society Papers, vol. 6, folder 8.

50. Indenture of Negro Judith, August 31, 1786.

51. Indenture of Nancy Burns, April 8, 1799, PAS, microfilm, series IV, reel 23.

52. Indenture of Sally a Negro, September 8, 1783, PAS, microfilm, series IV, reel 23.

53. Nash, *Forging Freedom*, 77–79

54. Catherine A. Herbert, "The French Element in Pennsylvania in the 1790s: The Francophone Immigrants' Impact," *Pennsylvania Magazine of History and Biography* 108 (1984): 451–70.

55. See Salinger, *"To Serve Well and Faithfully,"* 146.

56. See Nash and Soderlund, *Freedom by Degrees*, 174. The number of black indentured servants in Philadelphia between 1780 and 1790 totaled only 208. Between 1790 and 1800 there were a recorded 1,505 black indentured servants, according to the Pennsylvania Abolition Society. This jump was partially fueled by the transporting

of slaves from the French West Indies, as well as by the growing popularity of black indentured servitude at the end of the eighteenth century.

57. Ibid.

58. Pennsylvania Abolition Society Manumission Book C, 1795, microfilm, series IV, reel 20, Historical Society of Pennsylvania.

59. See Nash and Soderlund, *Freedom by Degrees*, 180–81, and Pennsylvania Abolition Society Manumission and Indenture Books, reels 20–24.

60. List of Refugees Returning to Santo Domingo from Philadelphia, 1798, Society Miscellaneous Collection, box 6A, folder 13, Historical Society of Pennsylvania. Although the race of the passengers is not indicated in the ship's records, the absence of a last name for a passenger implies that he or she had been a slave.

61. Case of Jean-Baptiste Lapointe v. Marie Louise and her Daughter Melanie, March 30, 1805, Pennsylvania Abolition Society American Convention Papers, Historical Society of Pennsylvania.

62. U.S. Bureau of the Census, *Heads of Families at the First Census of the United States Taken in the Year 1790: Pennsylvania* (Washington, D.C.: Government Printing Office, 1908).

63. *Philadelphia City Directory*, 1795, Historical Society of Pennsylvania.

64. Ibid.

65. Stansell, *City of Women*, 17.

66. *Minerva*, June 3, 1797.

67. Of the twenty-two women listed in the 1795 *Philadelphia City Directory*, nine were widowed. I am certain that there were many other examples of black women who worked in occupations that were not connected to domestic labor, but they are not represented in the directories of the 1790s because of their marital status. There were many women who assisted their husbands in their own businesses as bakers, fruiteresses, and tailors.

68. Deborah Norris Logan, Diary of Deborah Norris Logan, July 1822, vol. 5, Historical Society of Pennsylvania.

69. Elizabeth Drinker, Diary of Elizabeth Drinker, December 24, 1799, Historical Society of Pennsylvania.

70. Ibid., July 1804.

71. I will discuss the shift in hiring Irish and German women as domestics during the 1830s in chapter 4. The trend toward hiring white domestic servants displaced many black women workers in Philadelphia.

Chapter 3. Creating Black Philadelphia

1. Willie Lee Rose, *Rehearsal for Reconstruction: The Port Royal Experiment* (Indianapolis: Bobbs-Merrill, 1964). This work is an account of the first experiment in Reconstruction of the South following the Civil War, but there were many similarities between the experiences of freed slaves of the antebellum and postbellum eras. Rose's work examines the work of northern abolitionists who traveled to South Carolina to establish schools and to "train" recently freed black men and women in emancipation and citizenship. Philadelphia would become a national example, or a "rehearsal for Reconstruction," before the Civil War.

2. Harris, *In the Shadow of Slavery*, 140.

3. For more on the American Colonization Society, see George Fredrickson, *Black Image in the White Mind: The Debate on Afro-American Character and Destiny, 1817–1914* (New York: Harper and Row, 1971), 6–21. Also see E. L. Fox, *The American Colonization Society, 1817–1840* (New York: AMS Press, 1971).

4. James Forten to Paul Cuffe, January 25, 1817, in Winch, *Gentleman of Color,* 140–42.

5. For an overview of early eighteenth- and nineteenth-century women's lives, see Mary Beth Norton, *Liberty's Daughters: The Revolutionary Experience of American Women, 1750–1800* (Boston: Little, Brown, 1980); Cott, *The Bonds of Womanhood;* Carroll Smith-Rosenberg, *Disorderly Conduct: Visions of Gender in Victorian America* (New York: Knopf, 1985); and Ellen K. Rothman, *Hands and Hearts: A History of Courtship in America* (New York: Basic Books, 1984). Much of the work on family history often appears in local studies; see Nancy F. Cott, "Divorce and the Changing Status of Women in Eighteenth-Century Massachusetts," *William and Mary Quarterly,* 3rd series, 33 (1976): 586–614; and Cott, "Eighteenth Century Family and Social Life Revealed in Massachusetts Divorce Records," *Journal of Social History* 10 (1976–77): 20–43.

6. For new attitudes toward women's roles at the end of the eighteenth century, see Linda Kerber, "The Republican Mother: Women and the Enlightenment, an American Perspective," *American Quarterly* 29 (Summer 1976): 187–205; Ruth H. Bloch, "The Gendered Meanings of Virtue in Revolutionary America," *Signs* 13 (Autumn 1987): 37–58; and Merril D. Smith, *Breaking the Bonds: Marital Discord in Pennsylvania, 1730–1830* (New York: New York University Press, 1991).

7. Kerber, "The Republican Mother."

8. Kerber, *Women of the Republic,* 1–20.

9. For the "politics of respectability," see Evelyn Brooks Higginbotham, *Righteous Discontent: The Women's Movement in the Black Baptist Church, 1880–1920* (Cambridge: Harvard University Press, 1993). Although Higginbotham's work focuses on black churchwomen of the late nineteenth and early twentieth centuries, the paradigm of respectability, moral reform, and racial uplift is useful in understanding antebellum black churchwomen.

10. Nash, *Forging Freedom,* 29–31.

11. Roberts Vaux, *Memoirs of the Life of Anthony Benezet* (Philadelphia, 1817), 120–21, 138–40

12. Nancy Slocum Hornick, "Benezet and the Africans' School," *Pennsylvania Magazine of History and Biography* 99 (Winter 1975): 399–425.

13. Dr. Bray's Associates Minute Book, November 24, 1776, Society for the Propagation of the Gospel in Foreign Parts Photos, Library of Congress.

14. Nash, *Forging Freedom,* 22–23.

15. For discussions of women and early national education, see Cott, *The Bonds of Womanhood,* 110–15, and Mary Sumner Benson, *Women in Eighteenth-Century America: A Study of Opinion and Social Usage* (New York: Columbia University Press, 1935), 139–42. Cott demonstrates that the years following the American Revolution opened the doors of education to American women. Although it was most often restricted to middle-class whites, women's education was deemed a necessity for constructing the new republic. Philadelphia paved the way for the founding of schools for girls with Benezet's school in the 1750s and a handful of others during the 1780s.

Although the best-educated women were those who received private tutoring in the home, education became much more accessible.

16. W. E. B. Du Bois, *The Philadelphia Negro: A Social Study* (1899; rept., Philadelphia: University of Pennsylvania Press, 1996).

17. Harris, *In the Shadow of Slavery*, 48–52.

18. Gradual abolition, or the freeing of black men and women over the course of several decades, was one of the strategies adopted by early antislavery groups. As the majority of whites held the right to own property, including African slaves, as an inalienable right, the PAS and other antislavery societies throughout the North understood that most northern slave masters would free their slaves as it became economically feasible. See Robert William Fogel and Stanley L. Engerman, "Philanthropy at Bargain Prices: Notes on the Economics of Gradual Emancipation," *Journal of Legal Studies* 3 (1974): 377–401, and Fogel and Engerman, *Time on the Cross: The Economics of Negro Slavery* (1974; rept., New York: W. W. Norton, 1989). White antislavery activists in Philadelphia saw black education as a method that would prepare both whites and blacks for freedom.

19. Nash, *Forging Freedom*, 203.

20. See Du Bois, *The Philadelphia Negro*. According to Nash, the schoolhouse was built in Willing's Alley in 1773; Nash and Du Bois agree that the school educated more than 250 students. Following the Revolution, attendance rates for black students still remained fairly low. It appears as though the schoolhouse was closed, though the reason is unclear, and Benezet continued to instruct students in his home.

21. See Hornick, "Benezet and the Africans' School," 172–73.

22. Du Bois, *The Philadelphia Negro*, 84.

23. Pennsylvania Abolition Society Minute Book, 1790–1803, microfilm, reel 6, Historical Society of Pennsylvania. We can assume from the inclusion of her death notice in the obituary section of the local newspaper, as well as her appearance in the 1795 *Philadelphia City Directory*, that Harris was most likely very well known and respected by both blacks and whites. Harris's obituary appeared in the *Minerva* on June 3, 1797.

24. Gayraud S. Wilmore, *Black Religion and Black Radicalism: An Interpretation of the Religious History of Afro-American People* (Garden City, N.Y.: Doubleday, 1972).

25. See Nash, *Forging Freedom*, 95–97, and Richard Allen, *The Life, Experience, and Gospel Labors of the Rt. Rev. Richard Allen, to Which Is Annexed the Rise and Progress of the African Methodist Episcopal Church in the United States of America* (1833; rept., Nashville: Abingdon, 1960), 10–19.

26. Daniel Payne, *A History of the African Methodist Episcopal Church*, ed. Rev. C. S. Smith (Nashville: Publishing House of the A.M.E. Sunday School Union, 1891), 52.

27. Committee to Improve the Condition of Free Blacks Minute Book, Pennsylvania Abolition Society Collection, microfilm, reel 7, 100–101, 163–64, 191, 210–11, and Board of Education Minutes, I (1797–1803), 65, 76, 84–87. Also see Nash, *Forging Freedom*, 204.

28. William Douglass, *Annals of the First African Church in the United States of America, Now Styled the African Episcopal Church of St. Thomas* (Philadelphia: King and Baird, 1862), 119–21.

29. It appears as though this specific school for black children was short-lived and closed after only a few months.

30. PAS microfilm, reel 7; Board of Education Minutes, I (1797–1803), 65, 76, 84–87.

31. Douglass, *Annals of the First African Church,* 110–11.

32. PAS microfilm, reel 7; Board of Education Minutes, I (1797–1803), 84–87.

33. PAS microfilm, reel 7; Board of Education Minutes, I (1797–1803), 86–87. Many black children were not able to attend school for an entire day and were enrolled in half-day sessions.

34. Board of Education Minutes, I (1797–1803), 87.

35. Nash, *Forging Freedom,* 205.

36. "Address to the American Convention," 1804, Pennsylvania Abolition Society Papers, reel 29.

37. Nash, *Forging Freedom,* 209–11.

38. See Monroe Fordham, *Major Themes in Northern Black Religious Thought,* 1800–1860 (Hicksville, N.Y.: Exposition Press, 1975).

39. See Du Bois, *The Philadelphia Negro.* Public school education did not become universal for white Philadelphia residents until 1818. Black children were admitted to segregated public schools in 1822 with the opening of the Bird School, later renamed the James Forten School, located at Sixth and Lombard Streets.

40. "A Pioneer Negro Society, 1787," in Herbert Aptheker, ed., *A Documentary History of the Negro People in the United States* (1951; rept., New York: Citadel, 1994), 17–20. Also see Douglass, *Annals of the First African Church,* 19.

41. "A Pioneer Negro Society."

42. Bruce Dorsey, *Reforming Men and Women: Gender in the Antebellum City* (Ithaca: Cornell University Press, 2002), 7–9.

43. See Boylan, *The Origins of Women's Activism,* chap. 1. Boylan has compiled a tremendous amount of information regarding women's associations in New York and Boston.

44. Ibid., 13.

45. Sterling, *We Are Your Sisters,* 105. Sterling notes that no original documents from the earliest black women's organizations exist; however, the organizations are referenced in several notes and minutes of black women's groups of the 1820s.

46. "Beneficial Societies 1823–1838," PAS Papers.

47. Ibid.

48. Ibid.

49. Order Book, Daughters of Africa Society, 1821–29, Historical Society of Pennsylvania. Also see Sterling, *We Are Your Sisters,* 105–6.

50. Order Book, Daughters of Africa Society, 1821–29, July 2, 1822, minutes, entry 17.

51. Ibid., May 1, 1822, minutes, entry 12.

52. Ibid., July 5, 1822, minutes, entry 18.

53. Ira Berlin, *Slaves without Masters: The Free Negro in the Antebellum South* (New York: Pantheon, 1974), 306–8.

54. It appears that the Daughters of Africa disbanded in 1829. The existing Order Book records entries from 1821 to 1829.

55. "Special Organizations & Activities," Minutes and Trial Book, 1822–35, Mother Bethel A.M.E. Church, April 15, 1829, microfilm roll 8, Historical Society of Pennsylvania.

56. Ibid.
57. Ibid.
58. Ibid.
59. Ibid.
60. Ibid., November 25, 1829.
61. Ibid.
62. Ibid. An excuse probably would not have mattered to the committee, anyway.
63. Stansell, *City of Women,* 58–60. The same types of tensions erupted between neighbors in Irish neighborhoods in New York. Irish women used the courts, when possible, to settle disputes; however, physical violence often spilled over into the streets.
64. "Special Organizations & Activities," Minutes and Trial Book, October 6, 1823.
65. Ibid.
66. Ibid.
67. Ibid.
68. Ibid., August 19, 1823.
69. Ibid.
70. Ibid., July 22, 1829.
71. Ibid.
72. Ibid. It is unclear if Bell was married to another woman. I am assuming that he was not, for it most likely would have been mentioned in the records if he were.
73. Ibid., August 19, 1823.
74. Ibid.
75. Ibid.
76. Ibid., March 30, 1830.
77. Ibid.
78. Ibid.
79. Ibid., April 8, 1829.
80. Ibid.
81. Ibid.
82. Ibid.

Chapter 4. Voices from the Margins

1. Minutes of the Board of Managers, March 5 and April 2, 1840, Philadelphia Female Anti-Slavery Society, Historical Society of Pennsylvania.
2. Ibid., February 7, April 4, 1939; March 5, April 2, 1840.
3. For more on William Lloyd Garrison and the creation of the *Liberator,* see Henry Mayer, *All on Fire: William Lloyd Garrison and the Abolition of Slavery* (New York: St. Martin's Press, 1998), 127–66.
4. There is an immense amount of literature regarding the antislavery movement of the 1830s. Ronald G. Walters has attempted to broaden the understanding of the movement in his essay "The Boundaries of Abolitionism" in *Anti-Slavery Reconsidered: New Perspectives on the Abolitionists,* ed. Lewis Perry and Michael Fellman (Baton Rouge: Louisiana State University Press, 1979). Also see Herbert Aptheker, *Abolitionism: A Revolutionary Movement* (Boston: Twayne Publishers, 1989); James

McPherson, *The Struggle for Equality: Abolitionists and the Negro in the Civil War and Reconstruction* (Princeton: Princeton University Press, 1964); David Brion Davis, *The Problem of Slavery in Western Culture* (Ithaca: Cornell University Press, 1966); Gilbert Hobbs Barnes, *The Antislavery Impulse, 1830–1844* (New York: American Historical Association, 1933); James B. Stewart, *Holy Warriors: The Abolitionists and American Slavery* (New York: Hill and Wang, 1976); Dorsey, *Reforming Men and Women;* Leon Litwack, "The Abolitionist Dilemma: The Antislavery Movement and the Northern Negro," *New England Quarterly* 34 (March 1961): 50–73; Lawrence J. Friedman, *Gregarious Saints: Self and Community in American Abolitionism, 1830–1870* (New York: Cambridge University Press, 1982); John Stauffer, *Black Hearts of Men: Radical Abolitionists and The Transformation of Race* (Cambridge: Harvard University Press, 2002); and Berlin, *Many Thousands Gone.*

5. See Peter Kolchin, *American Slavery, 1619–1877* (New York: Hill and Wang, 1993), 93–133, 169–200.

6. Carol V. R. George, *Segregated Sabbaths: Richard Allen and the Emergence of the Independent Black Churches, 1760–1840* (New York: Oxford University Press, 1973), 79–81.

7. Ibid., 80–82.

8. For more on violence against abolitionists, see Julie Roy Jeffrey, *The Great Silent Army of Abolitionism: Ordinary Women in the Antislavery Movement* (Chapel Hill: University of North Carolina Press, 1998), 49–52, 211–12.

9. Jean Fagan Yellin, *Women and Sisters: The Antislavery Feminists in American Culture* (New Haven: Yale University Press, 1989), 44–50. See also Gerda Lerner, "Black and White Women in Interaction and Confrontation," in Lerner, *The Majority Finds Its Past: Placing Women in History* (New York: Oxford University Press, 1979), 94–103.

10. Anne M. Boylan, "Benevolence and Antislavery Activity among African-American Women in New York and Boston, 1820–1840," in *The Abolitionist Sisterhood: Women's Political Culture in Antebellum America,* ed. Jean Fagan Yellin and John C. Van Horne (Ithaca: Cornell University Press, 1994), 120.

11. Ira V. Brown, "The Cradle of Feminism: The Philadelphia Female Anti-Slavery Society, 1833–1840," *Pennsylvania Magazine of History and Biography* 102 (April 1978): 144–45.

12. *Proceedings of the Anti-slavery Convention, Assembled in Philadelphia, December 4th, 5th, and 6th, 1833* (New York: Dorr and Butterfield, 1833), 6–7.

13. Ibid.

14. Boylan, *Origins of Women's Activism,* sheds tremendous light on the earliest political, religious, and social organizations founded by women in the early republic and antebellum era.

15. Nancy Isenberg, *Sex and Citizenship in Antebellum America* (Chapel Hill: University of North Carolina Press, 1998), 15–17.

16. Susan Zaeske, *Signatures of Citizenship: Petitioning, Antislavery, and Women's Political Identity* (Chapel Hill: University of North Carolina Press, 2003), 151–61.

17. Minutes of the Philadelphia Female Anti-Slavery Society, 1833–1841, Historical Society of Pennsylvania, Manuscript Collection. Minutes from the first meetings appear to have been written at a later date, perhaps some time in the spring of 1834. The PFASS was founded on December 14, 1833.

18. The majority of women's antislavery societies were not interracial. Philadelphia and Boston were among the few urban cities to possess racially mixed organizations dedicated to abolition.

19. Sterling, *We Are Your Sisters*, chap. 10. Sterling describes the interaction between white and black female abolitionists in Boston and Philadelphia. Of particular interest are the letters between Angelina Grimké and Sarah Forten in which Grimké asked Forten to describe the effect that race prejudice had had on her life.

20. Minutes of the Philadelphia Female Anti-Slavery Society, December 14, 1833.

21. Minutes of the Philadelphia Female Anti-Slavery Society, January 9, 1845. Also see Julie Winch, *Philadelphia's Black Elite: Activism, Accommodation, and the Struggle for Autonomy, 1787–1848* (Philadelphia: Temple University Press, 1988), 85–92.

22. Minutes of the Philadelphia Female Anti-Slavery Society, microfilm edition, reel 30, January 9, 1845.

23. Sidney Kaplan, *The Black Presence in the Era of the American Revolution, 1770–1800* (Greenwich, Conn.: New York Graphic Society, 1973), 238–39.

24. Winch, *Philadelphia's Black Elite*, 73.

25. Ibid.

26. "The Petition of the Blacks in the City of Philada," ca. 1801, Cox-Parrish-Wharton Papers, vols. 2, 3, Historical Society of Pennsylvania.

27. Alan Kulikoff, "Uprooted Peoples: Black Migrants in the Age of the American Revolution, 1790–1820," in *Slavery and Freedom in the Age of the American Revolution*, ed. Ira Berlin and Ronald Hoffman (Charlottesville: University Press of Virginia, 1983), 147.

28. Winch, *Philadelphia's Black Elite*, 1–3.

29. Anna Davis Hallowell, ed., *James and Lucretia Mott: Life and Letters* (Boston: Houghton Mifflin, 1884), 114–15. For a detailed biography of Lucretia Mott, see Margaret Hope Bacon, *Valiant Friend: The Life of Lucretia Mott* (New York: Walker, 1980).

30. Hallowell, *James and Lucretia Mott*, 114–15.

31. Brown, "Cradle of Feminism," 146–47.

32. For a detailed biography of the Grimké sisters, see Gerda Lerner, *The Grimké Sisters from South Carolina: Pioneers for Women's Rights and Abolition*, rev. ed. (Chapel Hill: University of North Carolina Press, 2004). Also see Katharine Du Pre Lumpkin, *The Emancipation of Angelina Grimké* (Chapel Hill: University of North Carolina Press, 1974), 245.

33. Ruth Bogin and Jean Fagan Yellin, introduction to Yellin and Van Horne, *Abolitionist Sisterhood*, 9.

34. Ibid.

35. Minutes of the Philadelphia Female Anti-Slavery Society, December 14, 1833. Also see Brown, "Cradle of Feminism," 148.

36. Sterling, *We Are Your Sisters*, 120–21. Also see Winch, *Gentleman of Color*.

37. Debra Gold Hansen, *Strained Sisterhood: Gender and Class in the Boston Female Anti-Slavery Society* (Amherst: University of Massachusetts Press, 1993), 90–91.

38. Boylan, *Origins of Women's Activism*, 49.

39. Hansen, *Strained Sisterhood*, 90.

40. Boylan, *Origins of Women's Activism*, 49.

41. Winch, *Philadelphia's Black Elite*, 85–87.

42. Harris, *In the Shadow of Slavery*, 192.

43. Zaeske, *Signatures of Citizenship*, 151.

44. Minutes of the Board of Managers, December 1, 1834, Philadelphia Female Anti-Slavery Society.

45. Yellin, *Women and Sisters*, 3–20.

46. Angelina E. Grimké, *Letters to Catherine E. Beecher, in Reply to an Essay on Slavery and Abolitionism* (Boston: Isaac Knapp, 1838).

47. Blanche Glassman Hersh, *The Slavery of Sex: Feminist-Abolitionists in America* (Urbana: University of Illinois Press, 1978), 34.

48. Carolyn Williams, "The Female Antislavery Movement: Fighting against Racial Prejudice and Promoting Women's Rights in Antebellum America," in Yellin and Van Horne, *Abolitionist Sisterhood*, 165.

49. Sterling, *We Are Your Sisters*, 119–20.

50. Winch, *Gentleman of Color*, 10–11.

51. Ibid., 152–54.

52. Sterling, *We Are Your Sisters*, 119–20.

53. Winch, *Gentleman of Color*, 107–24.

54. Shirley J. Yee, *Black Women Abolitionists: A Study in Activism, 1828–1860* (Knoxville: University of Tennessee Press, 1992), 12–13.

55. Jean R. Soderlund, "Priorities and Power: The Philadelphia Female Anti-Slavery Society," in Yellin and Van Horne, *Abolitionist Sisterhood*, 75.

56. Yee, *Black Women Abolitionists*, 18–19.

57. Gerda Lerner, *Black Women in White America: A Documentary History* (New York: Pantheon, 1972).

58. Many young women, such as Margaretta, Sarah, and Harriet Forten, had no choice but to be educated in the home. It was not until the opening of Sarah Douglass's school in the mid-1830s that there would be institutionalized high school education for young black women.

59. Lerner, *Black Women in White America*.

60. Sterling, *We Are Your Sisters*, 127–28.

61. *Colored American*, March 1837.

62. Minutes of the Philadelphia Female Anti-Slavery Society, March 5, April 2, and April 9, 1840.

63. Ibid.

64. Ibid., December 14, 1833.

65. Ibid.

66. Ibid. The founding members of the PFASS were Anna Bunting, Leah Fell, Margaretta Forten, Mary Ann McClintock, Sarah McCrummell, Catherine McDermott, Esther Moore, Lucretia Mott, Rachel Passmore, Catherine Robinson, Mary Sharpless, Mary Sleeper, Lydia Thomas, and Lydia White.

67. Minutes of the Philadelphia Female Anti-Slavery Society, June 13, July 9, and September 10, 1835.

68. Fourth Annual Report of the Philadelphia Female Anti-Slavery Society, January 11, 1838.

69. Soderlund, "Priorities and Power," 77–78.

70. Zaeske, *Signatures of Citizenship,* 46.

71. Minutes of the Philadelphia Female Anti-Slavery Society, October 13, 1836; February 9 and May 18, 1837. Also see Soderlund, "Priorities and Power," 78.

72. Zaeske, *Signatures of Citizenship,* 46.

73. Deborah Bingham Van Broekhoven, "Let Your Names Be Enrolled: Method and Ideology in Women's Anti-Slavery Petitioning," in Yellin and Van Horne, *The Abolitionist Sisterhood,* 185.

74. *Liberator,* January 2, 1837.

75. Minutes of the Philadelphia Female Anti-Slavery Society, March 12, 1840; February 11, 1841. There was an even greater decline in several other women's antislavery societies along the northeastern seaboard. See Judith Wellman, "Women and Radical Reform in Antebellum Upstate New York: A Profile in Grassroots Female Abolitionists," in *Clio Was a Woman: Studies in the History of American Women,* ed. Mabel E. Deutrich and Virginia C. Purdy (Washington, D.C.: Howard University Press, 1980), 113–28.

76. Soderlund, "Priorities and Power," 78. Also see *Memorial of Sarah Pugh: A Tribute of Respect from Her Cousins* (Philadelphia: J. B. Lippincott, 1888), 22.

77. Zaeske, *Signatures of Citizenship,* 154.

78. Soderlund, "Priorities and Power," 83.

79. Sarah Forten to Elizabeth Whittier, Philadelphia, December 25, 1836, Elizabeth Whittier Papers, Clarke Historical Library, Central Michigan University.

80. N. Orwin Rush, "Lucretia Mott and the Philadelphia Antislavery Fairs," *Bulletin of Friends Historical Association* 35 (Autumn 1946): 69–75.

81. Soderlund, "Priorities and Power," 80–85.

82. Nash, *Forging Freedom,* 277–79.

83. Soderlund, "Priorities and Power," 84–85.

84. Minutes of the Philadelphia Female Anti-Slavery Society, March 1 and April 5, 1838.

85. Soderlund, "Priorities and Power," 76–77.

86. Vigilance committees were among the first public organizations with a purpose of protecting and assisting fugitive slaves. The Vigilance Committee in Philadelphia was led by Robert Purvis, and it thrived from 1838 until 1842. See Dorsey, *Reforming Men and Women,* 185.

87. Soderlund, "Priorities and Power," 77.

88. Sarah Forten to Angelina Grimké, Philadelphia, April 15, 1837, Weld-Grimké Papers, William Clements Library, University of Michigan.

89. Ibid.

90. Ibid.

91. Ibid.

92. It appears that there was segregation based on class in the churches of the black communities. Mother Bethel A.M.E. seems to have catered to a working-class black community. Many of its members had worked their way out of slavery and held many of the menial jobs in the city. Philadelphia's black elite apparently belonged to different churches: St. Thomas's Episcopal Church, Presbyterian denominations, or the Society of Friends.

93. Sarah Forten to Angelina Grimké, April 15, 1837.

94. Sarah Douglass to Sarah Grimké, 1838, quoted in Sterling, *We Are Your Sisters,* 130–31.

95. On the use of female slave testaments, see Margaret M. R. Kellow, "The Divided Mind of Antislavery Feminism: Lydia Maria Child and the Construction of African American Womanhood," in *Discovering the Women in Slavery,* ed. Patricia Morton (Athens: University of Georgia Press, 1996), 107–9.

96. *Minutes of the* Philadelphia Female Anti-Slavery Society, May 19, 1842; May 15, 1844. Also see Soderlund, "Priorities and Power," 80.

97. Soderlund, "Priorities and Power," 80.

98. Ibid.,105.

99. Harris, *In the Shadow of Slavery,* 201.

100. Soderlund, "Priorities and Power," 70.

101. Ibid.

102. *North Star,* September 29, 1848, cited in Frederick Douglass, *The Life and Writings of Frederick Douglass,* ed. Philip S. Foner (New York: International, 1950) 1:333.

Chapter 5. Writing for Womanhood

1. For more on antislavery newspapers, see Zaeske, *Signatures of Citizenship,* 38–40; also see Gerda Lerner, "Political Activities of Antislavery Women" in her *The Majority Finds Its Past,* 112–27; Yellin and Van Horne, *Abolitionist Sisterhood;* and Michael Warner, *Letters of the Republic: Publication and the Public Sphere in Eighteenth-Century America* (Cambridge: Harvard University Press, 1990).

2. *Freedom's Journal,* April 20, 1827.

3. Jocelyn Moody, *Sentimental Confessions: Spiritual Narratives of Nineteenth-Century African American Women* (Athens: University of Georgia Press, 2001), 9–14. Moody discusses sentimentalism and the spiritual autobiographies of several well-known nineteenth-century African American women, Jarena Lee and Zilpha Elaw among them.

4. Elizabeth McHenry, *Forgotten Readers: Recovering the Lost History of African American Literary Societies* (Durham, N.C.: Duke University Press, 2002), 41–50.

5. Du Bois, *The Philadelphia Negro,* 84.

6. Du Bois used the term "partly free" to refer to a mixed student body in which the parents of some children were able to offer financial contributions, whereas other students attended the school free of charge.

7. Du Bois, *The Philadelphia Negro,* 85.

8. Ibid.

9. Nash, *Forging Freedom,* 276–78.

10. Du Bois, *The Philadelphia Negro,* 84–89.

11. Ibid., 87.

12. Ibid., 199.

13. See Fordham, *Major Themes in Northern Black Religious Thought.*

14. Dorothy B. Porter, "The Organized Educational Activities of Negro Literary Societies, 1828–1846," *Journal of Negro Education* 5 (October 1936): 556–77. Also see McHenry, *Forgotten Readers,* 41.

15. *Freedom's Journal,* June 20, 1828.

16. Porter, "The Organized Educational Activities of Negro Literary Societies."

17. McHenry, *Forgotten Readers,* 58.

18. Joseph Willson, *Sketches of the Higher Classes of Colored Society in Philadelphia by a Southerner* (Philadelphia: Merrihew and Thompson, 1841), 108.

19. Ibid.

20. *Minutes and Proceedings of the First Annual Meeting of the American Reform Society Held in Philadelphia . . . 14th to the 19th of August,* 1837 (Philadelphia: Merrihew and Gunn, 1837), 42–43.

21. Porter, "The Organized Educational Activities of Negro Literary Societies," 557–58.

22. Ibid.

23. The New York African Clarkson Society was founded in 1829, one year after the founding of the Reading Room Society in Philadelphia.

24. Winch, *Philadelphia's Black Elite,* 130–31.

25. *Liberator,* April 14, 1832.

26. Winch, *Philadelphia's Black Elite,* 130–35.

27. Ibid., 175.

28. Edward Williams Clay's extremely racist sketches entitled "Life in Philadelphia" appeared during the late 1820s and early 1830s. The entire set can be found at the Library Company of Philadelphia. For more information about the series and its publication, see note 36 to chapter 6, below.

29. Yee, *Black Women Abolitionists,* 121.

30. See Zaeske, *Signatures of Citizenship,* 11–21.

31. Minutes of the Philadelphia Female Anti-Slavery Society, October 12, 1843.

32. See Erlene Stetson, ed., *Black Sister: Poetry by Black American Women,* 1746–1980 (Bloomington: Indiana University Press, 1981). The scholar Todd S. Gernes suggests that after 1834 Forten's literary contributions diminished; a stylistic analysis points to Eliza Earle, a virtually unknown white Quaker poet who also adopted the pen name Ada. See Gernes, "Poetic Justice: Sarah Forten, Eliza Earle, and the Paradox of Intellectual Property," *New England Quarterly* 71 (June 1998): 229–65. I have chosen to focus on Forten's poetry and essays before 1834 that are not contested by Gernes.

33. Sterling, *We Are Your Sisters,* 121.

34. Magawisca [Sarah Forten], "The Abuse of Liberty," *Liberator,* March 26, 1831.

35. Ibid.

36. Ibid.

37. Ada [Sarah Forten], "The Slave," *Liberator,* April 16, 1831.

38. Ibid.

39. Zillah [Sarah Mapps Douglass], "To a Friend," *Liberator,* June 30, 1832.

40. Ibid.

41. Zillah [Sarah Mapps Douglass], letter to the editor, *Liberator,* July 21, 1832.

42. Sterling, *We Are Your Sisters,* 164–65. Also see Jane Rhodes, *Mary Ann Shadd Cary: The Black Press and Protest in the Nineteenth Century* (Bloomington: Indiana University Press, 1998).

43. Sterling, *We Are Your Sisters,* 164–65.

44. Jeffrey, *The Great Silent Army of Abolitionism,* 191.

45. C. Peter Ripley et al., eds., *The Black Abolitionist Papers,* 5 vols. (Chapel Hill: University of North Carolina Press, 1985–92), 2:191–93.

46. Sterling, *We Are Your Sisters,* 170–71.

47. Jeffrey, *The Great Silent Army of Abolitionism*, 205–6. Also see Sterling, *We Are Your Sisters*, 159.

48. Darlene Clark Hine, ed., *Black Women in American History: From Colonial Times through the Nineteenth Century*, 4 vols. (Brooklyn: Carlson, 1990), 22–24.

49. Sterling, *We Are Your Sisters*, 159. William Still (1821–1902), an abolitionist, writer, and businessman, was born near Medford, in Burlington County, N.J. His father, Levin Steel, was a former slave who had purchased his own freedom and changed his name to Still. William Still would become one of the most outspoken and admired abolitionists and supporters of the Underground Railroad in the country.

50. Zillah [Sarah Mapps Douglass], "A True Tale For Children," *Liberator*, July 7, 1832.

51. Ibid.

52. Jeffrey, *The Great Silent Army of Abolitionism*, 206.

53. Sterling, *We Are Your Sisters*, 162.

54. Catherine A. Brekus, *Strangers and Pilgrims: Female Preaching in America, 1740–1845* (Chapel Hill: University of North Carolina Press, 1998), 143.

55. Jarena Lee, *Religious Experience and Journal of Mrs. Jarena Lee, Giving an Account of Her Call to Preach the Gospel* (Philadelphia, 1849), 4.

56. Ibid., 5.

57. See George, *Segregated Sabbaths*, 127–30. George gives a very positive representation of the relationship between the Reverend Richard Allen and Jarena Lee; by the time Lee approached Allen with her desire to preach, he had modified his views on the rights of women to participate in the church ministry. Allen accepted Lee as a woman preacher, though she was never ordained or given the same rights and privileges as her male counterparts. Lee often traveled with Allen to conferences as an unofficial member of the church delegation.

58. Zilpha Elaw, *Memoirs of the Life, Religious Experience, Ministerial Travels and Labours, of Mrs. Zilpha Elaw, an American Female of Colour; Together with Some Account of the Great Religious Revivals in America* (London, 1846), 1.

59. Zilpha Elaw was not set free until she was in her early thirties.

60. Elaw, *Memoirs*, 7.

61. Ibid., 14–15.

62. Rothman, *Hands and Hearts*.

63. Elaw, *Memoirs*, 14–15. See Cott, *The Bonds of Womanhood*, 78–83. Cott explores the influence of unhappy marriage on women in the early part of the century. Her term *marriage trauma* refers to the depression felt by many women, black and white, who were unhappy with their chosen spouses.

64. Elaw, *Memoirs*, 16.

65. Ibid., 15.

66. Ibid.

67. Lee, *Religious Experience*, 13.

68. Ibid.

69. Smith-Rosenberg, *Disorderly Conduct*, 23. Smith-Rosenberg examines nineteenth-century views toward women and illness. Menstruation, pregnancy, childbirth, lactation, and menopause were interpreted as part of the female experience, and women were thus depicted as weak and fragile creatures.

70. Lee, *Religious Experience*, 14.

71. Kerber, *Women of the Republic*, 144–46.

72. Ibid., 10–11. Following the American Revolution, women were to play a part in the construction of a new republic. It was the charge of women to raise and educate virtuous male citizens who would lead the republic to success.

73. Elaw, *Memoirs*, 57–58.

74. Ibid., 57.

75. Ibid., 58.

76. Lee, *Religious Experience*, 14.

77. Ibid., 18.

78. Ibid., 61.

79. From Lee's narrative, it appears as though James was born in 1816, which makes him her firstborn child. James Lee was in the care of Richard Allen from the age of thirteen until his apprenticeship at age fifteen. It is not known whether James was an apprentice and considered "free" or if he was an indentured servant.

Chapter 6. A Mental and Moral Feast

Epigraph: Cassey, Friendship Album of Amy Matilda Cassey.

1. In cities such as Philadelphia, Boston, and New York, gradual emancipation had erased the institution of slavery by the early decades of the nineteenth century. For more on gradual emancipation, see Melish, *Disowning Slavery*; Nash, *Forging Freedom*; and Harris, *In the Shadow of Slavery*.

2. For more on the capitalist transformation of the nineteenth century, see Christopher Clark, *The Roots of Rural Capitalism: Western Massachusetts, 1780–1860* (Ithaca: Cornell University Press, 1990); Charles Sellers, *The Market Revolution: Jacksonian America, 1815–1846* (New York: Oxford University Press, 1991); Mary Ryan, *Cradle of the Middle Class: The Family in Oneida County, New York, 1790–1865* (New York: Cambridge University Press, 1981); and Sean Wilentz, *Chants Democratic: New York City and the Rise of the American Working Class, 1788–1850* (New York: Oxford University Press, 1984).

3. Yee, *Black Women Abolitionists*.

4. Shirley Samuels, ed., *The Culture of Sentiment: Race, Gender, and Sentimentality in Nineteenth-Century America* (New York: Oxford University Press, 1992), 3–5. This collection of essays examines the functions of sentimentality in the nineteenth-century novel and women's magazines of the era. None of the essays examine personal correspondence, nor do they focus on the writings of the nineteenth-century African American elite.

5. Scholars such as Ann Douglas describe the sentimental novel written by and for women as "a corrupting means of self-indulgence and the epitome of consumerism." See Douglas, *The Feminization of American Culture* (New York: Alfred A. Knopf, 1977). Many feminist historians, however, have challenged this earlier critique of nineteenth-century sentimentalism. Mary P. Ryan, *Women in Public: Between Banners and Ballots, 1825–1880* (Baltimore: Johns Hopkins University Press, 1990), Linda Kerber, "Separate Spheres, Female Worlds, Woman's Place: The Rhetoric of Women's History," *Journal of American History* 75 (June 1988): 9–39, and Nancy Cott, *Bonds of Womanhood*, have offered an interpretation of the sentimental novel as a way in which women refuted the absolutism of separate spheres, transforming the

domestic sphere into an arena for political action and mobility. The sentimental novel was a tool for such work, specifically for the work of antislavery, suffrage, and temperance. Works such as Hazel Carby, *Reconstructing Womanhood: The Emergence of the Afro-American Woman Novelist* (New York: Oxford University Press, 1987), and Lori D. Ginzberg, *Women and the Work of Benevolence: Morality, Politics, and Class in the Nineteenth-Century United States* (New Haven: Yale University Press, 1990), have read sentimentalism as part of a popular feminist counterpolitics.

6. See Isabelle Lehuu, "Sentimental Figures: Reading 'Godey's Lady's Book' in Antebellum America," in Samuels, *The Culture of Sentiment*, 74–75.

7. Claudia Tate, *Domestic Allegories of Political Desire: The Black Heroine's Text at the Turn of the Century* (New York: Oxford University Press, 1992).

8. Ibid., 5.

9. From 1994 to 1999 the Library Company of Philadelphia purchased three of the four intact friendship albums belonging to African American women. The fourth album, maintained by Mary Virginia Wood Forten, is at the Moorland-Spingarn Library at Howard University.

10. See Catherine Kelly, *In the New England Fashion: Reshaping Women's Lives in the Nineteenth Century* (Ithaca: Cornell University Press, 1999), 80–95. Although Kelly focuses on rural white women of New England, she demonstrates the ways in which friendship albums were popular during the middle decades of the nineteenth century.

11. Smith-Rosenberg, *Disorderly Conduct*, 61.

12. Christine Stansell, "Revisiting the Angel in the House: Revisions of Victorian Womanhood," *New England Quarterly* 60 (1987): 466–83.

13. Kelly, *In the New England Mind*, 90–92.

14. Moody, *Sentimental Confessions*, 9–14. Moody discusses sentimentalism and the spiritual autobiographies of several well-known nineteenth-century African American women. She argues that sentimentality in literature seeks to create an emotional and moral alliance between the reader and text.

15. *The Annual Report of the Library Company of Philadelphia for the Year 1998*, 25. I would like to thank the staff of the Library Company of Philadelphia, in particular Phil Lapsansky and Erika Piola, for providing me with assistance during and after my fellowship.

16. Ibid., 27–30.

17. Ibid., 30.

18. Cassey Friendship Album, 3.

19. Ibid., 17.

20. Ibid.

21. Ibid., 10. This poem is undated, but there are several other entries written by Mary Forten dated 1833 and 1834.

22. Ibid., 18 (November 7, 1833).

23. Mary Virginia Wood Forten, Friendship Album of Mary Virginia Wood Forten, 1831–35, Moorland-Spingarn Library, Howard University, 4.

24. *Annual Report of the Library Company*, 1998, 31.

25. Cassey Friendship Album, 35 (January 1850).

26. Ibid.

27. *Annual Report of the Library Company*, 1998, 33.

28. Sterling, *We Are Your Sisters*, 121.

29. Cassey Friendship Album, 7. This entry was unsigned and undated, but it appears early on in the album, which indicates that it most likely was written in the early 1830s.

30. See Laurel Ulrich, *Good Wives: Image and Reality in the Lives of Women in Northern New England, 1650–1750* (New York: Alfred A. Knopf, 1982). Ulrich describes the many different expectations of a "good wife," from deputy husband to caregiver to business manager. Many black women subscribed to these values.

31. Cassey Friendship Album, 22. Although the undated entry was signed simply "Mary," it is quite probable that the author was Mary Forten.

32. Ibid.

33. See Ann duCille, *The Coupling Convention: Sex, Text, and Tradition in Black Women's Fiction* (New York: Oxford University Press, 1993), 3–4. Also see Claudia Tate's important *Domestic Allegories of Political Desire.* Tate provides a groundbreaking discussion of the representations of marriage and the family in nineteenth-century domestic fiction.

34. The expression of freedom through fashion was not specific to freed black men and women of the North. In her book *Labor of Love, Labor of Sorrow: Black Women, Work, and the Family from Slavery to the Present* (New York: Basic Books, 1985), Jacqueline Jones examines the expression of freedom through fashion during the years of Reconstruction in the South. A similar method of redefinition among black Philadelphians occurred throughout the antebellum years.

35. Although Jones's *Labor of Love, Labor of Sorrow* focuses on the ways in which newly freed slaves in the South expressed their new status through ornate attire during the 1860s and 1870s, a similar attitude is seen in 1830 Philadelphia.

36. Edward Williams Clay (1799–1857) was a well-known cartoonist of the early nineteenth century in Philadelphia. His extremely racist sketches entitled "Life in Philadelphia" appeared during the late 1820s and early 1830s; they mocked free blacks by making derogatory comments about their speech, dress, and alleged intellectual inferiority. These sketches were published by S. Hart and Son, publishers, which was a partnership between Sarah and Abraham Hart, Jewish owners of a Philadelphia stationery store who began to publish the series in 1829. The entire series of fourteen prints was reprinted in 1830 after Abraham entered a partnership with the respected Philadelphia publisher E. L. Carey. This complete set can be found at the Library Company of Philadelphia.

37. Nash, *Forging Freedom*, 254–55.

38. Although these images were extremely popular in Philadelphia, they were also very popular in the 1850s in England. Reproductions of "Life in Philadelphia" were published in London before the Civil War.

39. For more information about Edward Clay, see Nancy Reynolds Davison, "E. W. Clay: American Political Caricaturist of the Jacksonian Era" (Ph.D. dissertation, University of Michigan, 1980).

40. Clay, "Miss Minta," "Life in Philadelphia" (1829).

41. Ibid.

42. Clay, "Miss Minta," "Life in Philadelphia" (1830).

43. Phil Lapsansky, "Afro Americana: Meet the Dickersons," in *The Annual Report of the Library Company of Philadelphia for the Year 1993*, 17–24.

44. Ibid., 18. These dates are based on the entries of the albums.

45. Martina Dickerson, Friendship Album of Martina Dickerson, Library Company of Philadelphia, 57 (July 16, 1840).

46. Ibid., 35 (July 16, 1840).

47. Although the poem is not signed by Charlotte Forten, the initials C.F., which do appear, most likely refer to Charlotte Forten Senior as the author of the poem.

48. Mary Anne Dickerson, Friendship Album of Mary Anne Dickerson, Library Company of Philadelphia, 2. "The Mother's Joy" was probably written by Charlotte Forten in 1834.

49. Ibid., 22.

50. John A. Jones, "The Night of Death," November 1, 1857, in Martina Dickerson Friendship Album.

51. Daniel A. Payne, "Lines Occasioned by the Death of my Sainted Wife Julia Ann Payne, June 20th, 1849," in Cassey Friendship Album, 67–68.

52. Ibid.

53. Ibid., 68–68v.

54. A.W.W., untitled poem, June 2, 1855, in Cassey Friendship Album, 51. It is probable that the author of this sonnet is Anna Warren Weston.

55. Ibid.

56. William Lloyd Garrison, "The Abolition Cause," April 18, 1833, in Cassey Friendship Album, 12.

57. William C. Nell, "The Rights of Woman," in Mary Anne Dickerson Friendship Album, 34.

58. Adaliza Cutter Phelps, "For My Cousin's Album," quoted in Kelly, *In the New England Fashion*, 77.

59. Kelly, *In the New England Fashion*, 91.

60. Winch, *The Elite of Our People*, 10.

Conclusion

1. See Charlotte L. Forten, *The Journals of Charlotte Forten Grimké*, ed. Brenda Stevenson (New York: Oxford University Press, 1988).

2. Ibid., 103.

3. Du Bois, *The Philadelphia Negro*, 46, 47, 54. Also see Roger Lane, *Roots of Violence in Black Philadelphia*, 1860–1900 (Cambridge: Harvard University Press, 1986), 7.

4. Roger Lane, *William Dorsey's Philadelphia and Ours: On the Past and Future of the Black City in America* (New York: Oxford University Press, 1991), 286–87.

5. Ibid.

6. Sterling, *We Are Your Sisters*, 245.

7. Ibid.

8. Du Bois, *The Philadelphia Negro*, 39

9. Ibid., 58. In 1860, 3,621 African Americans lived in the Seventh Ward, and by 1870 there were 4,616 black residents. By 1890 that number had nearly doubled, reaching 8,861.

Bibliography

Manuscript Collections

African Methodist Episcopal Church Records (Mother Bethel). Philadelphia, 1822–51. Minutes and Trial Book. Historical Society of Pennsylvania.

Anti-Slavery Collection. Department of Rare Books and Manuscripts, Boston Public Library.

Cary, Mary Ann Shadd. Papers. Sophia Smith Collection, Schlesinger Library, Radcliffe College.

Cassey, Amy Matilda. Friendship Album of Amy Matilda Cassey, 1833–56. Library Company of Philadelphia.

Clay, Edward Williams. "Life in Philadelphia" series. Library Company of Philadelphia.

Cox-Parrish-Wharton Papers. Vols. 2, 3, 14. Historical Society of Pennsylvania.

Daughters of Africa Society. Philadelphia, 1822–38. Minutes and Order Book. Historical Society of Pennsylvania.

Daughters of Tapisco Society of Mother Bethel A.M.E. Church. Philadelphia, 1837–47. Minute Book. Historical Society of Pennsylvania.

Dickerson, Martina. Friendship Album of Martina Dickerson, 1840–46. Library Company of Philadelphia.

Dickerson, Mary Anne. Friendship Album of Mary Anne Dickerson, 1833–57. Library Company of Philadelphia.

Drinker, Elizabeth. Diary of Elizabeth Drinker. Historical Society of Pennsylvania.

Forten, Mary Virginia Wood. Friendship Album of Mary Virginia Wood Forten, 1831–35. Moorland-Spingarn Library, Howard University.

Historical Society of Pennsylvania, Miscellaneous Collection, box 6A, folder 13.

Logan, Deborah Norris. Diary of Deborah Norris Logan. Historical Society of Pennsylvania.

Pennsylvania Abolition Society. Papers. Historical Society of Pennsylvania.

Pennsylvania Abolition Society American Convention. Papers. Historical Society of Pennsylvania.

Philadelphia Female Anti-Slavery Society. Records, 1833–50, Minute Books, and Annual Reports. Historical Society of Pennsylvania.

Weld-Grimké Papers. William Clements Library, University of Michigan.

Whittier, Elizabeth. Papers. Clarke Historical Library, Central Michigan University.

Newspapers

Antislavery Examiner

Colored American, 1837–42; published in January and February 1837 as *Weekly Advocate*

Emancipator

Freedom's Journal

Genius of Universal Emancipation

Liberator

National Anti-Slavery Standard

North Star

Pennsylvania Freeman

Pennsylvania Gazette

Published Primary Sources

Allen, Richard. *The Life, Experience, and Gospel Labors of the Right Reverend Richard Allen, to Which Is Annexed the Rise and Progress of the African Methodist Episcopal Church in the United States of America.* 1833. Reprint, Nashville: Abingdon, 1960.

American Anti-Slavery Society. *Second Annual Report.* New York: William S. Dorr, 1835.

Andrews, Charles C. *The History of the New-York African Free Schools, from Their Establishment in 1787, to the Present Time.* New York: Mahlon Day, 1830.

Anti-Slavery Records and Pamphlets, 1834–44. Reprint, Westport, Conn.: Negro Universities Press, 1970.

"An Appeal to Women of the Nominally Free States, Issued by an Anti-Slavery Convention of American Women." 2nd ed. Boston: Isaac Knapp, 1838.

Delany, Martin Robinson. *The Condition, Elevation, Emigration, and Destiny of the Colored People of the United States.* 1852. Reprint, New York: Arno Press, 1968.

Douglass, Frederick. *The Life and Writings of Frederick Douglass.* Edited by Philip S. Foner. Vol. 1. New York: International, 1950.

Douglass, Rev. William. *Annals of the First African Church.* Philadelphia: King and Baird, 1862.

Elaw, Zilpha. *Memoirs of the Life, Religious Experience, Ministerial Travels and Labours, of Mrs. Zilpha Elaw, an American Female of Colour; Together with Some Account of the Great Religious Revivals in America.* London, 1846.

Forten, Charlotte. *The Journal of Charlotte Forten Grimké.* Edited by Brenda Stevenson. New York: Oxford University Press, 1988.

Garnet, Henry Highland. *The Past and Present Condition and the Destiny of the Colored Race: A Discourse Delivered at the Fifteenth Anniversary of the Female Benevolent Society of Troy, New York, February 14, 1848.* Reprint, Miami: Mnemosyne, 1969.

Grimké, Angelina E. *Letters to Catherine E. Beecher, in Reply to an Essay on Slavery and Abolitionism.* Boston: Isaac Knapp, 1838.

Hallowell, Anna Davis, ed. *James and Lucretia Mott: Life and Letters.* Boston: Houghton Mifflin, 1884.

Hazard's Register of Pennsylvania 7, 11 (March 12, 1831): 163. List of Expenditures of Beneficial Societies.

Heston, David. *Memoir of Old Elizabeth, a Coloured Woman, with a Short Account of Her Last Sickness and Death.* Philadelphia, 1866.

History of the Association of Friends for the Free Instruction of Adult Colored Persons in Philadelphia. Philadelphia, 1890.

Jacobs, Donald M., ed. *Antebellum Black Newspapers.* Westport, Conn.: Greenwood Press, 1976.

Lee, Jarena. *Religious Experience and Journal of Mrs. Jarena Lee, Giving an Account of Her Call to Preach the Gospel.* Philadelphia, 1849.

Loewenberg, Bert James, and Ruth Bogin, eds. *Black Women in Nineteenth-Century American Life: Their Words, Their Thoughts, Their Feelings.* University Park: Pennsylvania State University Press, 1976.

Memorial to the Honourable the Senate and House of Representatives of the Commonwealth of Pennsylvania, in General Assembly Met, from the "Colored Citizens" of This State, Residents of the City of Philadelphia. Philadelphia, 1855.

Nell, William C. *The Colored Patriots of the American Revolution.* 1855. Reprint, New York: Arno Press, 1968.

Payne, Daniel A. *History of the African Methodist Episcopal Church.* Edited by Rev. C. S. Smith. Nashville: Publishing House of the A.M.E. Sunday School Union, 1891.

———. *Recollections of Seventy Years.* 1888. Reprint, New York: Arno Press, 1968.

Philadelphia City Directories, 1795–1850.

Proceedings of the Anti-Slavery Convention, Assembled at Philadelphia, December 4th, 5th, and 6th, 1833. New York: Dorr and Butterfield, 1833.

Proceedings of the Anti-Slavery Convention of American Women, Held in the City of New-York, May 9th, 10th, 11th, and 12th, 1837. New York: W. S. Dorr, 1837.

Ripley, C. Peter, et al., eds. *The Black Abolitionist Papers.* 5 vols. Chapel Hill: University of North Carolina Press, 1985–92.

The Social and Economic Status of the Black Population in the United States: An Historical View, 1790–1978. Current Population Reports. Special Studies Series, No. 80. U.S. Department of Commerce, Bureau of the Census, 1790.

Society of Friends in the United States: Their Views of the Anti-Slavery Question and Treatment of the People of Color. Darlington, U.K.: John Wilson, 1840.

A Statistical Inquiry into the Conditions of the People of Colour, of the City and Districts of Philadelphia. Philadelphia: Kite and Walton, 1849.

Sterling, Dorothy, ed. *We Are Your Sisters: Black Women in the Nineteenth Century.* New York: W. W. Norton, 1984.

Still, Mary. "An Appeal to the Females of the African Methodist Episcopal Church, 1857." Philadelphia: Peter McKenna and Son, 1857.

Thomas, Isaiah, Jr. *Eccentric Biography, or Memoirs of Remarkable Female Characters, Ancient and Modern.* Worcester, Mass.: 1803.

Tregear, G. *Tregears Black Jokes.* London, 1830. (Complete collection located at the Library Company of Philadelphia.)

U.S. Bureau of the Census. *Heads of Families at the First Census of the United States Taken in the Year 1790: Pennsylvania.* Washington, D.C.: Government Printing Office, 1908.

Vaux, Roberts. *Memoirs of the Life of Anthony Benezet.* Philadelphia, 1817.

Wayman, Rev. A. W. *My Recollections of African M.E. Ministers.* Philadelphia: A.M.E. Book Room, 1881.

Webb, Samuel, ed. *History of Pennsylvania Hall, Which Was Destroyed by a Mob on the 17th of May, 1838.* Philadelphia: Merrihew and Gunn, 1838.

Wesley, Charles H. *Richard Allen, Apostle of Freedom.* Washington, D.C., 1935.

Willson, Joseph. *Sketches of the Higher Classes of Colored Society in Philadelphia, by a Southerner.* Philadelphia: Merrihew and Thompson, 1841.

Woodson, Carter G. *Free Negro Heads of Families in the United States in 1830.* Washington, D.C.: Association for the Study of Negro Life and History, 1925.

————, ed. *The Mind of the Negro as Reflected in Letters Written during the Crisis: 1800–1860.* 1926. Reprint, New York: Negro Universities Press 1969.

Secondary Sources

Abbot, George M. *A Short History of the Library Company of Philadelphia.* Philadelphia: Board of Directors, 1913.

Acornley, John H. *The Colored Lady Evangelist.* 1892. Reprint, New York: Garland, 1987.

Adams, Alice D. *The Neglected Period of Anti-Slavery in America (1808–1831).* Boston: Ginn, 1908.

Aptheker, Bettina. *Woman's Legacy: Essays on Race, Sex, and Class in American History.* Amherst: University of Massachusetts Press, 1982.

Aptheker, Herbert. *Abolitionism: A Revolutionary Movement.* Boston: Twayne Publishers, 1989.

————. *The American Revolution, 1763–1783.* New York: International, 1960.

————. *A Documentary History of the Negro People in the United States.* 1951. Reprint, New York: Citadel, 1994.

————. *The Negro in the Abolitionist Movement.* New York: International, 1941.

Bacon, Margaret Hope. *Valiant Friend: The Life of Lucretia Mott*. New York: Walker, 1980.

Barnes, Gilbert Hobbs. *The Antislavery Impulse, 1830–1844*. New York: American Historical Association, 1933.

Bearden, Jim, and Linda Jean Butler. *Shadd: The Life and Times of Mary Shadd Cary*. Toronto: NC Press, 1977.

Bell, Howard. "Expressions of Negro Militancy in the North, 1840–1860." *Journal of Negro History* 45 (January 1960): 11–20.

———. "National Negro Conventions in the Middle of the 1840's: Moral Suasion vs. Political Action." *Journal of Negro History* 42 (October 1957): 247–60.

Benson, Mary Sumner. *Women in Eighteenth-Century America: A Study of Opinion and Social Usage*. New York: Columbia University Press, 1935.

Berg, Barbara. *The Remembered Gate: Origins of American Feminism: The Woman and the City, 1800–1860*. New York: Oxford University Press, 1978.

Berlin, Ira. *Many Thousands Gone: The First Two Centuries of Slavery in North America*. Cambridge: Belknap Press of Harvard University Press, 1998.

———. *Slaves without Masters: The Free Negro in the Antebellum South*. New York: Pantheon, 1974.

Billington, Ray Allen. "James Forten: Forgotten Abolitionist." In *The Making of Black America: Essays in Negro Life and History*, edited by August Meier and Elliott Rudwick. 2 vols. New York: Atheneum, 1969.

Bloch, Ruth H. "The Gendered Meanings of Virtue in Revolutionary America." *Signs* 13 (Autumn 1987): 37–58.

———. "Sarah Parker Redmond: Black Abolitionist from Salem." *Essex Institute Historical Collection* 110 (April 1974): 120–50.

Boylan, Anne M. "Benevolence and Antislavery Activity among African American Women in New York and Boston, 1820–1840." In *The Abolitionist Sisterhood: Women's Political Culture in Antebellum America*, edited by Jean Fagan Yellin and John C. Van Horne. Ithaca: Cornell University Press, 1994.

———. *The Origins of Women's Activism: New York and Boston, 1797–1840*. Chapel Hill: University of North Carolina Press, 2002.

———. "Women in Groups: An Analysis of Women's Benevolent Organizations in New York and Boston, 1797–1840." *Journal of American History* 71 (December 1984): 497–523.

Brekus, Catherine A. *Strangers and Pilgrims: Female Preaching in America, 1740–1845*. Chapel Hill: University of North Carolina Press, 1998.

Brewington, M. V. "The State Ship *General Greene*." *Pennsylvania Magazine of History and Biography* 60 (1936): 229–41.

Bronner, Edwin. *William Penn's "Holy Experiment": The Founding of Pennsylvania, 1681–1701*. 1962. Reprint, Westport, Conn.: Greenwood Publishing, 1978.

Brown, Ira V. "Cradle of Feminism: The Philadelphia Female Anti-Slavery Society, 1833–1840." *Pennsylvania Magazine of History and Biography* 102 (April 1978): 143–66.

Bruns, Roger, ed. *Am I Not a Man and a Brother: The Antislavery Crusade of Revolutionary America, 1688–1788*. New York: Chelsea House, 1977.

Butler, Kathleen Mary. *The Economics of Emancipation: Jamaica and Barbados, 1823–1843.* Chapel Hill: University of North Carolina Press, 1995.

Carby, Hazel. *Reconstructing Womanhood: The Emergence of the Afro-American Woman Novelist.* New York: Oxford University Press, 1987.

Clark, Christopher. *The Roots of Rural Capitalism: Western Massachusetts, 1780–1860.* Ithaca: Cornell University Press, 1990.

Cott, Nancy F. *The Bonds of Womanhood: "Woman's Sphere" in New England, 1780–1835.* New Haven: Yale University Press, 1977.

———. "Divorce and the Changing Status of Women in Eighteenth-Century Massachusetts." *William and Mary Quarterly,* 3rd series, 33 (1976): 586–614.

———. "Eighteenth Century Family and Social Life Revealed in Massachusetts Divorce Records." *Journal of Social History* 10 (1976–77): 20–43.

Curry, Leonard P. *The Free Black in Urban America, 1800–1850: The Shadow of a Dream.* Chicago: University of Chicago Press, 1981.

Dannett, Sylvia. *Profiles of Negro Womanhood, 1619–1900.* 2 vols. New York: M. W. Lads, 1964.

Davis, Angela Y. *Women, Race, and Class.* New York: Random House, 1981.

Davis, David Brion. *The Problem of Slavery in Western Culture.* Ithaca: Cornell University Press, 1966.

Dill, Bonnie Thornton. "Race, Class, and Gender: Perspectives for an All-Inclusive Sisterhood." *Feminist Studies* 9 (Spring 1983): 131–50.

Dodd, Jill. "The Working Classes and the Temperance Movement in Antebellum Boston." *Labor History* 19 (Fall 1978): 510–31.

Dorsey, Bruce. *Reforming Men and Women: Gender in the Antebellum City.* Ithaca: Cornell University Press, 2002.

Douglas, Ann. *The Feminization of American Culture.* New York: Alfred A. Knopf, 1977.

Duberman, Martin, ed. *Antislavery Vanguard: New Essays on the Abolitionists.* Princeton: Princeton University Press, 1965.

DuBois, Ellen Carol. *Feminism and Suffrage: The Emergence of an Independent Women's Movement in America, 1848–1869.* Ithaca: Cornell University Press, 1978.

Du Bois, W. E. B. *Black Philadelphia: A Social Study.* Philadelphia: University of Pennsylvania Press, 1899.

———. *The Philadelphia Negro: A Social Study.* 1899. Reprint, Philadelphia: University of Pennsylvania Press, 1996.

DuCille, Ann. *The Coupling Convention: Sex, Text, and Tradition in Black Women's Fiction.* New York: Oxford University Press, 1993.

Dumond, Dwight L. *Antislavery: The Crusade for Freedom.* Ann Arbor: University of Michigan Press, 1961.

Dunn, Richard S. "Penny Wise and Pound Foolish: Penn as a Businessman." In *The World of William Penn,* edited by Richard S. Dunn and Mary Maples Dunn. Philadelphia: University of Pennsylvania Press, 1986.

Fogel, Robert William, and Stanley L. Engerman. "Philanthropy at Bargain Prices: Notes on the Economics of Gradual Emancipation." *Journal of Legal Studies* 3 (1974): 377–401.

———. *Time on the Cross: The Economics of Negro Slavery.* 1974. Reprint, New York: W. W. Norton, 1989.

Foner, Philip. *History of Black Americans from the Emergence of the Cotton Kingdom to the Eve of the Compromise of 1850.* Westport, Conn.: Greenwood Press, 1983.

Fordham, Monroe. *Major Themes in Northern Black Religious Thought, 1800–1860.* Hicksville, N.Y.: Exposition Press, 1975.

Frazier, E. Franklin. *The Negro Church in America.* New York: Schocken Books, 1964.

———. *The Negro Family in the United States.* Chicago: University of Chicago Press, 1939.

Fredrickson, George. *Black Image in the White Mind: The Debate on Afro-American Character and Destiny, 1817–1914.* New York: Harper and Row, 1971.

Friedman, Lawrence J. *Gregarious Saints: Self and Community in American Abolitionism, 1830–1870.* Cambridge: Cambridge University Press, 1982.

Genovese, Eugene. *Roll, Jordan, Roll: The World the Slaves Made.* New York: Pantheon, 1974.

George, Carol V. R. *Segregated Sabbaths: Richard Allen and the Emergence of Independent Black Churches, 1760–1840.* New York: Oxford University Press, 1973.

Gernes, Todd S. "Poetic Justice: Sarah Forten, Eliza Earle, and the Paradox of Intellectual Property." *New England Quarterly* 71 (June 1998): 229–65.

Giddings, Paula. *When and Where I Enter: The Impact of Black Women on Race and Sex in America.* New York: William Morrow, 1984.

Gilmore, Glenda Elizabeth. *Gender and Jim Crow: Women and the Politics of White Supremacy in North Carolina, 1896–1920.* Chapel Hill: University of North Carolina Press, 1996.

Ginzberg, Lori D. " 'Moral Suasion Is Balderdash': Women, Politics and Social Activism in the 1850's." *Journal of American History* 73 (December 1986): 601–22.

———. *Women and the Work of Benevolence: Morality, Politics, and Class in the Nineteenth-Century United States.* New Haven: Yale University Press, 1990.

Gregg, Robert. *Sparks from the Anvil of Oppression: Philadelphia's African Methodists and Southern Migrants, 1890–1940.* Philadelphia: Temple University Press, 1993.

Gutman, Herbert G. *The Black Family in Slavery and Freedom, 1750–1925.* New York: Pantheon, 1976.

Hansen, Debra Gold. *Strained Sisterhood: Gender and Class in the Boston Female Anti-Slavery Society.* Amherst: University of Massachusetts Press, 1993.

Hansen, Marcus Lee. *The Atlantic Migration, 1607–1860: A History of the Continuing Settlement of the United States.* Cambridge: Harvard University Press, 1940.

Harris, Leslie. *In the Shadow of Slavery: African-Americans in New York City, 1626–1863.* Chicago: University of Chicago Press, 2003.

Herbert, Catherine A. "The French Element in Pennsylvania in the 1790s: The Francophone Immigrants' Impact." *Pennsylvania Magazine of History and Biography* 108 (1984).

Herrick, Cheesman A. *White Servitude in Pennsylvania: Indentured and Redemption Labor in Colony and Commonwealth.* Philadelphia: J. J. McVey, 1926.

Hersh, Blanche Glassman. *Feminist-Abolitionists in Nineteenth-Century America.* Urbana: University of Illinois Press, 1978.

————. *The Slavery of Sex: Feminist-Abolitionists in America*. Urbana: University of Illinois Press, 1978.

Hershberg, Theodore. "Free Blacks in Antebellum Philadelphia: A Study of Ex-Slaves, Free-born, and Socioeconomic Decline." *Journal of Social History* 5 (Winter 1971–72): 183–209.

Hewitt, Nancy A. *Women's Activism and Social Change: Rochester, New York, 1822–1872*. Ithaca: Cornell University Press, 1984.

Higginbotham, Evelyn Brooks. *Righteous Discontent: The Women's Movement in the Black Baptist Church, 1880–1920*. Cambridge: Harvard University Press, 1993.

Hine, Darlene Clark, ed. *Black Women in American History: From Colonial Times through the Nineteenth Century*. 4 vols. Brooklyn: Carlson, 1990.

Hopper, Isaac T. *Kidnappers in Philadelphia: Isaac Hopper's Tales of Oppression, 1780–1843*. Compiled by Daniel E. Meaders. New York: Garland, 1994.

Hornick, Nancy Slocum. "Benezet and the Africans' School." *Pennsylvania Magazine of History and Biography* 99 (Winter 1975): 399–425.

Horton, James Oliver. "Freedom's Yoke: Gender Conventions among Antebellum Free Blacks." *Feminist Studies* 12 (Spring 1986): 51–76.

————. *Free People of Color: Inside the African American Community*. Washington, D.C.: Smithsonian Institution Press, 1993.

Horton, James Oliver, and Lois E. Horton. *Black Bostonians: Family Life and Community Struggle in the Antebellum North*. New York: Holmes and Meier, 1979.

Isenberg, Nancy. *Sex and Citizenship in Antebellum America*. Chapel Hill: University of North Carolina Press, 1998.

Jackson, John W. *With the British Army in Philadelphia, 1777–1778*. San Rafael, Calif.: Presidio Press, 1979.

James, Sydney. *A People among Peoples: Quaker Benevolence in Eighteenth-Century America*. Cambridge: Harvard University Press, 1963.

Jeffrey, Julie Roy. *The Great Silent Army of Abolitionism: Ordinary Women in the Antislavery Movement*. Chapel Hill: University of North Carolina Press, 1998.

Jennings, Francis. "Brother Miquon: Good Lord." In *The World of William Penn*, edited by Richard S. Dunn and Mary Maples Dunn. Philadelphia: University of Pennsylvania Press, 1986.

Johnson, Howard. *The Bahamas from Slavery to Servitude, 1783–1933*. Gainesville: University Press of Florida, 1996.

Jones, Jacqueline. *Labor of Love, Labor of Sorrow: Black Women, Work, and the Family from Slavery to the Present*. New York: Basic Books, 1985.

Jones, Maldwyn Allen. *American Immigration*. Chicago: University of Chicago Press, 1992.

Juster, Susan. *Disorderly Women: Sexual Politics and Evangelicalism in Revolutionary New England*. Ithaca: Cornell University Press, 1994.

Karlsen, Carol F. *The Devil in the Shape of a Woman: Witchcraft in Colonial New England*. New York: W. W. Norton, 1987.

Kellow, Margaret M. R. "The Divided Mind of Antislavery Feminism: Lydia Maria Child and the Construction of African American Womanhood." In *Discovering the*

Women in Slavery: Emancipating Perspectives on the American Past, edited by Patricia Morton. Athens: University of Georgia Press, 1996.

Kelly, Catherine. *In the New England Fashion: Reshaping Women's Lives in the Nineteenth Century.* Ithaca: Cornell University Press, 1999.

Kerber, Linda K. "The Republican Mother: Women and the Enlightenment, an American Perspective." *American Quarterly* 29 (Summer 1976): 187–205.

———. "Separate Spheres, Female Worlds, Woman's Place: The Rhetoric of Women's History." *Journal of American History* 75 (June 1988): 9–39.

———. *Women of the Republic: Intellect and Ideology in Revolutionary America.* New York: W. W. Norton, 1986.

Kolchin, Peter. *American Slavery, 1619–1877.* New York: Hill and Wang, 1993.

Kulikoff, Alan. "Uprooted Peoples: Black Migrants in the Age of the American Revolution, 1790–1820." In *Slavery and Freedom in the Age of the American Revolution,* edited by Ira Berlin and Ronald Hoffman. Charlottesville: University Press of Virginia, 1983.

Kutler, Stanley I. "Pennsylvania Courts, the Abolition Act, and Negro Rights." *Pennsylvania History* 30 (January 1963): 14–27.

Lane, Roger. *Roots of Violence in Black Philadelphia, 1860–1900.* Cambridge: Harvard University Press, 1986.

———. *William Dorsey's Philadelphia and Ours: On the Past and Future of the Black City in America.* New York: Oxford University Press, 1991.

Lapsansky, Emma Jones. "Feminism, Freedom, and Community: Charlotte Forten and Women Activists in Nineteenth-Century Philadelphia." *Pennsylvania Magazine of History and Biography* 113 (January 1989): 3–19.

———. " 'Since They Got Those Separate Churches': Afro-Americans and Racism in Jacksonian Philadelphia." *American Quarterly* (Spring 1980): 54–78.

Lehuu, Isabelle. "Friends, Wives and Strivings: Networks and Community Values among Nineteenth-Century Philadelphia Afro-American Elites." *Pennsylvania Magazine of History and Biography* 108 (January 1984): 83–102.

———. "Sentimental Figures: Reading 'Godey's Lady's Book' in Antebellum America." In *The Culture of Sentiment: Race, Gender, and Sentimentality in Nineteenth-Century America,* edited by Shirley Samuels. New York: Oxford University Press, 1992.

Lerner, Gerda. "Black and White Women in Interaction and Confrontation." In *The Majority Finds Its Past: Placing Women in History,* edited by Gerda Lerner. New York: Oxford University Press, 1979.

———. *Black Women in White America: A Documentary History.* New York: Pantheon, 1972.

———. *The Grimké Sisters from South Carolina: Pioneers for Women's Rights and Abolition.* Rev. ed. Chapel Hill: University of North Carolina Press, 2004.

Levy, Claude. *Emancipation, Sugar, and Federalism: Barbados and the West Indies, 1833–1876.* Gainesville: University Presses of Florida, 1980.

Litwack, Leon F. "The Abolitionist Dilemma: The Antislavery Movement and the Northern Negro." *New England Quarterly* 34 (March 1961): 50–73.

———. *North of Slavery: The Negro in the Free States, 1790–1860.* Chicago: University of Chicago Press, 1961.

Lumpkin, Katharine Du Pre. *The Emancipation of Angelina Grimké.* Chapel Hill: University of North Carolina Press, 1974.

Lutz, Alma. *Crusade for Freedom: Women of the Antislavery Movement.* Boston: Beacon Press, 1968.

Mayer, Henry. *All on Fire: William Lloyd Garrison and the Abolition of Slavery.* New York: St. Martin's Press, 1998.

McHenry, Elizabeth. *Forgotten Readers: Recovering the Lost History of African American Literary Societies.* Durham, N.C.: Duke University Press, 2002.

McPherson, James. *The Struggle for Equality: Abolitionists and the Negro in the Civil War and Reconstruction.* Princeton: Princeton University Press, 1964.

Melish, Joanne Pope. *Disowning Slavery: Gradual Emancipation and "Race" in New England, 1780–1860.* Ithaca: Cornell University Press, 1998.

Miller, Floyd J. *The Search for a Black Nationality: Black Emigration and Colonization, 1787–1863.* Urbana: University of Illinois Press, 1975.

Moody, Jocelyn. *Sentimental Confessions: Spiritual Narratives of Nineteenth-Century African American Women.* Athens: University of Georgia Press, 2001.

Morris, Thomas D. *Free Men All: The Personal Liberty Laws of the North, 1780–1861.* Baltimore: Johns Hopkins University Press, 1974.

Murray, Andrew E. *Presbyterians and the Negro—A History.* Philadelphia: Presbyterian Historical Society, 1966.

Nash, Gary B. *Forging Freedom: The Formation of Philadelphia's Black Community, 1720–1840.* Cambridge: Harvard University Press, 1988.

———. *Race, Class, and Politics: Essays on American Colonial and Revolutionary Society.* Urbana: University of Illinois Press, 1986.

———. *Red, White, and Black: The Peoples of Early North America.* Englewood Cliffs, N.J.: Prentice-Hall, 1991.

———. "Slaves and Slaveowners in Colonial Philadelphia." *William and Mary Quarterly* 30, no. 2 (1973): 223–56.

Nash, Gary B., and Jean R. Soderlund. *Freedom by Degrees: Emancipation in Pennsylvania and Its Aftermath.* New York: Oxford University Press, 1991.

Needle, Edward. *History of the Pennsylvania Abolition Society.* Philadelphia, 1848.

Newman, Debra L. "Black Women in the Era of the American Revolution in Pennsylvania." *Journal of Negro History* 61 (July 1976): 276–89.

Norton, Mary Beth. *Liberty's Daughters: The Revolutionary Experience of American Women, 1750–1800.* Boston: Little, Brown, 1980.

Palmer, Phyllis Marynick. "White Women/Black Women: The Dualism of Female Identity and Experience in the United States." *Feminist Studies* 9 (Spring 1983): 151–70.

Porter, Dorothy B. "The Organized Educational Activities of Negro Literary Societies, 1828–1846." *Journal of Negro Education* 5 (October 1936): 556–77.

Potter, David M. *The Impending Crisis, 1848–1861.* New York: Harper and Row, 1976.

Quarles, Benjamin. *Black Abolitionists.* New York: Oxford University Press, 1969.

———. *The Negro in the American Revolution.* Chapel Hill: University of North Carolina Press, 1961.

Rhodes, Jane. *Mary Ann Shadd Cary: The Black Press and Protest in the Nineteenth Century*. Bloomington: Indiana University Press, 1998.

Richards, Leonard L. *Gentlemen of Property and Standing: Anti-Abolition Mobs in Jacksonian America*. London: Oxford University Press, 1970.

Rose, Willie Lee. *Rehearsal for Reconstruction: The Port Royal Experiment*. Indianapolis: Bobbs-Merrill, 1964.

Rothman, Ellen K. *Hands and Hearts: A History of Courtship in America*. New York: Basic Books, 1984.

Rowe, G. S. "Black Offenders, Criminal Courts, and Philadelphia Society in the Late Eighteenth Century." *Journal of Social History* 22, no. 4 (1989): 685–712.

Ryan, Mary. *Cradle of the Middle Class: The Family in Oneida County, New York, 1790–1865*. New York: Cambridge University Press, 1981.

———. *Women in Public: Between Banners and Ballots, 1825–1880*. Baltimore: Johns Hopkins University Press, 1990.

Salinger, Sharon. *"To Serve Well and Faithfully": Labor and Indentured Servants in Pennsylvania, 1682–1800*. New York: Cambridge University Press, 1987.

Samuels, Shirley, ed. *The Culture of Sentiment: Race, Gender, and Sentimentality in Nineteenth-Century America*. New York: Oxford University Press, 1992.

Sellers, Charles. *The Market Revolution: Jacksonian America, 1815–1846*. New York: Oxford University Press, 1991.

Sernett, Milton C. *Black Religion and American Evangelicalism: White Protestants, Plantation Missions, and the Flowering of Negro Christianity, 1787–1865*. Metuchen, N.J.: Scarecrow Press, 1975.

Silcox, Harry C. "The Black 'Better Class' Political Dilemma: Philadelphia Prototype Isaiah C. Wears." *Pennsylvania Magazine of History and Biography* 113 (January 1989): 45–66.

Smith, Billy, and Richard Wojtowicz, compilers. *Blacks Who Stole Themselves: Advertisements for Runaways in the "Pennsylvania Gazette," 1728–1790*. Philadelphia: University of Pennsylvania Press, 1989.

Smith, Merril D. *Breaking the Bonds: Marital Discord in Pennsylvania, 1730–1830*. New York: New York University Press, 1991.

Smith-Rosenberg, Carroll. "Beauty and the Beast and the Militant Woman: A Case Study of Sex Roles in Jacksonian America." *American Quarterly* 23 (October 1971): 562–84.

———. *Disorderly Conduct: Visions of Gender in Victorian America*. New York: Oxford University Press, 1985.

Sobel, Mechal. *Trabelin' On: The Slave Journey to an Afro-Baptist Faith*. Westport, Conn.: Greenwood Press, 1979.

Soderlund, Jean R. "Black Women in Colonial Pennsylvania." In *African-Americans in Pennsylvania: Shifting Historical Perspectives*, edited by Joe William Trotter Jr. and Eric Ledell Smith. University Park: Pennsylvania State University Press, 1997.

———. "Priorities and Power: The Philadelphia Female Anti-Slavery Society." In *The Abolitionist Sisterhood: Women's Political Culture in Antebellum America*, edited by Jean Fagan Yellin and John C. Van Horne. Ithaca: Cornell University Press, 1994.

———. "Women in Eighteenth Century Pennsylvania: Toward a Model of Diversity." *Pennsylvania Magazine of History and Biography* 115 (April 1991): 163–83.

Soderlund, Jean R., et al., eds. *William Penn and the Founding of Pennsylvania, 1680–1684: A Documentary History.* Philadelphia: University of Pennsylvania Press, 1983.

Stansell, Christine. *City of Women: Sex and Class in New York, 1789–1860.* 1986. Reprint, Urbana: University of Illinois Press, 1987.

———. "Revisiting the Angel in the House: Revisions of Victorian Womanhood." *New England Quarterly* 60 (1987): 446–83.

Stauffer, John. *Black Hearts of Men: Radical Abolitionists and the Transformation of Race.* Cambridge: Harvard University Press, 2002.

Stetson, Erlene. *Black Sister: Poetry by Black American Women, 1746–1980.* Bloomington: Indiana University Press, 1981.

Stewart, James B. *Holy Warriors: The Abolitionists and American Slavery.* New York: Hill and Wang, 1976.

Tate, Claudia. *Domestic Allegories of Political Desire: The Black Heroine's Text at the Turn of the Century.* New York: Oxford University Press, 1992.

Trussell, John B. *The Pennsylvania Line: Regimental Organization and Operations, 1776–1783.* Harrisburg: Pennsylvania Historical and Museum Commission, 1977.

Turner, Edward R. *The Negro in Pennsylvania, 1639–1861.* New York: Arno Press, 1969.

———. *Slavery in Pennsylvania.* Baltimore: Lord Baltimore Press, 1911.

Ulrich, Laurel Thatcher. *Good Wives: Image and Reality in the Lives of Women in Northern New England, 1650–1750.* New York: Alfred A. Knopf, 1982.

Van Broekhoven, Deborah Bingham. "Let Your Names Be Enrolled: Method and Ideology in Women's Anti-Slavery Petitioning." In *The Abolitionist Sisterhood: Women's Political Culture in Antebellum America,* edited by Jean Fagan Yellin and John C. Van Horne. Ithaca: Cornell University Press, 1994.

Walker, Clarence Earl. *A Rock in a Weary Land: The African Methodist Episcopal Church during the Civil War and Reconstruction.* Baton Rouge: Louisiana State University Press, 1982.

Walters, Ronald G. "The Boundaries of Abolitionism." In *Antislavery Reconsidered: New Perspectives on the Abolitionists,* edited by Lewis Perry and Michael Fellman. Baton Rouge: Louisiana State University Press, 1979.

Warner, Michael. *Letters of the Republic: Publication and the Public Sphere in Eighteenth-Century America.* Cambridge: Harvard University Press, 1990.

Wellman, Judith. "Women and Radical Reform in Antebellum Upstate New York: A Profile in Grassroots Female Abolitionists." In *Clio Was a Woman: Studies in the History of American Women,* edited by Mabel E. Deutrich and Virginia C. Purdy. Washington, D.C.: Howard University Press, 1980.

White, Shane. *Somewhat More Independent: The End of Slavery in New York City, 1770–1810.* Athens: University of Georgia Press, 1991.

———. *Stories of Freedom in Black New York.* Cambridge: Harvard University Press, 1992.

Wilentz, Sean. *Chants Democratic: New York City and the Rise of the American Working Class, 1788–1850.* New York: Oxford University Press, 1984.

Williams, Oscar R. "The Regimentation of Blacks on the Urban Frontier in Colonial Albany, New York City, and Philadelphia." *Journal of Negro History* 63, no. 4 (1978): 329–38.

Wilmore, Gayraud S. *Black Religion and Black Radicalism: An Interpretation of the Religious History of Afro-American People.* Garden City, N.Y.: Doubleday, 1972.

Winch, Julie. *The Elite of Our People: Joseph Willson's Sketches of Black Upper-Class Life in Antebellum Philadelphia.* University Park: Pennsylvania State University Press, 2001.

———. *A Gentleman of Color: The Life of James Forten.* Oxford: Oxford University Press, 2002.

———. *Philadelphia's Black Elite: Activism, Accommodation, and the Struggle for Autonomy, 1787–1848.* Philadelphia: Temple University Press, 1988.

Woloch, Nancy. *Women and the American Experience.* 2nd ed. New York: McGraw-Hill, 1994.

Wulf, Karin. "Assessing Gender: Taxation and the Evaluation of Economic Viability in Late Colonial Philadelphia." *Pennsylvania Magazine of History and Biography* 121 (July 1997): 201–35.

Yee, Shirley J. *Black Women Abolitionists: A Study in Activism, 1828–1860.* Knoxville: University of Tennessee Press, 1992.

Yellin, Jean Fagan. *Women and Sisters: The Antislavery Feminists in American Culture.* New Haven: Yale University Press, 1989.

Yellin, Jean Fagan, and John C. Van Horne, eds. *The Abolitionist Sisterhood: Women's Political Culture in Antebellum America.* Ithaca: Cornell University Press, 1994.

Zaeske, Susan. *Signatures of Citizenship: Petitioning, Antislavery, and Women's Political Identity.* Chapel Hill: University of North Carolina Press, 2003.

Index

Introductory note: page numbers in italic type refer to illustrations.